# Going beyond the Pairs

# GOING beyond the PAIRS

## The Coincidence of Opposites in German Romanticism, Zen, and Deconstruction

Dennis McCort

State University of New York Press

Published by
State University of New York Press
Albany



Printed in the United States of America



For information, address
State University of New York Press,
90 State Street, Suite 700, Albany, NY 12207

Production and book design, Laurie Searl
Marketing, Michael Campochiaro

Library of Congress Cataloging-in-Publication Data

McCort, Dennis.
Going beyond the pairs : the coincidence of opposites in German romanticism, Zen, and deconstruction / by Dennis McCort.
p. cm.
Includes bibliographical references and index.
ISBN 0-7914-5001-5 (alk. paper) — ISBN 0-7914-5002-3 (pbk. : alk. paper)
1. German literature—History and criticism. 2. Romanticism—Germany. 3. Zen Buddhism. 4. Deconstruction. 5. Paradoxes. 6. Coincidence. 7. Polarity, Theory of. I. Title.

PT148.R65 M33 2001
830.9'145—dc21

00-046080

10 9 8 7 6 5 4 3 2 1

*For my wife, Dorothy,*

*and my children, Denise and Danny,*

*with love*

# Contents

# Acknowledgments

Two of the chapters have been adapted from previously published material. Chapter 3 originally appeared as "Kafka Koans" in *Religion and Literature,* Volume 23 Issue 1 (Spring 1991). Reprinted with permission of the University of Notre Dame. Chapter 5 originally appeared as "Hyakujo's Geese, Amban's Doughnuts and Rilke's Carrousel: Sources East and West for Salinger's *Catcher*" in *Comparative Literature Studies* 34 (3), pp. 260–78. Copyright 1997 by The Pennsylvania State University. Reproduced with permission of The Pennsylvania State University Press.

I wish to express my gratitude to the Thomas Merton Legacy Trust for permission to quote copiously in chapter 2 from the unpublished Merton notebook. My sincere thanks also go to Ms. Doroethy B. Leonard and Mr. Robert M. Briggs for permission to quote from Merrell-Wolff's two books, *The Philosophy of Consciousness without an Object* and *Pathways through to Space.*

Finally, it gives me joy to acknowledge my good friend, Dr. Robert G. Strickland, a true man of the Way, who well appreciates the fact that Zen is as at home with the intellect as anything else. So much of what has passed between us in many lively discussions over the years has, in one way or another, found its way into this book. To him a deep and grateful *gassho.*

# Overview

## THE DREAMING SUBJECT

The car rolls down the parking lot ramp at twilight, hitting bottom with a bit of a jolt. From there it circles the crowded lot tentatively, looking for a space. I feel a little better the instant I realize I am driving, better still on noticing my dad sitting next to me. He's been dead for only about four years and so still has some of that vigorous "just-been-living" look of the recently departed. Wife and children are seated in back, but they are only vaguely there, functioning as mere "accompaniment." This is clearly going to be a "front-seat" episode between Dad and me.

The lot is full, so I head back up the ramp. As I do, he reaches behind his lower back with closed fist and begins massaging. "Hurt?", I ask. He nods yes, continuing to rub. As we approach the top of the ramp, he leans toward me slightly and says *sotto voce,* as if to prevent their hearing but without their noticing, "I have to leave," by "leave" clearly meaning "die again, this time on *this* level." Overcome with sadness, I reply, "You don't have to do this, you know." But he insists, "Yes, I do," and I say, "Okay, Dad, you're the boss. Whatever you say."

We embrace each other (who's driving?), twice it seems, which adds a curious element of ceremony to the profoundly sad leave-taking, sadness and ceremony blending in a kind of mutual benediction. By now we are at the apex of the exit, atop not only the lot but, it seems, the dark-and-crowded-lot-become-world. From this sudden horizon I look away and up into the early evening sky, now in its most intensely ambiguous twilight, and behold a darkening dome pregnant with awe—vast, mysterious, inviting, writhing in ecstasy. Transfixed, I know I am gazing into the Source and realize instantly that everything, absolutely everything, is part and parcel of this Womb, shaped by It, born of It, kept by It, and dissolved back into It. It goes through all, permeating all with Its orgasmically free flow. It is what everything is and what anything means.

Dizzy with delight, I convey the glad tidings to my father. "Life is just a dream, Dad! It's all just a dream!" I chortle, still hugging him and acutely aware as I speak the words that I am speaking them from within a "dream." At the same time, the words also seem to issue from the writhing vortex of twilit Sky. But, most strange, they issue forth both audibly and visibly, as if the Sky has become a kind of articulate cosmic mouth whose speech is its writing and whose writing is its speech. As I continue to gaze upward, I revel in my inability to tell one of us from the other.

## THE CULTURAL OBJECT

If during a dream the idea occurs to one with overwhelming conviction that life is just a dream, is that a dream? Thus did my first "real-life" experience of the coincidence of opposites,[1] the subject of this study, some ten years ago leave an indelible impression; and, like any idea that shifts gears in one's psychic economy from intellectual formula to quasi ecstatic obsession, I began to discover it everywhere in culture: spread across broad canvases of art and scores of music, animating bodies of myth and religion East and West, tucked away in the subtler architecture of the most varied poetry and prose, energizing systems of philosophy and psychology, coordinating anthropological theories of group behavior, and gracing just about any other aspect of the human enterprise I happened to look at with a modicum of concentration. Was I projecting, or was the idea really that ubiquitous—indeed, in view of the transpersonal nature of the idea, was the question even relevant?

I had been practicing *zazen,* a form of Zen meditation, for about five years when the dream occurred. Though I had always found Zen lore fascinating—who could resist a religion that preferred raucous jokes and mind-bending riddles to painstaking exegesis and somber pronouncements on the nature of "Ultimate Reality"?—I also found its illogic frequently bewildering and, at times, intensely frustrating. "When Setcho hits the bottle, Ikyu stumbles home." What could possibly be the point of that? This ambivalence continued, with tiny occasional (and hence doubly frustrating) peeks of insight, until the dream finally took place, parting the curtain and revealing in radiant clarity what all the fuss and nonsense were about. Thereafter commenced my "tour" of a delightful obsession across the human cultural landscape, a tour culminating in the present volume.

If, despite the fierce and rampant secularism of modern life, religion still be the basis of human culture, then one should not be surprised to find the *coincidentia oppositorum* everywhere in cultural expression, for it is first and foremost a religious idea, an idea embodying man's ineradicable yearning for ultimate reconciliation, a final coming-to-terms with himself and his world. In today's poststructuralist parlance, everywhere man confronts difference yet hungers for identity. The psychological correlative of difference is tension, and man refuses to accept tension as fundamental to existence. Something there must be that liberates us from tension while yet in no way suppressing, idealizing, or otherwise falsifying the fact of tension, since this would simply be a psychological form of difference superimposed on the original fact and, in making us ignorant of the fact, would leave us worse off than ever. In other words, something there must be that reveals to us the impossible, yet necessary, congruence of transcendence and immanence.

This sort of perennial ruminating on the human plight has given rise in cultures the world over to an absurd idea: the idea of a coincidence or conjunction of opposites, for what else but a power greater than difference, a power nowhere in obvious evidence, could reconcile us to difference? What else but a force so far superior to difference—and to its descriptive principle of noncontradiction—as to leave difference intact while yet robbing it of the sting of endless tension could fulfill man's longing?[2] As Cirlot puts it, "In conjunction, then, lies the only possibility of supreme peace and rest" (62). Of course, some would say, extending St. Anselm's argument, that the sheer universality of so basic a longing reflects not only deep-seated human need but, equally, the deep-seated existence of what is longed for. Nature would not instill in us so profound a need without making it fulfillable.

Myths are one cultural expression of this absurd idea. They give imaginative glimpses of possibilities for success in man's struggle to overcome the fundamental contradictions that beset him—good versus evil (tales of Khidr in the *Koran*), innocence versus experience (Blake), mind versus body, spirit versus nature (Orpheus), male versus female (Euphorion in Goethe's *Faust* II). Or at least there once was a time when they did this—and did it for entire cultures—before the evolution of the rational-scientific consciousness in recent centuries gradually reduced them to quaint and clever subtexts of individual poets and novelists observable only by literary detectives. But anyone who peruses the major works of our century's great mythological scholars, say, Carl Jung's *Aion* (1951) or Joseph Campbell's *Masks of God* (1959) or Mircea Eliade's *Images and Symbols* (1969), can at least begin to recover a sense of the vital centrality of the *coincidentia oppositorum*—the metamyth of the overcoming of difference—to Western cultural traditions both pagan and Christian.

If, in Campbell's well-turned aphorism, "myths are public dreams, dreams are private myths," then mystics straddle the border between dream and myth for, as visionary channels of the Ineffable, their "dreams" are usually the creative font of a religious culture's collective imagination. Romanticism, in the "neo" vein of, say, Ernst Cassirer, reads the mystic as a vestige of prehistoric culture when no one had "visions" because everyone had "vision" and no one needed spiritual "insight" because what was to be seen was plainly evident to everyone. In an interesting book coming out of the neoromantic strain of the seventies counterculture, one Princeton psychologist named Julian Jaynes even went R. D. Laing one better in proposing that hallucinating schizophrenics were atavists of ancient mythic-eidetic man.[3] On this lapsarian view, then, mystics in postantique culture, whether surviving as lone wolves or sequestered in isolated sects, are leftovers from Paradise, unheard prophets, occasional strangers in an estranged land. As oddball counterpoints to the linear Aristotelian mind-set that shapes their culture, they preserve the myth of the *coincidentia oppositorum* with their "vision," not unlike the way Christian monks preserved the wisdom of the ancients during the "Dark Ages," only in this case the sacred preserve has by now become a global affair and a Westerner can as easily cite a Zen master or a Sufi adept as a Meister Eckhart or a Paracelsus for heterodox purposes.

Thus, in his splendid book on the Christian Trinity, the West's most dominant symbol of the coincidence of opposites, we have religionist David Miller citing Shibayama on the Zen art of flower arrangement:

> Zen man Rikyu once said, "In arranging flowers for a small room, one flower, or two, of single color, is to be lightly arranged." I like this remark very much. The word "lightly" is not light at all; in this one word we can detect . . . Zen insight. . . . When it comes to this point, there is no distinction between religion and art. They are identified; they are neither one nor two.

To which Miller adds his own "Christian Zen" insight:

> So, are they then a third? Of course, and of course not. Concerning the third one may not speak, for it is no-thing, since it is everything. This may be indeed why St. Augustine said, "Who can understand the omnipotent Trinity? And yet who does not speak about it, if indeed it is of it that he speaks? Rare is the soul who, when he speaks of it, also knows of what he speaks." (23)

Nevertheless, despite, or perhaps owing to, its unutterable nature, all religions do speak of it, as if the image of threeness were, as Miller puts it, "somehow fundamentally given" (21). Classical Hinduism has its own triad of ultimate reality in the deities Vishnu, Shiva, and Brahma, the first two representing various binary cosmic oppositions such as existence/annihilation, light/darkness, concentration/dispersion, and preservation/destruction, and the third the possibility of existence generated by the union of opposites. Parallel triune deities are to be found in the religions of Egypt (Osiris, Isis, Horus), ancient Greece (the theogony of Ouranos, Kronos, and Zeus), and the ancient Near East (Attis, Ishtar, and Tammuz). Even a nontheistic religion such as Buddhism has its doctrine of the Trikaya or three "bodies" of the one Buddha, namely, that of essence, of historical manifestation, and of the mutual bliss between them. Nor, apparently, is belief in a single god a hindrance to threeness, for, as Miller tells us by way of French scholar W. L. Duliere, an unmistakenly trinitarian sense of divinity is revealed in the iconography of iconoclastic Jewish monotheism (15–17).

In his speculation on the source of the symbol's universality, Miller cites literary critic Philip Wheelwright who

> finds the basis of trinitarian religious symbology in biology (the family pattern of father, mother, child) and in the geometry of human thought patterns (the beginning, middle, and end of linear thought structure; and the down-here/earth, up-there/sky, and in-between/atmosphere). It is into these modes of the "triadic archetype," as he calls it, that Wheelwright places Egyptian, Greek, Zoroastrian, Hindu, and Buddhist, not to mention Christian, images and ideas. (16)[4]

Leaving aside till later the forbidding question of whether the *coincidentia oppositorum* is an archetype, and if so, of what sort, I would only caution here in the matter of origins as to the virtual impossibility of avoiding circular thinking. Assuming for the sake of argument that archetypes are fundamental, and the *coincidentia oppositorum* the most fundamental archetype (a kind of psychospiritual meta-archetype), then it seems to make just as much sense to derive such things as thought patterns and even biology from *it* as the reverse. Considered on its own terms, the *coincidentia oppositorum* is prior to all phenomena—as Miller says, it is the no-thing that makes everything possible—so to root it in physical or mental structures would seem to betray the very materialist-evolutionist outlook that has, as the mystics tell us, beclouded it for the modern consciousness. Better for now, I think, to remain open on the issue.

Interestingly, it is not only in their cosmologies and formal religious institutions that innumerable societies through history have espoused the *coincidentia oppositorum,* but in their overall organization as well.

Anthropologist David Maybury-Lewis discusses a vast array of societies, ancient and contemporary, that have organized themselves on the principle of "moieties" or halves (usually according to complex rules of kinship) and view themselves as the divided consequence of a split or shattered cosmic principle. These societies based on "correlative cosmologies" (i.e., whose institutional structures and belief system are correlated) range from ancient Taoist China where kings and commoners alike were expected to act in alignment with "the Way" (the mysterious harmony of the universe) by balancing, sometimes in elaborate formal rituals, *yin* and *yang* energies; to contemporary sub-societies of Indonesia "that consider their own dualism to be the result of a shattered wholeness which they are constantly seeking to recreate" (4); to the moiety systems of the Australian outback which, like all aboriginal societies, "show an overriding commitment to dualism at the systemic level that is expressed in their cosmologies, their classifications, or their institutions" (6).

Of course, there are many exceptions, in the sense of dualistic societies that have not espoused the equilibrium or fusion or coincidence of opposing principles as ultimate redemption. The ancient Zoroastrians, and the Manichaean and Gnostic sects after them, although envisioning the world in terms of the interaction of Light and Dark or Good and Evil principles, rather construed the relationship as one of struggle than complementarity and looked forward to a final separation of forces through the eternal banishment of the negative. This outlook of cosmic conquest and exile has left its mark, and a deep mark at that, on Christianity, which in its "image of the self—Christ—lacks the shadow that properly belongs to it," as Jung has often pointed out. Jung further locates the source of the split in the refusal of overly intellectualist early Church fathers such as Irenaeus and Augustine to allow God the luxury of an ambiguous nature: "[N]either God nor Christ could be a paradox; they had to have a single meaning . . . . [T]he hybris of the speculative intellect had already emboldened the ancients to propound a philosophical definition of God that more or less obliged him to be the Summum Bonum" (*Aion* 45–46). Thus, in Christian culture it has been left to the late medieval and Renaissance secret societies with their occult alchemical philosophies, and to the occasional renegade mystic such as Eckhart or Böhme or Blake, to promulgate an "underground" vision of the *coincidentia oppositorum*. One might argue that the Christian West has been a predominantly "left-brained" culture in a predominantly "right-brained"—if indeed not "bilateral"—world-cultural history.[5]

Another vital faction closely allied to this Western "underground" movement of the *coincidentia* comprises the philosophers of German Idealism:

Fichte, Schelling, Schlegel, and, above all, Hegel. Here finally, if briefly, the idea had found a respectable home in the principle of dialectical logic. Not surprisingly, each of the Idealists, not to mention the extensive cluster of Romantic poets and thinkers invigorating university life in Berlin and Jena at the dawn of the nineteenth century, was immersed in the writings of the great German mystics of earlier centuries. Theirs was a true and potent marriage of mysticism and philosophy. Hegel in particular, with his deep hostility to Newtonian science and Enlightenment rationalism, was profoundly influenced by the dialectical ground of Böhme's mysticism, and that of Eckhart before him, creating, as Thomas Altizer tells us, "a dialectical logic, the only fully dialectical logic ever produced in the West" (28–29). Unveiling in his *Science of Logic* the key dialectical principle of negation *(Aufhebung),* inherited from the kenotic or "emptying-out" mysticism of Eckhart and Böhme and according to which a thing can pass over into its own opposite by annulling itself, Hegel gives a definition of the *coincidentia* that almost seems to justify the West's obsession with the verbal understanding of Mystery and surely comes as close as discursive language ever has to the thing itself. We must come to understand, with "*simple* insight," says the philosopher,

> that negation is just as much affirmation as negation, or that what is self-contradictory resolves itself not into nullity, into abstract nothingness, but essentially only into the negation of its *particular* content, that such negation is not an all-embracing negation, but is *the negation of a definite somewhat* which abolishes itself, and thus is a definite negation; and that thus the result contains in essence that from which it results—which is indeed a tautology, for otherwise it would be something immediate and not a result. Since what results, the negation, is a *definite* negation, it has a *content.* It is a new concept, but a higher, richer concept than that which preceded; for it has been enriched by the negation or opposite of that preceding concept, and thus contains it, but contains also more than it, and is the unity of it and its opposite. (qtd. in Altizer 29)

According to Franklin Merrell-Wolff, the subject of the sixth chapter of this book (q.v.), it was German Idealism with its subtle mystical understanding of dialectics that prepared the nineteenth-century Western mind to come to grips with the transpersonal philosophies and psychologies of Vedanta and Buddhism, systems in which the *coincidentia* had always been at home.

One other, peculiarly modern, underground "hideout" in the West for the *coincidentia* is the psychotherapist's office. I refer to therapists of a depth-psychological persuasion, and, even more narrowly, to Jungians. Freud we pass over in silence, notwithstanding hints and glints of binary thinking in such concepts as reaction formation, for he really took himself out of the running with his admission to Romain Rolland, doubtless made more out of pride in his own rational stability than out of sensed deficiency, that he could find nothing of the latter's "oceanic feeling" in himself.[6] As for Jung, however, one is tempted to view him as underground priest, presiding, in a German lent *gravitas* through generous sprinklings of hoary Neoplatonic "mantras" (*imago Dei, corpus mysticum, hieros gamos,* etc.), over the *mysterium conjunctionis* in the sanctuary of his consulting room. Certainly his entire vast enterprise is a tireless working-out of the idea of *conjunctio,* theoretically in his writings and practically in his efforts to guide his patients toward "individuation." The linchpin of Jungian analysis is binary opposition, the dynamic interplay of systems and subsystems of psychic forces, these forces distributed among at least three strata of relative consciousness, all clamoring for hegemony and all to be brought into concord in the process of individuation.

A key player in the grand Jungian drama of mediation called individuation is the archetype, and I suppose I must now take up the question, deferred above, as to whether the *coincidentia oppositorum* counts as one. Precisely put, the question would seem to be whether the *coincidentia* is equatable with Jung's self archetype which, as it manifests in myths and certain dreams, is characterized by Jung as "the *eidos* behind the supreme ideas of unity and totality that are inherent in all monotheistic and monistic systems" (*Aion* 34). My answer to this is a reluctant yes, reluctant for the following reason. Strictly speaking, the *coincidentia* is prior to all manifestation, being rather the eternal, dynamic threshold of manifestation, while yet comprehending anything that manifests. One must remember that, as soon as it assumes particularity through manifestation as an archetypal image, however lofty or powerful, it of necessity takes on a certain kind of bipolarity, becoming, so to speak, one vis-à-vis others (call it the one superior versus the many inferior archetypes) and thus is already less than the pleroma. I know Jung was well aware of this "paradox of manifestation," yet on occasion he forgets himself and writes carelessly of the self as if it were a *prima causa* and thus merely the *primus inter pares* of a descending order of archetypal causes:

> Wholeness is thus an objective factor that confronts the subject independently of him, like anima or animus; and just as the latter have a higher position in the hierarchy [of archetypes] than the shadow, so wholeness lays claim to a position and a value superior to those of the syzygy. . . . Unity and totality stand at the highest point on the scale of objective values. (*Aion* 31)

My own sense is that the *coincidentia,* or what Jung calls the self, is not itself a cause, even a first cause, but rather the condition of all causation, as of all other principles of relative existence. It is beyond causation even while comprehending causation—indeed, how else could it be a true *coincidentia oppositorum?* Perhaps calling it a meta-archetype, ontologically beyond the order of archetypes yet remaining "close" to them, would help to keep this important distinction in mind. In the end, it is the Great Abyss, in whose proximity even poles of archetypal power yearn to lose themselves in one another.

Turning to the arts, one may say that the *coincidentia* has always and everywhere been lavishly entertained in them, possibly because as forms that are, as the Germans say, *erdichtet* (made up, fabricated, hence "not true") they are allowed to "experiment" with values which, when argued for in tracts, instigate ideological dispute. Music is an especially "natural" medium for the *coincidentia* through its capacity for acoustical blending, particularly in its two (or more)-in-one polyphonic structures, and, in general, through its high degree of freedom from natural models and from the logical principle of noncontradiction under which the linguistic arts labor. In its power to commingle subtle interior values that in the other arts exist primarily through painstaking differentiation, music becomes for the Romantic Novalis, by virtue of a mysterious interior/exterior correspondence, a kind of "mystical Pythagoreanism," a harmony of the spheres grounding all of nature. It is, in Walter Pater's famous dictum, "the condition" to which all arts aspire.

More specifically, comparatist John Jones sees Western music of the classical period (Haydn, Mozart, and Beethoven), German Idealist philosophy, and English Romantic poetry as so many eddies in an evolutionary stream propelled by a kind of mutual dialectical thinking which he terms variously the "reconciliation of opposites" (159) and "unity in contrast and diversity" (170). The complex dialectical dynamics of sonata form in Beethoven's late string quartets, for instance, parallel the dialectics of Hegel, and both parallel the fusion of poetic imagination and nature envisioned in such Romantic lyrics as Wordsworth's "Immortality Ode" and Shelley's "Ode to the West Wind." I disagree sharply with Jones when he excludes the German Romantic poets from this dialectical stream (182). The first chapter of this book thoroughly refutes him on this. However, his analysis is compelling and enlightening as far as it goes. Summing up, he says, "Like the development and recapitulation of sonata form, the [English] Romantic poem, after the process of separation, fragmentation and 'alienation,' strives for reintegration and resolution. This analogy, while not exact or complete, is real" (178).

Of course, it is one thing to observe a gross global correspondence in dialectical features between music and literature around the turn of the eighteenth century in the West, and quite another to appreciate the labyrinthine complexity that a particular work of literature can reveal when considered *by itself* as an expression of the *coincidentia*. This complexity peculiar to literature has to do, in large part, with the dialectical interaction of denotative and connotative systems of meaning. But then, it would seem, as one gathers from much current literary theory, that this endlessly rich dynamic is itself embedded in two dialectically related levels of structure, superficial and deep. By superficial structures I mean potentially reconcilable thematic and formal oppositions that are deliberately built into the work; whereas deep structures involve some degree of the work's unawareness of its own "built-in" contradictions, as if it were a kind of "divided self," uneasy in its own presence. Since the issue here is linguistic in the most fundamental sense, it applies to the literature of any time and place, as do the implications for the *coincidentia oppositorum* that the linguistic issue reveals.

Superficial structurings of the *coincidentia* in a literary work are generally deliberate attempts to invoke the religious tradition in which the work is embedded. As we have seen, both East and West are grounded in essentially trinitarian world views, respectively Advaita Vedanta and Buddhism with their vision of a non-dual truth beyond the pairs and Christian trinitarianism with its tortured schism between aspects of the mystery that are "acceptable" (the Holy Trinity) and those that are anathema (God as origin of both good and evil). Thus we have, say, Prince Genji, the hero of the classic tenth-century Japanese novel, *The Tale of Genji,* holding forth on the subtle power of the literary romance (doubtless including the present one of which he is hero) to transcend the gulf between history/truth and fiction/illusion. This reflects the book's profound immersion in the non-dual philosophy promulgated in the great Mahayana Buddhist sutras originating in China in earlier centuries. Similarly, the traditional kenotic plot of a Western work such as Tolstoy's "The Death of Ivan Ilych," in which a proud protagonist is humbled by a cruel fate that ironically turns out to be the means of his redemption through love, clearly reflects the tripartite rhythm of the Christian myth of the Fall.[7] In both cases, however, the element of the *coincidentia* is "superficial," that is, it is more or less deliberately encoded into the work, in the first case as the explicit philosophical expression of a character, in the second as the work's structural dynamic.[8]

Far more elusive in terms of the *coincidentia* are the deep structures of a literary work that reveal it to be, on some level, a stranger to itself and that reveal the presumed authorial control of language to be an illusion. These are the fissured structures unearthed in recent decades by postmodernists, particularly deconstructionists, structures defined by the so-called aporia, understood as a basic rhetorical or logical contradiction lurking in all texts, literary or not. Interestingly, in the aporia we have the return of the aforementioned "underground" aspect of the *coincidentia,* only now the underground is not social but psychological (lurking deep in the text's "psyche") and "threatens" not only the values promulgated in self-defensive Western texts but in literary language—indeed, language of any sort—everywhere. It would seem that literary texts, like psychoanalytic man, have an unconscious, a repressed shadow side that may at any time rise up to undo "any proferred transcendental signified that supposedly exists outside the text—e.g. nature, Being, the unconscious, etc." (Gras 279). (Indeed, for deconstruction, texts, being language, are more fundamental than "man," a linguistic category posing as "a transcendental signified." Put round the other way, "man," like "nature" or "being," is always embedded in a text, an interpretation generated by language.)

The confrontation of rhetorical antagonists in the aporia of a literary work unleashes the anxiety of the undecidable moment. Two tropes, or a trope and a literal expression, claustrophobically attempt to occupy the same linguistic "space." In Paul de Man's famous example from Yeats's "Among School Children," the last line of the poem, "How can we know the dancer from the dance?", is torn between contradictory meanings: the one, rhetorical, implies a unity of dancer and dance and, by extension, a transcendental cosmic unity (the "Romantic" reading); the other, literal, demands, perhaps with great urgency, a way to tell them apart. Since, as de Man says, "the one reading is precisely the error denounced by the other," there can be no respectful coexistence of readings, nor can one reading prevail over the other, nor can they cancel each other out (*Allegories of Reading* 11–12.)

Thus, the aporia, in lifting the repressed literal reading of Yeats's line into awareness, uncovers a quasi Laingian anxiety over the threat of engulfment by an all-pervasive Romantic monism and a corresponding need to keep the boundaries of individual entities intact. This anxiety of engulfment is immediately superseded by the claustrophobic anxiety of undecidability, as the text realizes its entrapment between its own contradictory rhetorical modes. The poem, as de Man sees it, is mired in its own aporetic impasse, condemned to pinball back and forth between a rhetorical Scylla and Charybdis ad infinitem.

But I think de Man's horrific vision of a hell of eternal undecidability may be a bit premature, for such hells are precisely the temporary redemptive purgatories of the Zen koan, particularly the so-called *gonsen* koan of the Rinzai school that is meticulously framed to negotiate the slippery slopes of rhetorical and semantic ambiguity:

> A Monk asked Master Joshu: "What is Joshu?"
> "East gate, west gate, south gate, north gate," Joshu replied.

Again,

> "What is Tao?"
> "A bright-eyed man falls into a well." (Miura and Sasaki 55)

As Master Ummon says, "If you can penetrate directly into words and understand them thoroughly, everything, from vicious words to the inane disputations of the world, will be transformed into ghee of the finest flavor" (Miura and Sasaki 53). In "other words," when the literary text, through the consciousness of a sensitive reader, begins to become aware, not of the enfeeblement, but, quite the contrary, the empowerment of its own ambiguities, then a koan comes into being, an incendiary spirit of contradiction that, in the fullness of time, will combust into awakening to the *coincidentia oppositorum*.

A Western student of Zen once asked, "When the poem awakens, who is there to notice it?"

## THE ESSAYS

My study is made up of essays on the theme of the *coincidentia oppositorum*. The earliest of them grew more or less independently out of the cluster of my scholarly and teaching interests. It was only after completing two or three of them that it became clear to me that I *was,* in effect, composing variations on a theme. As I continued writing, I further noticed that this theme of the *coincidentia* tended to subdivide across the essays into a triangular cultural focus: German Romanticism, postmodernism, and the Eastern wisdom traditions, particularly Zen. Each point of the triangle, as one might expect, features prominently as a topic in the preceding cultural-historical survey of the main theme. In my studies over the past dozen or so years, it has gradually dawned on me that the *coincidentia* comes very close to being a common essence—or should I say essenceless essence or essence "under erasure"—to these three culturally disparate phenomena, and therefore a principle of considerable explanatory power for comparative culture.

To be sure, as I indicate in the conclusion of the last chapter, one could trace out broad historical connections among the three, Indian Buddhism splitting up into Eastern and Western directions in the early Christian centuries, going to China as Zen and to Rome as Neoplatonism, etc., and this would be an engrossing scholarly project. But, as Joseph Campbell was wont to say with respect to myths, historical influences between cultures pale in significance as an explanation of recurrent universal themes before the awesome fact of a common core of inner psychic structure. The core of this core for present purposes, the womb giving birth to these three dynamic cultural forces, is, I believe, the *coincidentia oppositorum*.[9] I hedged above in saying that the *coincidentia* comes "very close" to this lofty status, and that is because one of the three, postmodernism (particularly deconstruction), is, at least for now, in a kind of flirtatious relationship with it that stops short of being a full embrace. No doubt this has to do at least partly with a staunch psychological commitment to "difference" on the part of Derrida and de Man and, dare I say, an imperfect understanding of the nature of the Oneness or Identity implied in the idea of the *coincidentia*. This is a roundabout way of saying that mystical insight has not yet visited deconstruction, at least not openly and emphatically enough, though clearly it is not far away, as several of the chapters that follow are at pains to point out.

The seven chapters amount, then, at least in modest measure, to a three-way comparison. German Romanticism, Zen Buddhism, and postmodernism reveal themselves to be forms of each other on the basis of an inner attunement (still largely intuitive with deconstruction) to a radiant, fundamental guiding insight.[10] Each chapter touches at least two of the cultural triangle's three points; most touch all three. The Figure/Ground format of the book is itself a variation on the theme of dynamic opposition as centered in *coincidentia* or Interface (the more abstract "centering" discussion of chapter 4). The pairs of chapters on either side of the Interface (2 and 3, 5 and 6), each of which situates a modern Western author in this tricultural context of the *coincidentia,* flesh out the gestalt.

Accordingly, the opening chapter, on German Romanticism, treats that movement as a Figure or arresting individual feature emergent from this tricultural Ground. It is the single chapter in the collection that attempts, in some degree, to isolate one of the three cultural moments and study it, from the standpoint of the *coincidentia,* in some depth, in this way providing a context for the intercultural comparisons that follow. More specifically, *"Figure"* attempts to view German Romanticism, particularly in its early Jena phase, as an especially rich cultural manifestation of the *coincidentia oppositorum*—perhaps the last Western manifestation of such intensity in the past two centuries. The chapter characterizes the Romantic poets and critics as heirs to a German mystical tradition of the *coincidentia* extending at least as far back as

Meister Eckhart. My examination lingers on the aphoristic-philosophical prose of Friedrich Schlegel and Novalis but also highlights salient examples from Romantic artist-fiction.

At the same time, I attempt to use this perspective of the *coincidentia* as a strategy for settling a generational disagreement among scholars of Romanticism (call it the traditional millenialists versus the recent poststructuralists) as to the Romantics' ultimate aims and view of themselves. What, after all, *is* German Romanticism? What is it up to? What is the status of its presumed quest for spiritual transcendence, especially in view of the profound skepticism expressed in much current literary theory? My intent here is pointedly not to take sides with either scholarly camp but rather to show how the debate on Romantic transcendence "miraculously" resolves itself when one takes the Romantics' own embrace of the *coincidentia oppositorum* seriously.

There is, in the modern era, perhaps no worthier heir to the spiritual vision of the German Romantics than the poet Rainer Maria Rilke, and no more profoundly affected student of Rilke than Trappist monk Thomas Merton. The second chapter traces Merton's intense four-month preoccupation with Rilke during the mid-nineteen sixties. Using an unpublished notebook of Merton's, his only known extended exegesis on Rilke, as primary source, the essay views his relatively brief but profound involvement with the latter as a spiritual ordeal, a kind of Zen life koan, culminating in the monk's shattering realization of the long-sought, long-resisted Truth beyond contradiction, the *coincidentia oppositorum,* literally days before his untimely death.

Merton's private notebook provides a rare, almost day-to-day account of his inner struggle to recognize and, finally, come to terms with his own deep dis-ease before Rilke, a dis-ease deriving from long-standing inner conflicts that were themselves reflections of the inchoate shift in Western culture in the mid-sixties from modernism to postmodernism. Basically, Rilke's Orphic vision, penetrating as it did well beyond the rational-linguistic boundaries of essence and ontological level to a mystical substratum of no-boundary awareness, was an affront to Merton the essentialist Christian humanist but at the same time a fascination to Merton the mystical poet. The sustained four-month meditation on Rilke recorded in the notebook stoked in Merton various phases of a deep-seated conflict over his vocation and, in consequence, his world view: to wit, between the doctrinaire and the mystic; the mystic and the poet; the poet and the priest; the modernist and the postmodernist. For Rilke, grounded in the German Romantic tradition of the *coincidentia oppositorum* (a tradition relatively unfamiliar to the Francophile Merton), the boundaries between such pairs did not exist. Merton used Rilke's Orphic-poetic vision of the *coincidentia,* at first haltingly and intuitively but, with the passing weeks and spiritual support from the Zen philosopher Nishida's essay on "The Unity of Opposites," more and more deliberately, to come to this same no-boundary awareness. My essay presents Merton's relationship to Rilke as a progressive approach-avoidance dialectic, and thus, as the enactment of a genuine spiritual drama climaxing in the seeker's awakening to the *coincidentia.*

If Thomas Merton's grasp of "the world according to Zen" was explicit and somewhat "tainted" by formal study, Franz Kafka's was pure and intuitive for he most likely never heard of Zen. The unmistakably Zen-like style and spirit of his short fiction can be at least partly accounted for by his immersion in the lore of his Hasidic Jewish background. A vast anecdotal literature suffused with gallows humor and a zest for bizarre paradox is common to both traditions. It turns out, however, that virtually all traces of Hasidic lore in Kafka's writings are carefully hidden. He apparently found it necessary to do this, as Jofen has argued, "in order to identify himself as a German writer" (xii). However that may be, the resultant veiled or even suppressed quality of Kafka's Hasidism gives his short fiction a distinctly Zen flavor. His parables are particularly reminiscent of the koan, a traditional form of spiritual training in Rinzai Zen.

My reading of some of these parables as virtual koans in the third chapter argues the case for Kafka as basically a spiritual writer in quest of the *coincidentia oppositorum,* the goal of Zen Enlightenment. Such a reading also discloses Kafka's intent to portray the nature of the ego as delusive, a stance aligning him with the anatmic world view of Zen in particular and Buddhism in general. Further, it identifies him, as it does his Czech-German compatriot Rilke, as an important spiritual link between the ego-transcending Romantics and contemporary poststructuralists with their claims of individual identity as a delusion generated by language. All in all, the chapter presents Kafka as an intuitive Zen master for whom writing was a self-styled form of koan practice that occasionally provided him with deep glimpses into the no-self realm of the *coincidentia oppositorum.*

Precisely between the focal poles of my study's format, between the opening "close-up" of Romanticism *(Figure)* and the closing "longshot" encompassing Romanticism, Zen, and deconstruction *(Ground),* looms the *Interface* (chapter 4), the elusive common border binding together the members of any antinomy, belonging equally to both and wholly to neither. This essayistic Interface attempts to say something about the unsayable, to come as close as language allows to a postmetaphorical, unmediated view of this "interfacial" border reality of the *coincidentia oppositorum.* Of course, one finds it impossible to get any closer than the polarity on which language itself—and hence its subjective correlative, consciousness—rests, that of identity and difference. And so it would seem the chapter must content itself with exploring this primal precipitation, this virginal manifestation of the *coincidentia* in the world, asking the question, "Are things basically the same or different?" Yet, if asked with sufficient intensity, such a fundamental question can create a koan, and koans, as this study is at pains to point out, have this "sleight-of-mind" way of getting us past linguistic barriers. Consequently, in more specific terms, the chapter attempts to show how the Zen koan, principally cases one and three in the medieval Chinese collection *Mumonkan,* can illuminate the current Western debate between poststructuralist "differentialists" and "identity-traditionalists" through its insight into the wisdom of "not-two," a traditionally Eastern paradoxical expression of the *coincidentia.* A key question in the debate is the reducibility or irreducibility of what French cultural theorist Bernard Faure calls the "agonistic tension" of *différance.* Is the Buddhist *sunyata* an answer to this?

Arguably, no Western writer has made more creative use of the East to get beyond the impasse of the pairs of opposites than J. D. Salinger. Like Thomas Merton, Salinger was caught up in the postwar American interest in Eastern religion. Also like Merton, he seems to have discovered the *coincidentia oppositorum* as the dynamic matrix inspiring both the Zen and Rilkean spiritual visions, for, as I argue in chapter 5, his masterly *Bildungsroman, The Catcher in the Rye,* contains allusions to both that reveal it to be constructed precisely on this principle. Contrary to the prevailing view, there are definite allusions to Zen Buddhism in Salinger's fiction as early as *Catcher,* at least two allusions, but they are veiled and, in the novel's climactic scene at the Central Park carousel, fused with an image from the neo-Romantic Rilke's own "Karussell" that is itself veiled. In unveiling and linking these covert references to Zen and Rilke in Salinger's novel, my essay construes Holden Caulfield's crisis as psychospiritual in nature, more specifically, as the symbolic enactment of the struggle with a Zen koan, leading ultimately to Enlightenment, conceived here as the liberating *coincidentia* within Holden of innocence and experience, or the child and the man.

Franklin Merrell-Wolff was yet another American contemporary whose genius lay in a profound awareness of the *coincidentia oppositorum* as the common core of German and Eastern mysticism. Chapter 6 follows the absorbing intellectual and spiritual migration of this Harvard-trained philosopher and professorial dropout from West to East, from the thought of Immanuel

Kant, in whose meticulously discursive *Critique of Pure Reason* he nevertheless saw glimmers of mystical insight, to that of Shankara, whose Vedantic philosophy of the transpersonal Self struck him as the brilliant fulfillment of Kant's promise.

Sustained study of Shankara led to Merrell-Wolff's two great mystical "Recognitions," these providing the experiential basis for his subsequent writings in the philosophy of religion. My essay traces the progressive deepening of Merrell-Wolff's insight from the Heideggerean vision of an *Ursprache* fusing word and concept/experience to the final realization of "the High Indifference" (Merrell-Wolff's designation for the *coincidentia*), for him the long-lost "philosopher's stone" rediscovered, the fundamental state of consciousness promising final release for man from the anguish of bondage to the pairs of opposites, blending as it did even the ultimate subject-object binary, Self and Divinity, into "pure Being." The chapter concludes with a reflection on Merrell-Wolff's notion of philosophy as preparation for an inner combustion of consciousness allowing us to know in "another way" and a consideration of the vulnerability of his philosophy of mind to Richard Rorty's infamous "deconstruction" of the Western philosophical tradition.

The seventh and final chapter, "*Ground:* German Romanticism, Zen, and Deconstruction," summarizes and celebrates the triangular cultural focus of the whole, revisiting previously discussed themes and broaching new ones. Particular attention is paid to the strikingly similar heterodox perspective each of these three cultural moments holds with respect to such supernal Western values as self, time, and meaning. The chapter shows how each of the three (with deconstruction as yet more promise than realization), in its own unique style, deconstructs these values by showing their ontological interdependence with their own opposites. In this way each testifies to the *coincidentia oppositorum* as the matrix of an insubstantial or nonfoundational dialectically structured universe. In and of itself, no thing is real. The chapter ends where I think the book should end—right here at the beginning, only, to paraphrase the bard, "knowing the place for the first time."

A Western student of Zen asked, "When the book knows the place, who knows the book?"

1

# *Figure:* What Is German Romanticism *(noch einmal)*, *or* The Limits of Scholarship

> The world must be romanticized. This is the way to rediscover its original meaning. . . . By giving the base a lofty meaning, the ordinary an appearance of mystery, the known the dignity of the unknown and the finite an aura of infinity, I romanticize it.
>
> —Novalis

The mere idea of a coincidence of opposites can arouse in us inklings of the reality of the unseen, for we are stirred, even in spite of ourselves, by anything that bodes release from the prison of quotidian logic. Yet, to affirm the reality of the unseen, that is, to be a transcendentalist in Western academic culture at the turn of the century, is akin to being a liberal in current American politics: both positions are generally regarded as fraught with hope-fueled delusion and sentimental idealism. Consider, for instance, some recent post-structuralist re-visions of German Romanticism, which appear to have undermined that movement's lofty status in the annals of Western culture, a status that resides, in large measure, in its unabashed appreciation of the mystery of ontic unity. This undermining has taken two forms, one tendentious, the other well-intentioned. Paul de Man, echoing in *The Rhetoric of Romanticism* Nietzsche's deconstruction of traditional metaphysical verities, epitomizes the former trend in his outright excoriation of the Romantic vision of Paradise Regained: "The idea of innocence recovered at the far side and by way of experience, of paradise consciously regained after the fall into consciousness, the idea, in other words, of a teleological and apocalyptic history of consciousness is, of course, one of the most seductive, powerful, and deluded topoi of the idealist and romantic period" (267). The benign undermining is exemplified in Alice Kuzniar's *Delayed Endings: Nonclosure in Novalis and Hölderlin,* the title of which announces its intention to "read against the grain of" (9) what it regards as the misguidedly millenialist perspective of traditional scholarship with its superimposition on the Romantics of such ideals as closure, synthesis, and identity—in a word, the beatific *goldenes Zeitalter,* whether conceived as the end-stage of history *(futurus)* or as its sudden apocalyptic interruption *(adventus)*.[1] On this view, the Romantics were merely playing with the linguistic tropes and figures of traditional Pietistic transcendentalism as a way of ironizing the conventional essentialist mind-set. De Man would invalidate Romantic transcendentalism itself, Kuzniar the imputation of transcendentalism to Romanticism. Either way, should poststructuralism, at least as represented by these and other theorists,[2] carry the day, Romanticism would lose its transcendental dimension.

My aim here is neither to discredit the poststructuralist revisionists of German Romanticism ("differentialists") nor, as these remarks may seem to suggest, to credit the millenialists of tradition ("logocentrists"), but rather to take a fresh look at (*noch einmal,* revise!) certain fundamental aspects of Romanticism itself, and to do this through the focusing power of the primordial principle at issue in this study, a principle, I am convinced, that underlies and informs *all* important aspects of Romanticism: the *coincidentia oppositorum.* This principle, deeper even than the archetypes, has, as we have seen, many names conjured of many languages and cultures and, most important for present purposes, can be shown to be a leitmotif in the German mystical tradition stretching at least as far back as Nicholas Cusanus, who promulgated the Latin designation,[3] and Meister Eckhart before him. As the issue unfolds, as I reexamine Romanticism alongside highlights of its interpretative history, I believe the limitations inherent in both the revisionist and millenialist positions will become self-evident. A resultant irony, and one that will serve my aim, is that this very perspectival opposition, in becoming *itself* an enactment of the *coincidentia,* will indeed reveal what Romanticism is, but in a way neither scholarly camp could ever have imagined—that is, it will reveal Romanticism directly through its own dialectical wholeness, rather than through either of its signifying antagonists. The signifiers will become the signified.[4] Once this happens, what might previously have loomed as poststructuralism's dire threat to Romanticism's spiritual viability[5] should turn out to have been no more than a temporary obscuring of it.

If it be objected that I am assuming what I intend to "prove," I would only reply that the very issue of proof, as a required end of rationalist procedure, is precisely what Romanticism supersedes. If I could "prove" that Romanticism were the *coincidentia oppositorum,* it would not be. So I dispense with proof, accept my confinement within the hermeneutic circle and proceed along the interpretative rim of my subject.

## THE GERMAN MYSTICAL TRADITION

German spiritual literature is particularly rich in creative expressions of this fundamental experience of the coincidence or conjunction or unity of opposites. Certainly German Romanticism represented, not the initiation, but the brilliant if brief climax of the long spiritual development of a world view that was heterodox, though in no way opposed, to the predominantly rationalist outlook of the preceding and following eras. Like mystics in general, purveyors of this insight, if known to their societies at all, have been regarded as at best learned eccentrics and at worst demonic eruptions: thus it has been from the Dominican Meister Eckhart's gingerly cat-and-mouse game with Rome down to Friedrich Schlegel's complaint, in a more secular and liberal era, that he would have to give away a piece of candy with each issue of the *Athenäum* journal if he expected "the dull-witted bourgeoisie from Hamburg down to Swabia" to "get" his pithy aphorisms.

In the German tradition, the idea, or more precisely insight, that any pair of opposites, if known intimately enough, will resolve itself into unity can be traced back at least as far as Meister Eckhart in the late thirteenth and early fourteenth centuries. Whether heretically expounding God and man as two aspects of one Consciousness (or "Eye," to use his term) or peppering his sermons with incoherent ecstatic outbursts of "mystic-speak," Eckhart exuded the confidence of deep grounding in the *coincidentia oppositorum.* In one sermon, revealingly titled "Being is more than life," he expresses the illumination this way: "The whole scattered world of lower things is gathered up to oneness when the soul climbs up to that life in which there are no opposites. Entering the life of reason [read: insight or enlightenment], opposites are forgotten, but where this light does not fall, things fall away to death and destruction" (*Meister Eckhart* 173).

Not only did the renowned Cardinal and Church statesman, Nicolaus Cusanus (1401–1464), share Eckhart's vision of ultimate unity-in-difference, he also expounded that vision to the very limits of rational discourse and beyond in his tract, *De visione Dei* (1443), which represents the world as a vast network of contradictions and God as the abyssal point at which they all meet or coincide *(coincidentia oppositorum)*. The ensuing Renaissance and Baroque eras saw a burgeoning of the idea in the proliferation of secret religious societies with their elaborate, esoteric alchemical discourses, all aiming at a syncretism of metallic and human-psychospiritual transformation. As we know from the alchemical studies of Carl Jung and others, the *lapis* or stone became for Paracelsus and his magician-scientist contemporaries the objective correlative of that radiant spiritual pivot, extolled by the mystics, at which all boundaries become utterly porous (Jung, *Memories* 209–10).

The best of German Baroque poetry is mystical through and through, and the best of this best delights in conjuring a plethora of variations on the theme of the *coincidentia oppositorum*. Thus the great, though to us today largely inaccessible, alchemical systematizer, Jakob Böhme, in a simple album verse playing with the time/eternity antinomy:

> From stress and strife
> Will he be free,
> Who sees time
> As eternity.
> (M; Hederer 7)[6]

But it was the Baroque rhymed epigram, with its terse differential symmetry fusing form and idea, that provided the most nearly perfect form of expression for the mystery. In this the Silesian Angel, Angelus Silesius, had no equal:

> The bottom of my spirit cries aloud in ceaseless plea
> To the bottom of God's; tell me which deeper be.
> (M; Hederer 177)

Generally, historical surveys of German mysticism jump about a century and a half from the Baroque era to the Romantics, connecting the two with copious illustrations of Böhme's influence on the early Jena circle. Recent research has shown, however, that there is an important intellectual-historical link in the interim, a link that becomes especially compelling when we fix our focus on the particular spiritual principle under discussion here. In an excellent contribution to the scholarship on Johann Gottfried Herder, entitled *Herder and the Poetics of Thought*, Michael Morton analyzes an early essay of the renowned philosopher of history and mentor to the young Goethe, demonstrating his grounding in the tradition of the *coincidentia oppositorum*, a tradition that, according to the author, stretches back to Cusanus and, long before him, to the pre-Socratic Ionian philosopher Heraclitus. Morton calls Herder "a direct ancestor of such thinkers as Hegel and Nietzsche" (51), this by reason of his 1764 essay, "On Diligence in Several Learned Languages," the exposition of which occurs in three stages, "corresponding broadly to the pattern of thesis-antithesis-synthesis that, a generation later, becomes the characteristic framework, not merely of the Hegelian system, nor even solely of German Idealism, but of Romantic thought and sensibility generally" (28). In the third chapter of his book, Morton offers a reading of Herder's essay that shows how its subtle and paradoxical method of composition clearly prefigures the Romantic poets' playful deconstruction of the presumably irreducible identity/difference antinomy: "Unity seems to restore itself by means of its own disruption. The return to unity, lost in the process of historically necessary differentiation, can be achieved only by sustaining differentiation" (Allert 248).

## THE JENA CIRCLE

An Eastern metaphor much favored by Westerners for that state of consciousness most conducive to the realization of the *coincidentia oppositorum* is that of "the razor's edge." This is, of course, the *Bhagavad Gita*'s arresting image of the subtle and often painful difficulty involved in attaining that absolute equanimity of mind necessary to the realization of spiritual illumination. The idea is that, in order to embrace the entire universe (i.e., become cosmically conscious), one must inwardly withhold commitment to any particular aspect of it—one must sit on the razor's edge. To be sure, the steely discomfort of this seatless seat says much about man's profound need to come down securely on one side or the other of any issue that may confront him at any time. Things, it seems, must always be "decided" this way or that. Yet it is precisely this most human drive for settlement or fixity (or, in the parlance of deconstruction, "closure") that must, finally, be relinquished if man is to realize what Nietzsche, in a moment of neo-Romantic illumination, called "the transvaluation of values," that is, the equal and absolute value of everything. Such a realization would be synonymous with Cusanus's definition of God as the *coincidentia oppositorum,* the power beyond all duality capable of reconciling all oppositions, since every opposition is another mask or permutation of the ground-conflict between what is valued (self) and what is rejected or disowned (other).

August Wilhelm Schlegel clearly implies Jena Romanticism's non-negotiable commitment to this radically nondiscriminatory spirit of the *coincidentia oppositorum,* which is, in effect, a "commitment to everything," in the Vienna lectures (*Vorlesungen über dramatische Kunst und Literatur* [1808]) when he says, in the context of artistic appreciation, that

> [o]ne cannot be a true connoisseur without universality of spirit, i.e., without that flexibility that puts us in a position, even as we disavow personal preference and blind habituation, to ensconce ourselves amidst the peculiarities of other peoples and times, to sense these directly from within their own center. (M; 162)

In the remaining pages of this chapter, we will see how the underlying principle of the *coincidentia oppositorum,* this elusive equipoise on the razor's edge of subject-object consciousness, channels great spiritual and aesthetic power into the quintessentially Romantic attitude of openness, an attitude that, taken on the purely conceptual level, might strike one as little more than a banal echo of Enlightenment humanitarian tolerance.

The early German Romantics experienced themselves as possessed by a "Sehnsucht nach dem Unendlichen" [longing for the Infinite] (A. W. Schlegel). This quest for Ultimate Reality, nurtured by an inner awareness of its imminence, is the hallmark of what William James called the "religious sense," and justifies the Romantics' inclusion in any history of Western religious movements. But it was no mere sense of boundless expanse that the Romantics were after, no "empty Absolute where everything is one," as Hegel derisively characterized the vain efforts of formal logic to grasp the dialectic (qtd. in Altizer 30). Nor did the Romantics conceive of the Infinite as some diaphanous, all-pervasive cosmic substance. In fact, the point is that they did not lead with the faculty of conceptual thought at all, rather they *experienced* the Infinite holistically from the deepest, subtlest regions of the mind, regions where mind and body shade into one another, as a sense of the fundamental balance of things, and specifically, a balance assuming trinitarian form and function. (Indeed, this sense of mind/body interface was itself an instance of this balance.) "My dear man," observes one of Novalis's interlocutors, "you're obviously no chemist, otherwise you'd know that through genuine mixing a *third element* arises, that is both at once and more than either one by itself" (M; *Werke* 312; emphasis Novalis's). The mixing of the two did not "produce" the third but rather *revealed* it as an ontologically prior matrix.

On the chemical analogy, ultimate reality was for the Romantics one, but a one that constituted the bond between two. Not just air, but the atmosphere fusing heaven and earth; not just love, but the love between man and woman; not just "romantische Poesie," but its mediating function "between the depicted [object] and the one depicting [subject]" (M; F. Schlegel 93). The Absolute was thus fundamentally trinitarian, a three-in-one that was equally a one-in-three, the third term confounding all description since it was the connection between things and could therefore not be a describable thing itself. Yet this indescribable no-thing of the Romantics' inner experience was to them more "real" than the things composing so-called reality, just as the science of the day was beginning to attribute greater reality to such invisible forces as electricity, heat, and magnetism than to the visible bodies they suffused.[7] This emergent "reality of the unseen" within and without (where was the border now?) awakened in the Jena circle an intimate intuition of the world's abysmal mystery. A most incisive formulation of this intuition, one giving powerful expression to the precisely trinitarian nature of the mystery, is the following of Novalis, in which the third term is characterized as a "hovering" *(Schweben),* that is, "neither this nor that" or, in the Hindu negational expression, *neti neti:*

> All being, being *per se* is nothing but a being-free—a *hovering* between extremes, which must needs be united and separated. From this luminous point of hovering all of reality streams forth—in it all things are contained—Obj[ect] and subject are [constituted] through it, not it t[hrough] them.
>
> I-ness or the productive power of imagination, the *hovering*—determines, produces the extremes between which the hovering takes place—This is an illusion, but only in the sphere of common under-standing. Apart from that it is something utterly real, for the hovering, its cause, is the source, the *mater* of all reality, indeed is reality itself. (M; *Novalis Schriften* 2: 266)[8]

All of this was the fruit of the Romantics' intrepid self-inquiry, guided, to be sure, by an ambitious program of reading and intellectual exchange. The proto-dialectical mystical insights elaborated in the writings of Plotinus, Böhme, and Spinoza, for example, could only have encouraged members of the early circle to probe themselves more deeply.[9] But it was the direct looking into self, the exploratory ardor of Novalis's "Geh in dich hinein!" [Go into yourself!], that was paramount. We know from Oskar Walzel that the Romantics carried on an intensive regimen of experiments in self-contemplation or introspection (12). They were probably the first modern thinkers to entertain seriously the theory of an unconscious mind (Huch 81; Walzel 64–65; Ellenberger 202–10). Historian of psychiatry Henri Ellenberger goes so far as to hold the entire fields of modern dynamic psychiatry and depth psychology unthinkable without the foundation of "interest that was shown by Romanticism for all manifestations of the unconscious: dreams, genius, mental illness, parapsychology, the hidden powers of fate, . . . the psychology of animals" (200). But the speculation and theorizing of the Romantics always remained grounded in the confidence of inner experience, for they had done nothing less than tap an archetype, the primordial trinitarian archetype of the *coincidentia oppositorum,* and in so doing appropriated for their art, quite apart from its manifest religious or secular content, the empowering vision of all the major religions of the world.

It would appear then that the Romantics, with their profusion of dialectical systems of thought, paradoxical aphorisms, and multivalent symbols, were, in effect, "reinventing religion" for themselves by means of an ingeniously improvised depth psychology, literally rediscovering the transcultural archetypal wellsprings of the received Christian orthodoxy. Thomas Altizer makes this point with specific reference to two figures closely peripheral to our subject, Blake and Hegel, each of whom in his own way evolved a radically new *Heilsgeschichte* out of a seminal insight into the *coincidentia oppositorum*. Altizer summarizes the single apocalyptic moment beheld by both poet, in his *Jerusalem,* and philosopher, in his *Phenomenology:* "By moving through an actual death of its original form, every opposite will dialectically pass into its other: this self-annihilation will wholly dissolve the original identity of each opposite, and this process of the negation of negation will draw all the estranged contraries of a fallen Totality into a final coincidence of the opposites" (218).

## ROMANTIC PANORAMA

I want to suggest that it is precisely this apocalyptic moment, epitomized in the cosmologies of Blake and Hegel, that Friedrich Schlegel is urging upon his fellow poets in his celebrated essay, "Rede über die Mythologie." The ripeness of conditions for a leap into the transpersonal depths of mind, where the gods are at home, and still deeper into the dynamic trinitarian matrix ("those principles of eternal revolution" [M; 129]) that is their source, is what Schlegel is implying when he says, "[M]an is just beginning to become aware of his divine power" (M; 128). Not a mythology limited to sensory experience, as in antiquity, does Schlegel envision, but one grasping the fundamental triadic-dialectical principle generating *all* phenomenal reality, a metamythology therefore, that would realize "how it is of the essence of mind to determine itself and, in eternal alternation, to go out of itself and come back into itself" (M; 123–24). Since the *coincidentia oppositorum* was experienced as a kind of base-line gravitational field of the psyche capable of accommodating any culturally determined content, the new mythology would literally be a source of inexhaustible inspiration, giving powerful shape to any experiential particulars that came within its orbit:

> The new mythology must . . . be fashioned from the deepest depths of the mind; it must be the most artful of all works of art, for it is to contain all others, to be a new bed and vessel for the old eternal *Ur*-source of poetry, even to be the endless poem that conceals the seeds of all other poems. (M; 122)

As *sine qua non* for the revitalization of poetry, Schlegel was advocating what Jung, more than a century later, would posit as the goal of his analytic psychology and of human evolution in general: self-realization.

The extent to which the other Romantics, in and beyond the early circle, caught the spirit Schlegel was at pains to articulate and were actually able to plumb their own inner depths to create "metamythologically" out of this triadic-archetypal foundation of mind is astonishing. Eminently citable examples abound, some obvious, others subtle. The obvious ones would include the entire dialectical-philosophical arc of Fichte, Schelling, Müller, and Hegel, all of whom drew inspiration from the idea of a synthesis of polar opposites, even if, in Fichte's case, the inspiration was negative (no synthesis, but *unendlicher Progreß* toward one). Among the subtler, but no less compelling, manifestations of the archetype would be A. W. Schlegel's dyadic view in the Vienna lectures of the Romantic era as both historical phenomenon (essentially, the post-antique Christian order, especially the late medieval to early modern era) *and* the transhistorical consciousness that sees "classical" and "Christian" as conceptually interdependent (165): hence Romanticism, as it were, remains "itself" even as it embraces its own "other." (How close this is to Derrida's nature/culture antinomy!)[10] Then there is the acknowledgment by both Schlegels that this dialectical "Grundkraft" is prior even to distinctions between internal-individual and external-collective reality: "The whole play of vital movement is based on identity and difference. Why shouldn't this phenomenon repeat itself even in the history of humanity at large?" (M; A. W. Schlegel 165).

Examples from the literary side would include Wackenroder's many depictions of both the successful and failed struggles of artists to come to terms with the repressed poles of self: Raphael finally liberates the long-slumbering "Madonna within" (prefiguring Goethe's late-Faustian "eternal feminine" and even Jung's third- or fourth-stage anima); the effete composer Josef Berglinger fails to assimilate "Leben," in the form of the Philistine courtiers surrounding him. As for Novalis, the "Hymns to the Night" live and breathe through the mystical reversal of innumerable pairs: night/day, inner/outer, ascent/descent, life/death, East/West, classical/Christian, personal/transpersonal, and so on

E. T. A. Hoffmann's greatest tale, "The Golden Pot," turns on a vision of the poet as the instrument of that Wisdom that is not opposed to ignorance. And Eichendorff's entire *oeuvre* seems a magnificently obsessive flirtation with the diaphanous boundary between pagan eros and Christian agape, typically allegorized in the rhythmic tension between a seductive nocturnal and a bracing matinal nature.

In each case, the Romantic sensibility is drawn to the protean spirit of the archetype in which a given term—madonna, wisdom, agape—seems to be both itself and the link between itself and its other. In the climax of Hoffmann's "modern fairy tale," for example, the wise old archivist/salamander Lindhorst vanquishes his mortal foe, the sorceress Liese, not with a killing blow but a transforming embrace: he smothers her in the thick, warm folds of his princely mantle. Thus, a reconciliation and, as such, a victory for a "higher third term" (the poet Anselmus, around—that is to say, *within*—whom this cosmic agon takes place) rather than for either faction. Of course, when the poet, whose soul is the object of the struggle, "wins," all of nature wins, for what is the poet but the arrival of nature at a condition of total self-awareness.[11]

In his classic elaboration of the mystical consciousness in *The Varieties of Religious Experience,* William James expresses beautifully this shifting identity of triangular forces that inspired the Romantics: "It is as if the opposites of the world, whose contradictoriness and conflict make all our difficulties and troubles, were melted into unity. Not only do they, as contrasted species, belong to one and the same genus, but *one of the species,* the nobler and better one, *is itself the genus, and so soaks up and absorbs its opposite into itself*" (298; italics James's). James, who incidentally was well schooled in German idealist philosophy, seems here almost to have had Lindhorst's absorbent mantle in mind.

## FOCUS: NOVALIS AND FRIEDRICH SCHLEGEL ON THE SELF

It is not difficult to argue from interpretations of the imaginative forms of literature to the Romantics' embrace of the *coincidentia oppositorum* as a potent source of aesthetic and spiritual inspiration, since such argument benefits from the fundamentally indeterminate nature of all interpretation. In the particular case of poetic or literary interpretation, the act of interpreting must be considered at least as creative as it is discoverative. (Indeed, in the spirit of the present inquiry one might well ask what the relationship is between these two modes of consciousness.) On the other hand, if we limit our focus to such nonimaginative forms as the aphoristic fragment and the essay, forms in which members of the Jena circle address the wide range of issues that concern them in direct and prolific exposition, the variable of interpretation is minimized, baffling and abstruse though many of the utterances remain. In many cases one need only point out what is manifestly there to convey an indelible sense of the *coincidentia oppositorum* as of the very stuff and substance of "Romantic reality"—by which I mean *all* reality, not just its aesthetic aspect (unless, of course, one broaden the scope of "aesthetic" to include all reality, as the Romantics themselves did).

For this reason I would like in this section to limit discussion primarily to the prose fragments, particularly the pivotal aperçus of Friedrich Schlegel and Novalis. Allow me, moreover, to sharpen the focus still further by confining discussion to a single theme, the theme of self, which was an intense preoccupation of both thinkers, as indeed of the early circle generally. It is also a theme that, doubtless by reason of its elusiveness and subtlety, continues to spark the interest of scholars of Romanticism today.[12]

The most important thing to know about the German Romantics' understanding of the self is that for them there *was* no self in the sense of a discrete conscious being or entity. Rather, they conceived of—and, in their best moments, experienced—the self as a relationship, indeed, as the very spirit of relationship. In Brentano's exquisite verse, "Alles ist freundlich wohlwollend verbunden" [Everything's joyously interconnected]. This wondrous sense of *Verbindung,* of the primordial interconnectedness of things, was the realization of self, which is to say, Self. Relationship was more real to the Romantics than the terms of relationship, the links between things ontologically prior to the things linked. (Which means, incidentally, that in thus "limiting" our discussion here to the Romantic concept of self, we are in paradoxical effect "opening up" the discussion to that mysterious "what?" that scintillates between *any* pair of opposites. Upon reflection a dizzying irony begins to emerge, not unlike the intended effect of the facing mirrors of F. Schlegel's famous *Athenäum* fragment 116: one has the oddly buoyant sense of finding one's ground by losing it.). Needless to say, this perspective confounds our ordinary view of the world, the view constituting what Schlegel called the "mechanischer Geist" or dualistic mind, which assumes connections or relationships to be derivative of substantial preexisting entities. But the Romantics knew from patient introspection that this was no more than a habit of conventional consciousness, which accords greater reality to the palpable objects of sense and less to the "empty air" between them. The "empty air" it was, though, that fascinated the Romantics, the typically overlooked "space" or "gap" between things, for the reason that their meditations had shown them that the emptier the mind is of its own content, the more radiant—which is to say, conscious—it becomes. This meant that the "light" of consciousness dimmed according as objects entered into it, as if, in a giddy reversal of common sense, so-called objective existence represented a subtraction from an absolutely conscious plenum, which, if fully realized, would have no (necessary) content at all. As Novalis has it, "The outer world is the shadow world; it casts its shadow over the realm of light" (M; *Werke* 327).

Those who read the Romantics as otherworldly escapists[13] generally follow the equation only this far, failing to accompany them in the next, and crucial, step of insight, which is that any sought-after *nirvana* of absolute consciousness would itself necessarily be a "content" or object, in contradistinction to the *samsara* of the relative world of objects, and hence would not be absolute at all. By definition, what exists by virtue of distinction cannot be absolute. The Romantics recognized, in other words, that the human mind was its own trap since it could only function by an act of differentiation in which one of the two terms at issue was necessarily excluded/rejected/repressed (Derrida would say "deferred"). One especially striking simile used by Novalis in the "Pollen" fragments to convey a sense of this functioning of ordinary consciousness by way of repression is that of the flautist's finger stops, that is, the enforced silencing of some notes precisely in order to express others:

> Certain inhibitions resemble the touches of a flautist, who, in order to bring forth different tones, will keep now this, now that opening shut and will thereby seem to create deliberate couplings of mute and ringing openings. (M; *Werke* 325)

This dynamic view anticipates several conceptions of human-consciousness-as-structured-by-exclusion proferred by later thinkers, to wit: Hegel's autonomous negation; Jung's intro/extraversion dynamic; and, as mentioned, Derrida's *différance,* by which the signifier indefinitely "defers" meaning.

For the Romantics any given moment of consciousness, however noble or sublime, always and of necessity left something out. The most fundamental omission, however, and one implicit in every conscious discrimination, was "the other," that which was experienced as not-self. But then, these two were themselves a binary, were they not, the result of a primordial splitting of mind, so that the true self must have more to do with this mind prior to splitting, prior to the rise of consciousness, than with the I/Not-I binary constituting consciousness. In other words, the true self was to be found on the borderline between I and Not-I, that is, in the *coincidentia oppositorum.*

Here, then, in the vital seam between self and other, self and world, subject and object, lay that absolute freedom of the True Self for which the Romantics yearned, not in some remote ethereal sphere within or without. Indeed, the very pursuit of an "inner" as opposed to an "outer" self or vice versa was an expression of that privileging or preferential desire of the binary rational consciousness that necessarily entailed bondage. Strictly speaking, the "rational" pursuit of a self chained one to two ghosts, the unattainable preferred and the inescapable rejected. This is why it is precisely *between* "within" and "without," in the very interstices of desire, that Novalis locates the Self in the "Pollen":

> The seat of the soul is to be found there where inner world and outer world touch. Where they interpenetrate, it is in each point of the interpenetration.[14] (M; *Werke* 327)

The Self was realized through penetration, and essentially what was penetrated was the illusion of an interior world as situated over against an exterior one. A leap of the mind out of itself had to be ventured, a leap from the privileged part with which one had identified to the dialectical whole that one *was*. Once made, one found oneself in a condition sometimes characterized by Novalis as *Ekstase* (the ecstasy of "standing outside" the confines of the personal or egoic self) and, at others, as *Interesse:* "Interest is taking part in the suffering and activity of a being. A thing interests me when it succeeds in moving me to this taking-part" (M; *Werke* 330–31). (One notes here Novalis's deft—and characteristic—use of Latin and Greek-derived, rather than Germanic, terms to convey a sense of the awe or gravity entailed by any dislocation of the sense of conventional identity.) For Novalis the Self was *Interesse,* literally an *inter esse* or "being between" ego and other that enabled one to "take the part" that the other was into oneself. This triangular or three-in-one dynamic of the True Self transformed separating barriers into connecting borders. Thus did consciousness expand.[15]

To speak of self is, for Novalis, to speak the language of paradox, in particular the paradox of ecstatic reciprocity. One gets a most disarming sense of the exquisite dynamism involved in the reciprocal interpenetration of opposites in the following in which Novalis affirms/negates the self as that which is always "becoming other" and the other as that which is always "becoming self." The True Self's elusion of any limiting essence is brought home not only by the statement's meaning but, perhaps more importantly, by its very rhythm, almost as if the writer were using a primitive erotics of rhythm to undermine our overly civilized obsession with "meaning" as the linguistic analogue of "essence," both these latter here exposed as phantasmic dead ends in the tortuous, delusion-prone quest for Self. This quasi-orgasmic rhythm, it will be noted, evokes the mathematical sign for infinity. Thus, Novalis's German: "Ich kann etwas nur erfahren, in so fern ich es in mir aufnehme; es ist also eine Alienation meiner selbst und eine Zueignung oder Verwandlung einer andern Substanz in die meinige zugleich" [I can only come to know something to the extent that I take it into myself; it is therefore at once an alienation of my self and an appropriation or transformation of another substance into my own] (M; Hardenberg 341). Gail Newman certainly has in mind this fundamental boundlessless of the Self in Novalis when she describes the relationship between Heinrich von Ofterdingen and Mathilde in the poet's *Bildungsroman* as a dialectical hovering the vibrational frequency of which tends toward absolute fusion: "Novalis posited the process of hovering *(Schweben)* between subjective and objective moments as the most authentic form of subjectivity, yet the two moments tend to conflate entirely at important points in his work. The two selves involved in the lovers' discourse become almost literally one self" (66).

In light of our earlier discussion of the ontological significance of the term *schweben* for Novalis, Newman's observations suggest the synonymousness for the poet of Self and Reality or Being outright. More particularly, they suggest an affinity of Novalis's mystical insight with the Buddhist metaphysical doctrine of the *sunyata,* the great fertile Void that is forever bodying forth and reabsorbing all discrete phenomena. In a kind of widening gyre, the fixed boundary that is ego can become the permeable border that is Self, which can itself "hover" freely between dynamic triangularity, the subtlest state of phenomenal existence, and Nothing. Even the *coincidentia oppositorum* itself, it would seem, when it exists as a phenomenon in pointed contradistinction to its own possible nonexistence, is a product of Itself. The Self as the absolute identity of these two, of existence and nonexistence or *samsara* and *nirvana,* is the cornerstone of Eastern mysticism. (In the concluding chapter we will observe Novalis's flirtation with this most basic phase of the Self's hovering in his fragments on time.)

The recent—and, as it strikes me, forced—efforts of scholars, alluded to at the opening of this chapter, to deny the transcendental status of the Self in Romanticism are based on the false conclusion (though one that is by now virtually unquestioned in our scientistic academic culture) that the Self's relative inaccessibility to ordinary conceptual consciousness means inaccessibility *outright* and therefore, in effect, nonexistence. But it is clear that neither Novalis nor Friedrich Schlegel sees it this way. What they *do* see is the necessity for what dialectical philosophers of consciousness from Hegel through Marx to Althusser have identified as "a move of the critique" in order to realize transcendence (Harland 95–96). This means that thought itself must actually experience its own inadequacy to the issue of Self. It must see that it is itself a mere function of Self, that Self comprehends *it* but never the reverse. Coming up thus hard against its own limits, thought abdicates, as it were, and in so doing, clears the ground for a "move of the critique," a move, that is, of consciousness, backward behind itself, so to speak, to a more comprehensive dimension, as if the eyes had suddenly jumped back to catch a glimpse of themselves. This move or leap of consciousness is the manifestation of the Self, which is both the one glimpsing and the one glimpsed, that is, the dialectical unity of subject and object. That all this occurs quite beyond the pale of logical thought, with its exclusionary unidirectional movement, has confounded the current demythologists of Romanticism who themselves cannot fathom, that is to say "think," a Self not dominated by thought.

But it is just such a "thought-free" Self (which, by the way, does not mean "vacant of thought"), realizable through an inner leap, that Novalis and Schlegel deftly imply through the occasional use of "meta" language. Novalis speaks of an "Ich seines Ichs" which he identifies with the "transzendentalen Selbst" (*Werke* 329), and Schlegel is partial to expressions such as "Philosophie der Philosophie" (87) and "poetische Poetik" (88) to suggest that the True Self functions qualitatively rather than quantitatively, that is, it inspires philosophy or poetics without necessarily "adding" to them, since all "additions" are necessarily confined within the domain of thought. Paradoxically, the Self must be free of the partial, incremental, hence, necessarily incomplete nature of thought if it is to "complete," that is, illuminate thought.

Schlegel's metalanguage also aims to suggest the Self's simultaneous transcendence of and immanence within its own conscious functions. Jaffé notwithstanding, transcendence for the Jena Romantics in no way signals aloofness or insulation from that which is transcended. *Das Ideale* is not sealed off from *das Reale* in some remote metaphysical Shangri-la. Rather, true transcendence is the freedom to *be with* the world, which is to say, with the content of one's own consciousness, whatever it may be. (Hence, Wackenroder's tragic-because-overly-sensitive musician, Josef Berglinger, is to be taken as the subject of a cautionary tale and not in any sense as an elite exemplar of true Romantic devotion to art.) This is the only way to understand Schleiermacher's famous definition of religion as "being one with the Infinite in the midst of the finite." And it is why Schlegel rejects any form of censorship on principle and does not hesitate to recommend the literary exploration of even the most repugnant of human impulses, for the blackest of hearts is always already transfigured when viewed in the light of the Self:

> If, out of psychological interest, one writes novels or reads novels, then it is quite illogical and petty to wish to avoid even the most long-drawn-out and detailed dissection of unnatural desires, ghastly torments, hair-raising infamy or disgusting sensual or spiritual decadence. (M; 94)

Here the themes of thought and beauty touch, as we see in the Romantic Self the coalescence, not only of thought and no-thought, but also of beauty and ugliness, an aesthetic apotheosis not unlike that of Kafka's hideous sirens with their sterile wombs (symbolizing perhaps his profound ambivalence toward his "call" to writing) who could not help it "that their lament sounded so beautiful." It is precisely within the sterile womb that the most exquisite beauty may gestate. As with single terms, so too with polarities: thought/no-thought, beauty/ugliness, the Romantic Self does not favor one over another (to do so would unilateralize the dialectic) but manifests itself indiscriminately, as it were, in the interstices of any pair, or pair of pairs.

The notion of the Self as coupling or marriage is, if possible, even more pervasive in Schlegel than Novalis. This becomes evident once one grasps that the myriad antinomies with which Schlegel plays in the *Athenäum* fragments are to be understood as dynamic, transparent, mutually interpenetrating phases of the illumined consciousness rather than discrete and sedentary "bookends" holding upright a linear world of volumes. Thus, *real* and *ideal, Absicht* and *Instinkt, Historiker* and *Prophet, System* and *kein System, Sympoesie,* and the "zwei befreundete Gedanken" [two befriended thoughts] that provide the alchemy for "witzige Einfälle" [flashes of wit] (89–94) are all seamless correlates of Mind, not composite spheres "out there" or "in here" (further correlates).

But *what* mind, *whose* mind, one demands. The very questions assume dichotomies (individual/collective, personal/impersonal, possessor/possessed) that are themselves categorical structures of the delusive binarist mind (again, "mechanischer Geist," in Schlegel's expression). There is for Schlegel just Mind, just Consciousness, just Self, all connoted for him in the term "organischer Geist" (102, 104), the ground-zero dialectical mind of *Genie* that infinitely supersedes its own lower "human, all too human" stages, "chemischer Geist" (wit) and "mechanischer Geist" (intellect) (102), which are by nature given to "a one-sided . . . ideal. . . . [B]ut the antitheses to these are missing" (M; 104). In the Romantic Self both thesis and antithesis are always present; indeed, each exists solely to "present" the other in an ongoing "mutual saturation of all forms and all substances" (M; 106). The delusive mind, be it *mechanisch* or even *chemisch* (an evolved intermediate consciousness enjoying occasional flashes of illumination, somewhat like a flickering lightbulb not yet firmly screwed in), exists by virtue of the repression of the antithesis (cf. Derrida's *différance*); the Enlightened Mind or Self heralds the return of the repressed, culminating in an embrace ("mutual saturation," or perhaps even deconstruction's "aporia," that luminous moment in which a text is reunited in the reader's mind with its own negation or anti-text).[16]

It should be clear from the foregoing excursus on the Romantic Self that German Romanticism is in fundamental accord with those *Weltanschauungen,* religious or quasi-religious, that deny the validity of an autonomous individual ego, such as Buddhism with its pivotal anatmic or no-self doctrine. In fact, one might view Romanticism as a link between very ancient and very modern, indeed postmodern, perspectives on the ego, historically situated as it is between Buddhism and the recent "death-of-the-author" proclaimed by deconstruction, an intellectual-spiritual force that has probably yet to tap fully its own resources of mystical insight.[17] Derrida's and de Man's insistence on regarding all foundational Western values (self, essence, truth, etc.) as decentered and their obsessive fascination with undecidability and aporia, dialectical phenomena so seemingly akin to Novalis's "hovering" and Schlegel's "mutual saturation," give one pause to wonder just how new deconstruction really is. If one object that deconstruction keeps its focus narrowly trained on the self-negating gestures of language, while the purview of Romanticism is cosmic, I would simply cite Harland's observation that "Derrida expands his theory of language into a philosophy of the world *as* language" (141). In any case, as I hope to demonstrate more fully in the concluding chapter of this book, we are far from closing our accounts with the subtle and complex relations that seem to obtain between these two heterodox Western paradigms.

## SCHOLARSHIP AS ENACTMENT OF ROMANTICISM

Once one comes to appreciate fully that for the Romantics *das Reale* and *das Ideale* are neither separate nor merely linked (both dualistic positions) but *absolutely identical,* then the scholarly debate between the traditional millenialists and the current poststructuralists over Romantic transcendence begins to take on the surreal contours of an Escher engraving: Is it black geese that are flying East or white geese that are flying West? No matter which position one takes, the counterposition is forever disturbing one's barely settled view. At some point the theoretical debate begins to wobble and soon collapses in on its own insubstantiality. In that moment the irony of ironies is realized as the debate, heretofore like all scholarly argument a quest for a "truth" or "meaning" or "understanding" not quite yet in view, is transformed into the very enactment of Romantic "hovering." In a stunning manifestation of the *coincidentia oppositorum,* the debate itself has become what it presumed to be pointing to; the signifier has become the signified. Now the debate is a dance, and the dance can go on forever, *being* Romanticism even as it forever falls short of *meaning* it.

It will be clear by now why, at the outset of this essay, I remained noncommittal in the scholarly debate over "Romantic transcendence." To have taken a position would have been to violate the very spirit of Romanticism which is the spirit of the *coincidentia oppositorum*. Romantic transcendence consists in this very freedom within—or better yet, freedom as—the dialectical dance of transcendence and immanence, conditions now revealed to be in some mysterious way both different and identical. Romanticism is, in the end, all about the exhilarating emancipation from any and all positions, a dynamic a-positionality which alone fully discloses the bedrock "reality" of any given position, which is empty. But then this emptiness is fullness itself; kenosis is plerosis. And so it goes, on and on.

Even to affirm, as I do here, that Romanticism is the lively and enchanting dance of a-positionality is to run the risk of reifying the unreifiable.[18] Older scholars such as Gero von Wilpert who stress above all the sheer undefinability of Romanticism seem to me to come closest to the spiritual mark (525).[19] If it be objected that this amounts to an intellectual nihilism that abrogates the obligation of scholarship to do all it can to establish the "facts of the matter," I can only reply that a closer look will reveal it to be rather a humility that brings one up hard against the existential limits of factual scholarship. But then, to be truly humbled by one's own scholarly ignorance is already to have taken a small step into that condition of Mind known, at a certain Western cultural-historical juncture, by the name of Romanticism. Scholarship that thus reveals its own limitations has served its purpose well indeed.

2

# Merton's "Rilke," Rilke's "Merton": From an Unpublished Notebook

> A poet is someone who has been struck by lightning at least once. A great poet has been struck about seventeen times.
>
> —Seamus Heaney

It is no exaggeration to observe that, in the poetry of Rainer Maria Rilke, German Romanticism comes of age. With the possible exception of Nietzsche's *Zarathustra,* nowhere is the Jena Romantic quest for the *coincidentia oppositorum* more profoundly realized than in the *Duino Elegies* and *Sonnets to Orpheus,* cycles launched by Rilke in paroxysms of inspiration in a castle on a cliff overlooking the Adriatic more than a century later. And, in an expansion of the sphere of influence some forty years after that, the spiritual power burgeoning from Rilke's verse drew into its orbit the mind and heart of American Trappist monk Thomas Merton, who late in life spent a few months grappling with the sonnets' and, particularly, the elegies' elusive paradoxes. In the course of his labors, Merton grew more and more uneasily aware that, in seriously taking on Rilke, he was getting much more than he had bargained for, for the German poet had the temerity to "exhume" in intensified form many troubling spiritual, theological, and philosophical issues the monk thought he had long ago laid to rest (but had merely "buried alive")—not to mention raising a few new ones.

On the basis of his private unpublished notes, this chapter traces the fascinating evolution of Thomas Merton's intense relationship to Rainer Maria Rilke over a four-month span in the mid-1960s. It shows the course of that relationship to have been shaped by a stunning ambivalence, a consuming psychospiritual dialectic culminating finally in Merton's liberating experience of the *coincidentia* shortly before his death. What begins as curiosity and attraction quickly darkens into a nervous defensiveness as Rilke's transessential Orphic vision, at once Romantic and pre-postmodern, challenges the monk's cherished conclusions and assumptions about the nature of spirit and poetry, and, ultimately, his own identity. Yet at the same time, guided and fortified by his contemplation of the Zen philosopher Nishida's essay on "The Unity of Opposites," Merton occasionally drops his guard long enough to experience sudden flashes of insight into the poet's sublime intent. These insights bring him into an almost unwitting consonance with a spiritual vision normally threatening to his Catholic world view. Courageously the monk perseveres in this stressful ambivalence, this existential "being buffeted about" by the pairs. At first the ambivalence is only implicit, reflected in his oscillating hot-and-cold reactions to Rilke's work and life, but finally Merton becomes aware of the problematic complexity of his own response to the poet as he focuses his attention on three passages in the first "Duino Elegy" that contain explicit images of the identity of opposites. His contemplation of these images leads him ever more deeply into the mystery of the *coincidentia.*

The subtitles of the chapter sections cue the conflictual phases of the relationship as it lurches fearfully yet inevitably toward epiphany. In the end it is clear that Rainer Maria Rilke was for Thomas Merton a spiritual gift disguised as a problem, a late and timely form (appearing as it did just a few years before his untimely death) of what Zen would call his life koan.

## BACKGROUND

It is hard to think of a modern writer in the West whose work is a busier conduit of global intellectual-historical crosscurrents than that of Thomas Merton. From ancient to modern, sacred to secular, East to West, there seems scarcely a philosopher, critic, artist, or poet of any consequence who has not found his way into one of the great monk's innumerable vehicles of self-expression, be it essay, tract, journal, notebook, diary, novel, poem, or even audio and video tape. As rich primary materials continue to appear in print even now, almost thirty years after Merton's death, it is all the secondary "production" can do to keep up.[1] It turns out, for example, that in the few years before his untimely death in December 1968 Merton corresponded with the Syracuse University library staff and was moved to give the library a small collection of partly published, partly unpublished personal papers dating from the last five years of his life (Keenan 157).

By far the most interesting part of the collection for the researcher is a group of ten unpublished notebooks filled between 1963 and 1967. Along with sketches of projects, rough drafts of some of his own poems and translations of others', these spiral binders contain occasional handwritten notes made in response to a profusion of quotations recorded from the works of various writers and thinkers whom Merton was studying in his last years. Prominent names among those most frequently quoted include Simone Weil, Maritain, Schiller, Eckhart, Sartre, Artaud, Faulkner, Kafka, and, at length, Camus. The chronologically fourth of these notebooks, covering the period from November 1965 to late February 1966, should be of particular interest to Merton scholars because it features his only known extended exegesis of a great modern poet, Rainer Maria Rilke, whose dense and difficult German verse presented the polyglot Merton with one of his greatest linguistic and literary-critical challenges.

Here is Merton, so at home in the Romance and classical tongues, armed now with bilingual dictionaries, translations, and commentaries, negotiating heroically and with great skill the Teutonic labyrinth of Rilke's highly idiosyncratic syntax and opaque neologisms. Over the course of some one hundred twenty pages of notes, Merton tackles head-on both the "Duino Elegies" and the "Sonnets to Orpheus," two of the most demanding lyric cycles in all of German spiritual literature. Interspersed with critical observations, casual speculations, and questions are rough but complete verse translations of five of the "Sonnets." One gets a clear sense of the poet's sensitivity in translating the verse of a kindred spirit, however ill at ease he may otherwise have been in German, from his rendering of Rilke's terse lyric, "Rose, O reiner Widerspruch, Lust/ Niemandes Schlaf zu sein unter soviel/ Lidern": "Rose, O pure/ Contradiction/ Longing to be nobody's/ Sleep under so many/ Lids."[2]

Kindred spirits though they be, we must remember to take the term not only in its ordinary meaning of honest affinity but also in its more opaque sense of the mysterious kinship that always exists between a self(-image) and its alter ego. For the construction of Rilke that emerges from these notebook pages is a fascinatingly complex and at times even contradictory one, and certainly reveals as much about the note taker as his subject. For this reason I have chosen in these pages to read the notebook essentially as equal parts autobiography and critique. Indeed, we have here a most intimate personal account of a man as he reveals himself to be a kind of "work in progress" toward the *coincidentia oppositorum,* driven to spiritual epiphany by the "insoluble problem" of Rainer Maria Rilke.

Inasmuch as these notes are Merton's unguarded preliminary impressions of Rilke, hastily written down during actual periods of study, riddled with crossings-out, connecting arrows, and recurrent self-questionings as to whether he has grasped Rilke on this or that point, they do not have anything like the stylistic polish, argumentative consistency, or self-assured tone we are used to from such finished contemporaneous journals as, say, *Conjectures of a Guilty Bystander* (1965). But they are for that reason all the richer in terms of authorial spontaneity and self-revelation. One is even tempted to say there is a paradox here in that we intuit more of Rilke's poetic power through the private stammerings and uncertainties flowing from the fountain pen of a man of Merton's stature than we might have, had the notebook found its way to print via the usual editorial "repair." In the pages that follow, then, it seems fair to say we will be examining more a mutual, and a mutually illuminating, than a one-way relationship; we will be examining "Rilke's 'Merton'" no less than "Merton's 'Rilke.'"

## IN FEAR OF RILKE

What leaps out at the reader of Merton's notebook, and fascinates, is the palpable tension of ambivalence. As the primary focus of attention, Rilke seems virtually to generate two Mertons, one who fears him and one who reveres him, neither knowing quite what to make of the other. While it is obvious that Merton shares the general opinion of Rilke as one touched with a rare poetic and spiritual genius, it is also clear that he is at times made uncomfortable by that genius, and for reasons, as we shall see, that explain a great deal about the dialectic between his own interior life and his intellectual-historical situation. We find, for example, a curious incongruity between his admiring general description of Rilke to the monks, in one of his taped Sunday afternoon talks, as a poet operating "on a deep level,"[3] "an angelic poet . . . filled with prophetic speech" (CC AA2076, side 2) and some of the private remarks jotted down in his notebook around the same time, remarks that betray a nervous uncertainty over the sweep of Rilke's spiritual insight. Take, in particular, his response to the fifth "Sonnet to Orpheus," part 1, which exalts that god's transformative power. After writing down a rough translation, as follows:

Set up no memorial stone. Only allow the roses
Each year to bloom for his sake.
For it is Orpheus. His constant changing
Into this and this. We should not care

To find another name. Once for all
It's Orpheus, when it sings. He comes & goes.
Is it not much, if he sometimes a day or two
Overcomes the outer Rose-shell?

How you need to grasp the fact that he must vanish.
Though he himself is anxious in his vanishing.
Just when his word overcomes the Here-ness,
He is already there where you cannot follow.
The lyre's fence of strings does not constrain his hands.
He obeys where he has already passed on.[4] (108)

Merton appends elliptically: "This sonnet—a key to his phenomenology—his idea of the poetic instant—creative inwardness not the grasp of a secret and static *essence* but of 'Orpheus' in his passing." And immediately thereafter: "Here R[ilke] is indeed disquieting in a way—his spiritistic aspect" (108; emphasis Merton's).

What does Merton mean by Rilke's "spiritistic aspect" and why should he find this "disquieting"? What I want to do here is suggest answers to these and similar questions raised by the notebook that I believe give us a dramatic yet accurate portrait of Merton as a man caught up in a nexus of longstanding inner conflicts, conflicts that were at once intellectual, psychological, and spiritual, and, in that strange way of insoluble conflicts that grip the whole man, intensely fertile. "Spiritistic" is Merton's way of characterizing Rilke's Orpheus-symbol, lexically an oddly theological adjective and yet one quite properly emphasizing the unfixed, endlessly protean nature of the poetic consciousness. Since the poet is forever moving toward, in the sense of creatively assimilating, that which he encounters, he can be said to have—or rather, to *be*—no discrete self; he is, as Keats put it, "forever filling some other body." Or as Merton writes here: the poet is "'Orpheus' in his passing." This particular sonnet dwells, with an exclusivity verging on obsession, on this elusive, will-o'-the-wisp quality of poetic vision; it is perhaps the one thing that cannot be rationally "bottled." That which man cannot in some way trap with his intellect makes him anxious, and that which makes him anxious tends to obsess him. Thus, the poem portrays what is traditionally rhapsodized as the soaring freedom of the poetic consciousness from the all-too-human point of view as a spectral object of dread.

Of course, Merton gives a close rendering of this human perspective in all its benighted anxiety in such turns of translated phrase as "[s]et up no memorial stone . . . [h]ow you need to grasp the fact . . . anxious in his vanishing . . . where you cannot follow." And it is just here, I think, in his faithful recreation of Rilke's portrayal of our dis-ease with the fact of poetic inscrutability that Merton's own dis-ease, or "disquiet," arises. Poet though, or shall we say because, he himself be, Merton is not at all at ease with the notion that the poet's "creative inwardness [is] not the grasp of a secret and static *essence* but of 'Orpheus' in his passing." To put it in terms of Merton's peculiar position in his own intellectual-historical milieu, this is Merton the Christian essentialist humanist covertly at odds with Merton the proto-post-structuralist poet.

To put it in Goethean terms, this is Merton sensing that he holds, and is therefore caught between, mutually exclusive world views, one of whose ordering principles is *Dauer,* the other *Wechsel.* His disquiet reflects his anxiety over being swept up in the great intellectual-historical paradigm shift of his—and *our*—time, one in which all thoughtful humanist scholars continue to find themselves embroiled: the shift, with all its attendant horrific birth-pangs, from modernism to postmodernism. Notwithstanding his mystical bent, his liberal theological views, and his generous reaching-out to the religious Other (e.g., *Zen and the Birds of Appetite; The Asian Journal*), part of Merton remained to the end the more or less doctrinaire Catholic monk with a respect for theological distinctions and a spiritual-emotional investment in such traditional essences as "soul," "human nature," and "God," conceived of as "*a* God."

But if Merton's moral allegiance was with the essentialist tradition of his Catholic faith and of the culture at large, both grounded in the rational psychology of Aristotle and Aquinas, his poet's heart belonged to the nascent postmodern "world without a center," a world in which all hallowed categorical values were suddenly, and traumatically, problematic. The stable "soul" of old, no less than its modern psychologized model, the "self," was becoming the phantom signified; "human nature," or even "man" were suddenly found to be mere metaphors; and "God," already reeling from the Death-of-God theology of the early '60s, was now being unmasked as a construction of ideology. In sum, the curtain before which the Ozzian illusion of eternal verities had so long cast its spell was being lifted to expose a wizardless self-working set of levers called language.

True, Merton finished his notebook some two years prior to the publication in 1967 of Jacques Derrida's three key books (*La Voix et le phenomene,*

*De la grammatologie,* and *L'Ecriture et la difference*), an event considered by many to have singlehandedly changed French structuralism into poststructuralism (Gras 277); and some three years prior to the two ensuing "capping events," the Paris student riots of May 1968 and the first international deconstructionist symposium held at the Johns Hopkins University in Baltimore in the fall of the same year. But Merton was already clearly sensing the tremors at least as early as 1964. Francophile and fluent in French as he was, he had read Roland Barthes's two early seminal works, *On Racine* and *Essais Critiques* (both 1964), and was intrigued by Barthes's assertions as to the nonreferential nature of literary language, a notion that would culminate four years later in the provocative *Writing Degree Zero,* a book reviewed by Merton with enthusiastic approval in September 1968 (Merton, *Literary Essays* 140–46). Thus, by the time he began his notebook jottings on Rilke in November 1965, Merton was already quite at home with the idea that poetic language, if not indeed *all* language, was concerned only with its own utterance, its own unfolding. What did not sit at all well with him, I would argue, was the idea's immediate and unavoidable implication: that if language is systemically self-contained, what it presumes at its noblest to articulate, e.g., spiritual values and verities, becomes inaccessible and, consequently, ontologically problematic. This, I believe, is precisely the "spiritistic aspect" of Rilke's sonnet that Merton finds "disquieting," for, among other things, Rilke's Orpheus-symbol is meant to suggest, as Merton well recognized, a fundamental Reality, channeled through the absolute fluidity of poetic language, in which all boundaries are dissolved, including the boundary by which alone we are enabled to speak of "*a* God."

Beyond the spiritual insight afforded by his own personal capacity, Rilke also had more than a century of German Romantic tradition to support him in his own anxious broaching of this awesome sphere of no-boundary awareness. The precedent provided by such mystical poets as Novalis and Brentano, and by such neo-Romantic thinkers as the Nietzsche who wrote *Zarathustra,* was certainly a profound comfort to him in his own inner explorations. On the other hand, of the several Western European cultural traditions, the cosmopolitan Merton was probably least at home in German Romanticism and so could not easily invoke its support of his own burgeoning postmodernist vision.[5]

All this implies, I must confess, two bold presuppositions on my part which it is time to state outright. The first, aesthetic, is that religious or spiritual poetry is always fundamentally "Romantic," the term understood in the sense of the perennial nature of the spiritual project in which the German Romantics felt themselves to be caught up. By this I mean that "deep" poetry, regardless of cultural-historical circumstance, always aims, deliberately or not, at that ultimate ontological synthesis so fervently sought by the German Romantic poets and known in the world's Wisdom traditions variously as the Kingdom of God, or the Pure Land, or, put subjectively, Illumination, or Enlightenment, or *satori*. The second presupposition, historical, is that postmodernism is, surface incongruities (even seeming contradictions) notwithstanding, in many important ways a reincarnation of the no-boundary world view of German Romantic Idealism. It is no accident that Foucault's and Derrida's *engagement* is above all with the thought of Hegel, Nietzsche, and Heidegger, each in his own way rooted deeply in the dialectical intellectual style of the early Jena Romantics. There is much in common between the deconstructionist notions of *différance* and aporia and the dialectical energies animating certain "decentered" Romantic notions, such as Schlegel's concept of *Symphilosophie,* or Schelling's view of the interplay of *Geist* and *Natur,* or Novalis's notion of the self as a *Schweben* (hovering) between *ich* and *du.* [6] The objection that postmodernism abhors metaphysics usually rests on the assumption that Romanticism exalts it,[7] an assumption that reads the latter movement superficially as a monolithic and millenarian quest for Presence (e.g., F. Schlegel's imminent "goldenes Zeitalter") and ignores the key Romantic attitude of irony that dialectically "deconstructs" any such presumed quest with the flash of insight that what is being quested after is, lo and behold, already here.[8]

This brings us back to our main point, which is that the relative inaccessibility to Merton of this understanding of German Romanticism as a forerunner of postmodernism left him somewhat unprepared psychologically for Rilke's Orphic, or proto-postmodern, vision. What appealed to him in Barthes concerning the non-referential nature of literary language disquieted him in Rilke where its implications of metaphysical or cosmic delusion were clearly manifest. It is just possible that Merton's anxiety on this score is reflected in the one—quite significant—translating error he made in an otherwise flawless effort. The last line of Rilke's sonnet reads: "Und er [Orpheus] gehorcht, indem er überschreitet" (*Werke* I, 490), which Merton renders wrongly and ineffectually as: "He obeys where he has already passed on." In mistranslating the conjunction *indem* and the verb *überschreitet* Merton totally misses the thundering paradox that ends the poem as it captures Orpheus's essenceless essence. Accurately translated, the line reads: "And he obeys by transgressing." The god is truest to himself (most *gehorsam*) when he violates the very notion of self or nature. It is Orpheus's nature *to have no nature* and, indeed, to *überschreiten*, that is, to "step beyond" or deconstruct, all putative discrete "natures," not excluding "*the* Divine Nature," the instant he encounters them. Orpheus is the transessential mythical embodiment of the *coincidentia oppositorum*. One is left to wonder whether Merton's error was, in origin, simply intellectual, in my view not very likely considering his discerning linguistic sense, or, more tellingly, psycho-spiritual, the symptom of a shrinking-back from a Truth sensed to be overwhelming.

To say that he was made nervous by the depth and power of Rilke's mystical insight into the *coincidentia* is by no means to do Merton a disservice, for he was a gifted mystic himself and his anxiety is to be taken, I think, as that of a believer who is deeply immersed in the Mystery and thus in a continual struggle to integrate its awesome implications into his rational theological understanding. Merton's nervousness before Rilke is therefore in the deepest sense just another mask of the struggle with self, with the perennial "zwei Seelen," to paraphrase Goethe's Faust, "die in meiner Brust wohnen." (The irony of putting it this way in light of the very de-centering at issue here does not escape the present "author.") The Zen Buddhist tradition, to which the mystic in Merton felt strongly drawn, makes a sharp distinction between a practitioner's early *kensho* experience, which is fleeting, and the total integration of that experience into "everyday mind," which is the project of "innumerable lifetimes."

It is in this implied context of spiritual growth through self-struggle, the struggle with a strangely attractive-repulsive alter ego, this struggle itself a prototype of an inchoate shift in the intellectual-cultural paradigm, that many of Merton's rather disparaging notes on a poet he clearly respects are to be taken. One can discern in them a number of intellectual-psychological strategies employed by the monk to keep Rilke's sensed spiritual power at bay, to keep his genie "in the bottle," as it were, though perhaps with the cork just barely inserted. Thus, for instance, his tendency to interpret Rilke's *Innerlichkeit* (inwardness), a kind of catch-all label of '40s and '50s commentators for the poet's obvious spiritual quality, in a demeaning way as a kind of fixated emotional self-absorption. With apparent approval he cites caustic critics such as Hans Egon Holthusen (*Der späte Rilke*, 1949) for whom "R's work [was] concerned 'with one theme only—with feeling as the measure of all being and all knowledge'" (5). The common midcentury view of Rilke's poetry as an apotheosis of feeling was but a short step from the charge of narcissism, a charge only aided and abetted, alas, by Rilke's doting on the symbol of Narcissus (though from anything but the conventional psycho-pathological perspective on the myth).[9] Thus, Merton characterizes the above-quoted "Rose, O reiner Widerspruch" as a "self-contained 'handful of inwardness,'" prefacing this with the remark: "Here is the whole question: whether Rilke was really able to get beyond a Narcissistic inwardness" (50–51).[10]

As if trying to build a case in his own mind for Rilke's mysticism as a grandiose cloak for what is at base merely "neurotic deficiency" (104), Merton piles paraphrase on paraphrase of Holthusen and like-minded critics: "God ceases to be transcendent [and] becomes a creature of man's feeling" (5); "Both the greatness & the limitation of his manner of writing lie in its radical subjectivism . . . a personal myth here replaces religion . . . 'a myth of omniscient and omnipotent feeling'" (7). The noted philosopher of religion Romano Guardini (*Rainer Maria Rilkes Deutung des Daseins,* 1953) is enlisted in the diagnosis of Rilke's crippling limitations in the sphere of interpersonal love: "R. was limited psychologically and was inhibited in interpersonal love.—'Certainly R. gained from this weakness an added sensitiveness to life which he would otherwise have lacked! This must not blind us however to the fact that R's view is *fundamentally false*'" (106; emphasis Merton's). Then, as if wishing to mitigate the harshness of such a pronouncement, Merton adjudges as "judicious, sensitive and fair" a more thoughtful speculation of Guardini's: "Underlying his [Rilke's] ideas on the subject [of love] there is something more profound—an experience & a demand which were doubtless connected with his inability to love but were also rooted in a fundamentally religious impulse" (107).[11]

The project of demystifying the mysticism of a poet who happened to be radically anti-Christian, the reduction of that mysticism to psycholgical aberration, could only be hindered by the views of a critic such as Erich Heller for whom the validity and maturity of Rilke's spiritual insight were not an issue; indeed, who dubbed Rilke "the St. Francis of the Will to Power" (*Disinherited Mind* 105). To Heller's assertion, noted by Merton, that "theirs [i.e., Nietzsche's and Rilke's] are the only personal accounts we possess in modern literature of states of inspiration," Merton adds the cynical, if hilarious, qualifier: "(until the psychedelics came along!)" (52). In a similar mood, comparing Heller's brief *for* Rilke's mysticism with Guardini's *against* it, Merton ends his reflection on a text of the latter's with a terse dismissal of the former: "The more we study passages like this the more we see Heller is all wet" (104). While it is only too easy to second guess Merton's critique of the critics from the vantage point of today, yet one cannot help but remark that Erich Heller's essays on Rilke still belong on the bookshelf of any serious Rilke scholar, while the books of Holthusen, Guardini, and so many others who share their reductionism languish unread in the dusty Dewey-decimal section of most research stacks. Did Merton make a genuine effort to open himself to Rilke's spiritual vision, with all its personal idiosyncrasies, or was he more often preoccupied with making the case against someone sensed, however dimly, as a threat?

Other strategies that strike the reader of these notes as defensive include an insistence on the "purely" psychological, as opposed to religious, significance of Rilke's most important prose work, the autobiographical novel of his Paris years, *Die Aufzeichnungen des Malte Laurids Brigge* (1910): "Start with parable of the prodigal—end of Malte LB. (Obviously insuffient as a religious statement, but it is not intended as one. It is purely human and psychological.)" (9). In another place Rilke is granted mystical status but of an order far below that of someone like Eckhart: "Two kinds of mysticism. The higher is the 'abyss' mysticism. See Ruysbroeck, Eckhart." Accounting for this second-class status is, again, Rilke's stunted capacity for interpersonal love which, Guardini persuades him, led to his having "lost sight of the essential meaning of love!— This meant an 'inner vacuity' which even infected his relation to God" (106). Elsewhere, commenting on the first part of Rilke's early lyric collection, *Das Stundenbuch* (1905), Merton makes an amusing comparison of the poet's "inferior" mysticism to the oftentimes artificial zeal of the young monks under his spiritual direction at Gethsemani: "Book of Hours.- note that the 'inwardness' and the 'converse with God' are definitely wilful and forced. 'Novice' piety! Lack of surrender. Using and 'having' God. 'Willing' God" (39). Although Merton notes some "progress in Pt II" on the poet's part toward a less possessive attitude to God, citing as case in point the powerful "Du musst nicht bangen, Gott" [You need not fear, my God] (M; 39), essentially for him the question remains "whether Rilke was really able to get beyond a Narcissistic inwardness."

But by far the most interesting and revealing intellectual attempt by Merton to come to terms with the whole question of Rilke's spiritual legitimacy occurs in an extended passage located just short of midway in the notebook. It is in this passage, I believe, that the confessional autobiographical aspect of Merton's relationship to Rilke, what we might call his "projected personal agenda," is most apparent. It needs to be quoted in full:

> Question of Rilke as 'mystic' is irrelevant.
> In him the contradiction between poetry and mysticism was lived (not resolved). He decided on being a poet and was completely, authentically a poet & nothing else—a poet & *not* a mystic.
>
> The question is not was he an authentic mystic but was he an authentic poet.
>
> This question is not taken seriously enough because it is assumed that all poets are easily 'authentic poets' which is not the case. Most poets have a bit of a gift & play around with it, but

> they are not fully and completely poets & do not really develop the poetic vision & live as poets (seers & singers). (Same with painters. Cezanne was a painter.)
>
> We assume R. quite naturally did what was "easier", & only question the "harder" achievement. Is it any "easier" to be a poet than to be a mystic?
>
> Is it not possible that by his poetic authenticity he has a religious value & points [to] where he himself did not go?
>
> *He dared to remain ambiguous.* (51; emphasis Merton's)

Here we have a most vivid expression of an inner conflict with which Merton doubtless wrestled for his entire adult life: that between the mystic and the poet, or between the religious and the secular seer. For what strikes us in these particular jottings is his insistance, with reference to Rilke, on keeping the categories of "poet" and "mystic" strictly separate and their simultaneous refusal in his mind to remain so: on the one hand, Rilke "lived the contradiction between poetry and mysticism," daring "to remain ambiguous"; yet on the other, there was no such contradiction in Rilke at all: "He decided on being a poet and was completely, authentically a poet & nothing else—a poet & *not* a mystic." I think Merton's confusion here is best understood as reflecting his chronic inability to bring about any final reconciliation between these two fundamental poles of his own identity. Merton vacillated between his Catholic need to secure for himself an untaintedly religious self-definition (priest, spiritual mentor, contemplative), this the polar opposite of his alter ego Rilke who was "a poet & *not* a mystic," and his deeper, truer sense of himself as one in conflict over the issue, a conflict also projected here onto Rilke.

But there is no indication that Rilke was troubled by this issue, that he felt himself to be living such a contradiction or to be walking any perilous tightrope strung out over tensely adjacent sacred and secular spiritual realms. As for mystical literature per se, he had little use for it, lumping it together with systematic philosophy as irrelevant abstraction.[12] It is unlikely that the category *mystic* had any personal meaning for him (though what the term *mystical experience* generally refers to certainly did), or that it played any part in his understanding of the poet's mission.

In other words, in Rilke the sacred and the profane were not at odds, and for the same reason that the current transition from the modernist to the postmodernist era would have passed for him without strife (indeed, he would have shuttled back and forth between the two with delight): the German Romantic tradition. The Novalis who pronounced, "Poet and priest were at one time one," and the Nietzsche who had his Superman intone, "I am the one in whom all contradictions are united," were part of the literary-cultural air Rilke breathed. In fact, the early Romantics had made it part of their collective agenda to re-sacralize poetry which they felt had fallen into a kind of secularist-intellectualist stasis since the days of the great Baroque mystic, Jakob Böhme.[13] Of course, for them this "fall" of poetry, as an aspect of the Fall itself, was basically a matter of a lapse in consciousness, having nothing to do with any decline in so-called "objective quality." For the Romantics—and for their heir, Rilke, in whom one could say that their vision came of age—poetry was intrinsically sacred and could only *appear* to be less than that through a prosaic dimming of the overall poetic consciousness of a culture.[14]

On the other hand, Thomas Merton did indeed live what was for him "the contradiction between poetry and mysticism." As biographers' accounts of troubled discussions of the issue with his superiors during the early monastic years reveal, he vacillated between regarding his own writing as something akin to a basic need and as a self-indulgence with potentially deleterious spiritual consequences.[15] One of his coping strategies was to hierarchize the poetic and the mystical, with the latter as "top dog." An example of this would be the rhetorical question (perhaps more anguished than rhetorical) posed in the notebook excerpt quoted above, ostensibly about Rilke: "Is it not possible that by his poetic authenticity he has a religious value & points [to] where he himself did not go?" The poet would thus seem capable of rising to the level of a kind of second-order seer, though yet barred, as such, from the domain of deep mystical revelation.[16] Whether Merton thought of himself in these terms strikes one as an obvious and yet, ultimately, imponderable question. One *could* give an autobiographical reading to the central paragraph in the above excerpt, in which he gives an unmistakably sacerdotal description of the poetic vocation, as a possible clue that he did regard himself this way, at least at times: "Most poets have a bit of a gift & play around with it, but they are not fully and completely poets & do not really develop the poetic vision & live as poets (seers & singers)." Certainly in his own eyes Merton was both poet and priest, and did his best to live the austere life he saw as quintessential to both callings. Whether this poet-priest identity effectively meant for him something less than true mystical initiation, we can only wonder.

Adding the evidence of this "unmonitored," hastily filled notebook to the mix of other discussions of the issue, one would have to conclude there is no simple summing-up of the contours of the poet-versus-mystic dilemma in Merton's scheme of values, nor any final reconciling of mind and heart to be found. Quite the contrary, the Merton who penned these notes is like a Rinzai Zen student in the grip of a powerful "life koan," plumbing the depths of the unfathomable by assuming all possible roles, positions, and perspectives in turn, moving even into the teeth of contradiction. Take, for example, his tendency in other sections of the notebook, sections on subjects other than Rilke, to leave the issue of mysticism per se aside and affirm *poiesis,* the pure creative in-seeing of the poet, as the principle by which "one must approach reality" (92). Here Merton seems to align himself with the views of the contemporary Japanese philosopher, Nishida Kitaro (1870–1945), who, after Rilke, is the subject of his most sustained attention in the notebook, occupying about one-quarter of the pages.

Nishida's philosophy of "immediate experience" is grounded in Zen meditation; yet it has been significantly shaped by a profound understanding of the Western rationalist religio-philosophical tradition (he read both English and German fluently). Despite the occasional question or doubt, that philosophy finds great favor with the already Zen-inclined Merton, who reviews and takes detailed notes here on two key essays: "The Intelligible World" and "The Unity of Opposites," both appearing in a volume of translated works used by Merton, entitled *Intelligibility and the Philosophy of Nothingness* (1958). What is interesting here in light of the present discussion is Merton's enthusiasm for Nishida's exalting precisely of *poiesis* as the key to mystical understanding, a notion that, oddly enough, reminds him explicitly of Rilke, this after having denied Rilke, precisely *as poet,* mystical capability. After summarizing Nishida's basic position that the world, as a creative process generated by the unity of opposites, is always moving "from formed to forming," Merton concludes by quoting the philosopher's view of the world as "essentially a world of poiesis." On this Merton comments in brackets, "This is Rilke exactly!" (85).

On several other occasions as well, Nishida's "world of mystic intuition, unapproachable by word or thinking" (qtd. p. 77) strikes Merton as a world shared by Rilke. Opposite quotation of the philosopher's aesthetic view that "[s]ubjective activity of the personality has the highest degree of objectivity when perfect harmony of the outward & inward has been achieved in a beautiful form," Merton writes in shorthand, "of Rilke" (66–67), probably having in mind the poet's project in the *Neue Gedichte* (1907) of achieving a contemplative fusion with the object of poetic description: Rilke's "Panther" is more than a panther—it is nature's mystical awakening to itself through the poet.[17] To Nishida's assertion that "the intelligible world [i.e., the highest realm of consciousness] transcends our thinking," Merton nods his assent with a corresponding metaphor of the Ineffable from the first "Duino Elegy": "Die ununterbrochene Nachricht, die aus Stille sich bildet" [The uninterrupted communication, formed of stillness] (M; 68–69). And, in interpreting the philosopher's characterization of the religious disposition as one in which "[t]he conscious self disappears & so does all content which was intended by it," Merton refers to none other than Rilke's most un-Narcissistic notion, psychoanalytically speaking, of the "poetic instant":

> For Rilke the ideas of 'pure event' & willingness to change are inseparable. The poetic instant, the pure event, is the moment when the new emerges. Yet how define that moment? It is seen at the moment of death. But what is the *moment* of death? For R. it is not a chronological moment but a moment in the will when the decision for the unknown is ripened & falls off the tree. (77–78; emphasis Merton's)

It is interesting how mystically insightful Rilke becomes when Merton happens to be using him as a lens here and there to clarify for himself the subtleties of Nishida's thought; yet how strangely and confidently the poet, and his vocation, are cast into pre- or submystical exile when they themselves become the objects of focus.

I think it prudent at this point to summarize discussion of this central aspect of the notebook by asking, one final time and in light of the foregoing reflection, the question *why*. Why was Merton, ordinarily so magnanimous toward the religious Other, unwilling to acknowledge explicitly the profundity of Rilke's spiritual vision, especially in view of such readily forthcoming implicit acknowledgment in the notes on Nishida? The answer, as we have seen, is complex, made up of a number of not unrelated personal-psychological, intellectual-cultural, and even spiritual motives. His own mystical proclivities notwithstanding, part of Merton remained grounded in the essentialist articles of faith undergirding Catholic-Christian tradition. He continued to need the consolations of Queen Theology with her reassuring assertion of discrete psycho-spiritual entities and ontological levels such as "the godhead," "the soul," and the eternal non-identity of these two. On encountering the Janus-faced genius of a spiritual poet such as Rilke, whose mature work both crystallized the transpersonal—indeed transessential—aspirations of the early Romantics and anticipated by some fifty years the "neo-Romantic" ironization of all traditional logocentric thought that has come to drive postmodernism, Merton, understandably, reacted with ambivalence. The mystic was fascinated but the traditionalist, unaccustomed to the philosophically seditious binocular focus of German Romanticism,[18] drew back.

All of this was further complicated by Merton's personal struggle with the two never-quite-compatible faces of his self-image: the priest cum mystic and the poet, the sacred and the secular. If Merton took himself—uneasily—

as mystic-poet, he took his alter ego Rilke just as uneasily as poet-mystic, and one may presume at least a modicum of psychological projection to be going on in the Rilke-sections of the notebook. Merton's lifelong uncertainty about the subtle inner relations of these near-twin facets within himself made it difficult for him to appreciate with clear consistency a poet such as Rilke in whose sensibility the aesthetic and the religious are a simple, seamless whole.

One additional factor, alluded to above in passing, deserves further mention here, and that is the matter of Rilke's radical anti-Christianity—or more precisely, Merton's reaction thereto. The question, of course, is what role, if any, Rilke's lifelong animus toward the Catholicism of his upbringing played in determining Merton's ambivalent attitudes regarding his spirituality. Did the ecumenical Merton, even in spite of himself, let this cloud his judgment of Rilke in any way? Again, on the basis of the notebook, and the taped Sunday talks on Rilke evolving out of it in Spring 1966, the answer is, on first glance at least, tantalizingly ambiguous. On tape, which he knew to be for public consumption, Merton, it seems, was prepared to overlook a great deal and to keep the brunt of his doubts to himself, whereas in the privacy of the notebook there is clearly some agonizing over the matter. Taped statements of astonishing generosity coming from the mouth of a Catholic priest (e.g., "Rilke can get away with it [i.e., blasphemously insisting that 'God needs us']. And we need to let a person like Rilke get away with it" [CC AA2078: "Love and the Search for God," side 2].) are countered—or shall we say undermined—by soul-searching questioning and uneasy rationalizing in the notebook.

Much of the latter is in reaction to Rilke's infamous letter of December 17, 1912, from Spain to his friend and patron, Princess Marie von Thurn und Taxis. In this letter, which Merton read in Guardini, Rilke gives full vent to what he (Rilke) calls "einer beinah rabiaten Antichristlichkeit" [a near-rabid Anti-Christianity] (M; Rilke and Thurn und Taxis 245). In poor physical health at the time and unable to shake a lingering depression only exacerbated by the rigors of travel during the rainy season, Rilke spares no sarcasm in describing to the princess only the most questionable and controversial aspects of Spanish Christianity in the regions he has recently visited, such as Andalusia, Cordoba, and, at the time of writing, Ronda. Excoriating a religion that, he insists, refuses to recognize its own exhaustion (as evidenced by all the empty churches), Rilke concludes "[t]he fruit is sucked out . . . so we should just spit out the rinds." Indeed, even the era of its greatest energy (the Inquisition) was anything but glorious: its stock-in-trade was murder: "[T]hat was the version of Christianity practiced here." After shaking his head at the crosses set up in Andalusia to memorialize victims of the Inquisition, the poet goes on to rail against what he considers the arrogance, bordering on blasphemy, of the Gothic-style cathedral in Seville and, most venomously, against the inferiority of a religion that cannot do without an intermediate "telephone" to God (Christ); after all, the very human founder of the "other" religion in Spain, Mohammed, managed quite nicely, thank you, to set up a direct line to God for his followers (M; Rilke and Thurn und Taxis 245–51).

Basically, Merton's reaction to the letter is a strategy of rationalization no doubt meant to mitigate the extreme harshness of Rilke's critique. Yes, Rilke insists he has turned "rabidly anti-Christian & speaks of Xtianity as obsolete," but, Merton counters (to himself?), "read the whole letter. 1) He is sick. He is exhausted from travel. He is depressed. 2) This is a particular aspect of his depression, a revulsion precisely against the symbols of Xtianity in Spain as he saw them" (117). Thus, it is not really Rilke but the bad temper of ill health that is speaking here; and (by way of damage control) even if it *is* Rilke, the condemnation is limited to *Spanish* Christianity. Then Merton tries to minimize the import of the entire outburst by contextualizing it: we should note the exuberant letter from Toledo written a month earlier in which the poet speaks "about his lamentation being ordered to a whole in which 'praise swells up behind all heaviness'" (117). Apart from the question whether Merton is sensitively picking up here in the letters on a mood swing or intermingling of moods in Rilke (depression in a matrix of euphoria), it is clear that he is also at pains to put the best possible light on a grim situation. This leads him in one instance to an observation that would never have survived the prepublication editor's blue pencil: "Note—this is a negative mood—but [note] the positive aspect of the same feeling toward the 'dead' [victims of the Inquisition] in [Duino] Elegy I. The youthful dead. Here they are a different kind of dead I guess!" (116). They are indeed: it is only their state that these hapless victims could be said to have in common with the "jungen Toten" of Rilke's first Elegy. Wearily, Merton summarizes and concludes with a gesture of concession: "Rilke in depression struggles to free himself from a mood of disintegrated and futile images that only perpetuate his misery & depression & seek [?] something that will really integrate him. Obviously Andalusian Christianity—or his mother's, or Italian etc. could not do it" (117).

With respect to Rilke's anti-Christian sentiments, however, it is not such hyperemotional tirades, vented privately to friends, that are most upsetting to Merton, but rather the mature and inspired pronouncements of the poet of the "Elegies," pronouncements that cannot easily be dismissed as momentary aberrations. In particular, Merton is bothered by the mystical seer's celebration of the *nunc stans,* that is, the Abiding Present or all-encompassing Here-and-Now that opens up from and indeed subsumes the zones of time and space that order conventional experience. Thus Rilke's famous utterance in Elegy Seven: "Hiersein ist herrlich" [Being here is marvelous] (M; *Werke* I, 466). Or his glorification, in the eighth, of the animal, able to be at one with the moment because unburdened by past or future: "Und wo wir Zukunft sehn, dort sieht es Alles/und sich in Allem und geheilt für immer" [And where we see future, there it sees All/and itself in all and healed forever] (M; *Werke* I, 471). The ability of the mystic to transcend time and space is, of course, perennial, and, being mystically inclined himself, one would not expect Merton to be particularly troubled by Rilke's expression here; but we have here, I believe, another instance of Merton's "two souls," that of the mystic and that of the essentialist, jockeying for position, as it were. What happens is that Merton allows Guardini's shallow essentialist reading of Rilke on this point to taint his own. Guardini takes Rilke's celebration of "Hiersein" as an implicit rejection of the Christian Kingdom of Heaven as a specifically future event. And Merton, for the moment at least taken in by this, wonders fretfully, "Is Guardini right in his accusation that R. consistently 'secularizes' in the sense of downgrades, degrades (blasphemously) the Xtian idea of the supernatural?" (119). Had the mystic in Merton not been "ambushed" by Guardini's ill-considered polemicism, he certainly would have recognized that, far from taking issue with anything, Rilke is here speaking from a vantage point that celebrates all "issues" at once, not excluding "past" travails and "future" glories.

It should be noted, however, that there is another, quite different "Rilke contra Christianity" passage in the notebook in which the mystic in Merton does get the upper hand and align with the mystic in Rilke. In the midst of his musings on "Elegy One," Merton suddenly comes out of the shadow of Guardini's interpretation and, as he lets go for a shining moment of his defensive posture, we find the alterity disappearing from the alter ego:

> As in his dealings with things, nature etc., so here too in his earthly concept of the holy [in "Elegy One"]—R. regresses knowingly to the pagan, the pre-Xtian, not rejecting the truly Xtian but the abstractness and irrelevance of the falsely spiritualized, the 'ethicized' bloodlessness of conventional Xtianity (implicit infidelity to the N[ew] T[estament]). (107)

Here Merton is able to appreciate that the sweep of Rilke's Dionysian ("pagan, pre-Xtian") gesture of affirmation, like that of his mentor Nietzsche, far outreaches any particular sectarian act of exclusion or rejection.

Perhaps the psychological significance of Rilke's anti-Christianity for Merton's conflicted attitudes toward his spirituality can best be grasped through a comparison with a figure contemporary to Rilke, also a favorite of Merton's, who appears briefly in the notebook: the Spanish poet and philosopher Unamuno. Merton has no problem with Unamuno's particular brand of anti-Christianity, termed by the latter "agonic Christianity," because it is an expression of that poet's "[e]xtreme individualism" which is "certainly a falsified perspective, though much truth [is] here nevertheless" (96). Indeed, Unamuno's "individual cristianismo," in which "every man [is] for himself" and is "centered on his own death & his own salvation" (98), is even humored by Merton as a kind of shallow adolescent rebellion: "Here his individualism makes it impossible for him to see personality as it really is—he is not 'agonic' enough—see Nishida. The [personal] identity created by deeds bypasses the deep self-contradiction, response to God, confrontation of neighbor in agape, etc." (98). Set against Nishida's genuine metaphysical depth, which pursues agon or contradiction to the very heart of reality as a cosmic-generative principle, Unamuno's religious rebellion strikes Merton as egocentric, hence trivial. And of whom was Merton so often reminded in his reflections on the Japanese philosopher? Rilke. Again we see an oblique reflection of Merton's secret respect for, perhaps even awe of, Rilke's vision, not the cranky, myopic vision of an exhausted traveler under the weather, nor the posturing vision of the youthful Russian monk-persona in part one of *Das Stundenbuch,* a calculated snubbing of his mother's low-church "rosary-bead Catholicism" the egocentricity of which Merton easily spotted, but the spiritually seasoned, diamond-hard vision conjured by a voice that could intone, with a vatic assurance reminiscent of Novalis: "Nirgends, Geliebte, wird Welt sein, als innen" [Nowhere, Beloved, will there be world but within] (M; *Werke* I, 467). Of this voice and this vision Merton is in awe, and it is precisely this awe, grudging and half-suppressed as it is, I would argue, that makes Rilke's anti-Christianity so psychologically problematic for Merton. If someone as obviously blessed with spiritual insight as the mature Rilke could dismiss a large part of the monk's religious self-identity as a tired irrelevancy, what then?

## IN AWE OF RILKE

In his most excellent study of the transition from modernism to postmodernism in Western culture, *Prophets of Extremity: Nietzsche, Heidegger, Foucault, Derrida* (1985), Allan Megill offers a fascinating portrait of Freud based on what he takes to be a striking contradiction in the master's personality. Freud, Megill argues, preaches rationalism but practices something suspiciously akin to postmodernism. More specifically, while Freud represents psychoanalysis as the rational-scientific investigation of the patient's reported introspection (dreams and associations thereto) in pursuit of an ultimate psychological truth the discovery of which should lead to the latter's deeper personal integration, nevertheless, in practice as an interpreter of dreams, Freud behaves as if *there were no such ultimate truth*, no such psychic *Ursprung,* to be found, or as if it would not matter much even if there were. The basis for Megill's argument is that Freud's belief in an airtight psychic determinism, modeled on the determinism in physics that reigned supreme in the nineteenth century, caused him to see *all* behavior as equally symptomatic, so that it really was not necessary to "track anything down": "In short, psychic determinism justifies the practice of entering into an understanding of the psyche at points far along the interpretive chain. . . . Far from being highlighted, the 'really real,' the 'thing itself,' tends to disappear" (Megill 328). Viewed in this light, Megill observes, Freud has become a kind of ironic cult hero in certain truth-eschewing postmodernist circles because what he does "well accords with the whole postmodern valuation of interpretation for interpretation's sake." Indeed, to his postmodernist readers Freud's masterwork, *The Interpretation of Dreams,* "would remain a work of genius even if every statement in it were proved wrong" (Megill 328–29).

By and large, we have up to now been examining one of an inverse pair of Mertons, the Merton whose *explicit* allegiance, like that of Megill's Freud, was to the rationalist pursuit of objective truth. As we have seen, this hallowed Western mindset, oriented to an extra-mental truth held to be discoverable, caused the monk no small anxiety upon encountering the proto-postmodern labyrinth of Rilke. But also as with Freud, there is the other "implicit" Merton, the playful visionary whose practice precisely *as an interpreter* (not of dreams but of poems, their waking analogues) reveals itself on occasion to be stunningly attuned to Rilke's subtlety. This Merton is capable of awe before spiritual genius regardless of its provenance. With both "readers," sober generalities and self-protective gestures give way, more or less unwittingly, to those bold incursions of creative thought that typically occur when consciousness momentarily allows the categorical boundaries between the pairs of opposites to slacken. Caught up in the spirit of play that lies at the heart of all interpretation, each, for a while at least, blissfully forgets about the defense of his own ideological territory, in the one case scientific, in the other religious.

The commonality to these two men in particular of a contradiction so fundamental is the more striking in light of the profound differences in their world views. It is as if the contradiction were at bottom a psychodynamic dialectic and as if the *form* of this dialectic, whether it be called "modernist/postmodernist" or identified by some more perennial and familiar label (say, Enlightenment/Romantic or Derrida's "rabbinical/poetic"), were more fundamental to human consciousness than the *content* of any espoused ideology or world view. Seen in this light, Freud and Merton stand a good deal closer to each other than one would ordinarily expect of a "serious" scientist and a "serious" mystic. The differences in their respective proto-postmodern sides are mainly those of a superficial stylistic nature as imposed by the forms of writing we happen to be examining here. Whereas Freud, working as he did in the rhetorically expansive, inviting form of the case history, could entertain his "implicit" side lavishly, spinning out dazzlingly Byzantine interpretations of dreams presented by Dora or the Wolf Man, Merton gives us only such terse, interpolated glimpses of the "crypto-postmodernist" as one might expect from the vernacular, reactive format of the private notebook teeming with quotations recorded from favorite writers.

In fact, these glimpses are at times so terse as to be perhaps more tantalizing than satisfying. Such is the case, for example, with Merton's reaction to the well-known letters of January 1912 in which Rilke elaborates his reasons for foregoing the great personal emancipation promised by psychoanalysis. Though plagued by periods of intense anxiety and depression his whole adult life, Rilke nevertheless refused the solace of the analytic couch and for reasons that perhaps only a fellow poet, and a religious one at that, could truly appreciate. Merton quotes variously from the *Selected Letters:*

> [I]t is precisely my, if one may say so, piousness [before life] which holds me back from this intervention [i.e., psychoanalysis], from the great clearing up which life does not do—from this correcting of all the pages of my life hitherto written. . . .
>
> The fact is . . . I could not allow myself the loop-hole of psychoanalysis unless I were really determined to start a new (if possible uncreative) life on the other side of it. . . .
>
> I still feel bound with infinitely strong ties to what has been begun, to all the happiness & misery that it [life] entails, so that strictly speaking I can wish for no change, no intervention from outside, no relief save that which is inherent in endurance & ultimate triumph.
>
> If my devils were driven out my angels would also receive a slight, a very slight (shall we say) shock, & you see I cannot let it come to that pass at any price. (49)

To this Merton appends the following note to himself: "For full understanding of Rilke & analysis—see in context of the big city-hospital—inauthentic death idea. Analysis would 'disinfect' his tone (make it smell of the big impersonal hospital)" (48). Merton's remark is penetrating in its use of the metaphor of medical disinfection to convey his appreciation of the poet's horror of any cultural-mechanical tinkering or tampering with his capacity for "pure experience," no matter how "therapeutic."[19] But what makes the remark ingenious is its oblique allusion to the opening hospital sequence in *Malte Laurids Brigge* with its atmosphere of sterile alienation, demonstrating that Rilke probably did in fact equate psychoanalysis in his own mind with a kind of abhorrent psycho-spiritual sterilization that must needs be the death of any poet.

However, the issue of Merton's terseness and of tantalizing things left unsaid becomes truly compelling only in the brief closing remark of this note to himself: "His reward [for declining psychoanalysis] was the *Duino Elegies*!" (48). This particular comment, written on the left-hand page of the notebook, just to the left of Rilke's above-quoted words as recorded on the right-hand page on the inseparability in creativity of "devils" and "angels," and thus, we may infer, in precise response to it, raises a host of questions concerning Merton's "implicit" views on creativity and morality which one can only wish he had elucidated further. In sanctioning Rilke's decision to keep his devils for the sake of his creative angels, is Merton taking a position close to that of Jung, who in his critique of Christianity insisted that the Satanic or Shadow archetype, as a reservoir of blocked creative energy, must be somehow liberated and integrated into the lopsidedly benign Christ (i.e., self) archetype? Is the mystical Merton, who could well appreciate the fundamental, even intimate, interdependence of good and evil, emerging here out of the dialectically sensitive moralist who asserted in the *Conjectures,* "To imprison ethics in the realm of division, of good and evil, right and wrong, is to condemn it to sterility, and rob it of its real reason for existing, which is *love*" (166)? Is Merton here perhaps even echoing, however faintly, the radical-Christian Blake, the presider over "The Marriage of Heaven and Hell," who "went walking among the fires of hell, delighted with the enjoyments of Genius, which to Angels look like torment and insanity" (*Portable Blake* 252)?[20] If so, then like his "explicitly" heretical predecessor, the "implicit" Merton viewed evil not as an ontological, and hence not as a moral, issue, but as a problem of the relative nature of all human values, and therefore as a problem of limited consciousness, or of what the far-seeing psychologists of the Eastern Wisdom traditions call *avidya* (Ignorance).

Moreover, this "poetic" view of good and evil as a dialectical dynamic of consciousness in which each pole attains expression precisely at the expense of the other brings both Merton and Rilke intriguingly close to the "deferral" or "suppression" aspect of Derrida's psycholinguistic understanding of *différance*. Making the point in *Speech and Phenomena* that the opposite meanings of the

Greek *pharmakon* (poison and remedy) exist not merely by virtue of any static "difference" between them but also, and especially, by virtue of their dynamic reciprocal "deferral," Derrida says, "On the one hand, [differer] indicates difference as distinction, inequality, or discernibility; on the other, it expresses the interposition of delay, the interval of a *spacing* and *temporalizing* that puts off until 'later' what is presently denied" (qtd. in Harland 138). What Derrida sees as operating on the circumscribed level of semantics, Rilke and Merton see as operating in the creative consciousness at large. As a poet himself, Merton was sensitive to the difficult and delicate balancing act of a continuous alternating deferral of devils and angels that Rilke felt a sacrosanct commitment to sustain in order, through their carefully modulated interaction, to realize his creative gift to the utmost.

A much clearer, more explicit illustration of a pre-postmodern sympathy between these two poets may be seen in Merton's comments, early in the notebook, on Rilke's "Ninth Duino Elegy" and on the earlier lyric, "Kindheit." Here Rilke takes up the theme of language (or, in the latter instance, pictorial representation) and its implication in the Fall. Merton quotes the line, in mid-elegy, that cues the theme: "Sind wir vielleicht hier um zu sagen: Haus etc." [Perhaps we are here in order to say: house etc.] (M; 10). The entire verse sequence runs as follows:

> Sind wir vielleicht *hier*, um zu sagen: Haus,
> Brücke, Brunnen, Tor, Krug, Obstbaum, Fenster, —
> höchstens: Säule, Turm . . . . aber zu *sagen*, verstehs,
> oh zu sagen *so,* wie selber die Dinge niemals
> innig meinten zu sein.
>
> [Perhaps we are *here* in order to say: house,
> Bridge, fountain, gate, jug, fruit tree, window, —
> at best: column, tower . . . . but to *say* them, y'see,
> ah to say them the *way* even the things themselves never
> in their heart of hearts intended to be.] (M; *Werke* I, 474)

Merton comments:

> Two conceptions of Adam 'giving names' to the animals:
>
> 1) The static & conservative. He named them once for all. Essences were established in the past and cannot change.
>
> 2) Adam is every man & the world is paradox where every man has to discover for himself new aspects of an inexhaustible creation. . . .

> The perception of real relatedness *(wirklicher Bezug)* can only be the perception of our [deep] relatedness, not of an abstract relation of "man" to things (the "closed" defining gaze that "traps" beings—9th Elegy). (10)

Needless to say, Merton is here in complete sympathy with the second notion of language, as affirmed by Rilke. This is poetic language, the language of Orpheus, which reveals rather than isolates (thereby concealing) the things it names, language that, in *saying* things (Rilke's emphatic "*sagen*"), actually creates them, bringing them in some mysterious way to full, vibrant life. In this—sacred—language there is no gap between word and thing, signifier and signified, rather, both exist in a seamless continuum of Being. This is the pristine language, the *Ursprache,* pined after by Heidegger in his nostalgic lament that no language has truly been up to the task of philosophy since ancient Greek. It is a mystical sense, or sensibility, of language as forever evoking Presence or Being as it goes about its natural, effortless function of naming. It is a sense of language inherited by both Rilke and Heidegger from German Romanticism with the insistence of that movement on viewing all works of literature, indeed all texts of any kind, as *ein endloses Buch* (one endless book).

Implied by and foreshadowed in all this is the postmodern value of interpretation for its own sake, of reading as a creative form of play in which we do not laboriously read "back against" the grain of the text in pursuit of a meaning presumably re-presented therein but "take off," as it were, from the text in a "forward" direction in order to "spin out" our own chapters of "the never-ending story." (It is no accident that the German verb *spinnen* can have the vernacular meaning of "be mad or crazy.") True, postmodernism eschews "Presence," but then, Romanticism only upholds it when seen as inseparable from its complement, Non-presence. It is only the Presence that is not opposed to Non-presence that the German Romantics are interested in, the Presence without a name, unless that name come out of the spirit of Rilke's latter sense of language in "Elegy Nine," a sense shared by Merton (the postessentialist Merton schooled in Barthes but, above all, grounded in his own experience). In that case, *any* name will do since the poet is one who has found his way out of the prisonhouse of language in which every word is a straitjacket and every "essence" a cell. In poetic or Orphic language all "things"—and here words too are things—are forever flowing into and out of one another and hence *do not exist* in the circumscribed way we think they do. Rather, they exist in a way "even the things themselves never in their heart of hearts intended to be."

One might refine the above objection by asserting that postmodernism, particularly deconstruction, denies the existence of the signified, of any final resting place of meaning. In this case the signified becomes the Signified, or

Presence experienced as Meaning, the ultimate goal of language. Again, the response is that this is perfectly consonant with Romantic philosophy of language. Although I stated above that poetic language, for Romanticism, closes the gap between signifier and signified, it would have been more precise to say that it exposes this gap as a delusion, as a necessary pretended or virtual space between inseparable poles the virtual nature of which has somehow been forgotten. For the poetic consciousness there *is* no such gap: words and things, be those things objects "out there" or meanings and associations "in here," are, like God and his masks, an eternal dynamic interface. No need for any "resting place" of meaning here. The endless movement, or rather flow, of the signifier carries its own built-in repose. One suspects that the curiously puckish tone in which Derrida "laments" the interminable nature of linguistic process reflects a (barely) secret delight he takes in some such understanding as this. Would he not agree that we are better off imagining this endless movement, this eternal pursuit by the hound of language of its own tail, as playfully circular or infinitival ( $\infty$ ) rather than drearily linear, whether in a recessive or lateral direction? This is the same quantum leap in perspective that enabled Novalis to turn the depressing scenario of history's "unendlicher Progreß" proffered by his philosophical mentor Fichte into his own ecstatic vision of time and eternity as shot through with each other.[21]

Interestingly, on the next page of the notebook Merton cites a passage from Rilke's *Tuscan Diary* (1898) in connection with this poetic experience of "things":

> I feel that more and more I am becoming the disciple of things (not merely their listener), a disciple who adds, through comprehending questions, intensity to their answers and confessions, & who, enticing them to spend their advice & wisdom, learns how to reward their generous love with the disciple's humility. (11)

What catches the attention here, apart from the moving quality of the reverence expressed in the passage itself, is its published source: not an edition of Rilke but a quotation from Erich Heller's *The Disinherited Mind.* After citing Heller, Merton adds parenthetically: "Heller says that as in Renaissance painting 'things' came into their own & their shapes were accorded recognition, so in Rilke & Nietzsche they acquired new names" (11). Merton's overall ambivalence toward Rilke's spirituality is reflected, I believe, in the variability of his attitude toward Heller in the notebook. Here he cites with apparent approval a perspective on Rilke's mystical empowerment of language offered by a critic whom he would only weeks later brand as "all wet" for making the larger, more sweeping case in favor of Rilke's mystical vision.

In "Kindheit," a wistful lament of the loss of innocence contained in the *Neue Gedichte* (1907), Rilke imagines the transition from childhood to adulthood as a gradual yet inexorable slippage from the bliss of pure experience ("was einem Ding geschieht und einem Tiere" [as bestowed upon a thing or animal] [M; *Werke* I, 267]) into a morass of confusion engendered by the interpolation of images of experience into experience itself. As grownups we

> . . . wurden so vereinsamt wie ein Hirt
> und so mit großen Fernen überladen
> und wie von weit berufen und berührt
> und langsam wie ein langer neuer Faden
> in jene Bilder-Folgen eingeführt,
> in welchen nun zu dauern uns verwirrt.
>
> [. . . became as isolated as a shepherd
> and burdened by enormous distances
> and as if called to and bestirred from afar
> and slowly like a lengthy brand-new thread
> sewn into that vast quilt of images,
> in which to linger now it dizzies us.] (M; *Werke* I, 267)

Merton's comment reveals a fellow poet's sympathy with Rilke's depiction of the Fall as an alienation both from and through language. Gradually the soul becomes entangled in images, in apparent signifiers (as they would later come to be called) that have fooled it into accepting them as re-presentations of a "True Reality" forever "calling to it from afar":

> *Kindheit*—the simplicity of childhood experience (The child is like a 'thing' or a 'beast'—but becomes full of images & now we are bewildered by these.) (15)

One might well expect a Christian poet to respond sympathetically to Rilke's casting of the human dilemma in terms of lapsarian myth since German Romanticism, the cultural "soil" of Rilke's poetic genius, has often been viewed as a secularized version of Christian salvation history or *Heilsgeschichte*. Anti-Christian though he was in any explicit sense, Rilke never wavered from a basically lapsarian view of human nature. Some of his most potent recurrent symbols—the child, the animal, the lovers—are invocations of precisely this lost State of Grace, this natural communion with "things," from which, as beings now imprisoned in a maze of signs, we have fallen away. Thus, to the anguished question as to the cause of our exile posed in "Elegy Eight,"

Wer hat uns also umgedreht, daß wir,
was wir auch tun, in jener Haltung sind
von einem, welcher fortgeht?

[So who has turned us around, such that
no matter what we do, we are in the attitude
of someone leaving home?] (M; *Werke* I, 472)

Merton responds with a melange of phrasal translations from various parts of the elegy that render some of Rilke's densest, most evocative language of spiritual loss. Clearly Merton's singling-out of just these phrases for translation (especially the intensely nihilistic "niemals Nirgends ohne nicht"), powerfully leitmotivic as they are, and his spirited accompanying comment issue from that corner of his mystic's soul able to affirm Rilke's vision of loss, and, above all, of that which has been lost, without reservation:

> *Gegenüber sein*. 8th Elegy.
> 'Turning the child around.' so he no longer looks at openness ["das Offene"] !! . . . away from the 'pure unsuperintended element', 'Never nowhere without no' . . . . Who turned us around? Great question of 9th [i.e., 8th] Elegy (which is also key to all he says about 'beasts', 'faces', etc.) (9–11)

It is not unlikely that Merton recognized the hallowed lineage in German esoteric literature of the image of the "turn-around" or inversion of spiritual vision that Rilke twice invokes in the "Eighth Elegy" ("Nur unsre Augen sind/wie umgekehrt" [But our eyes are/As though turned around] [l. 2–3] and, toward the end, the above-quoted "Wer hat uns also umgedreht"). Its ultimate source is probably Eckhart's mystical Eye through which God and man view each other, but the epiphanic aspect of the image as such is more strongly emphasized in Böhme's theosophical "umgewandtes Auge," suggesting our beholding of God as an "eye-opening" or "vision-transforming" event. We know from Merton's letter to the Sufist, Abdul Aziz, written in December 1964 (that is, less than a year before his recording of these notes), that, thickets of esoteric jargon aside, he was enjoying a period of submersion at that time in Böhme's mythological-alchemical universe,[22] and so probably recognized instantly Rilke's lapsarian twist on the revered image: the turn of the eye that interests the poet here is not the final one toward but the prior one away from God (*Umkehrung* as *per*version), leaving us with a sense of sight that perceives space, outer or inner, as that which separates rather than joins things: "*Gegenüber sein* . . . 'Never nowhere without no.'"[23]

But it is above all on "Duino Elegy One" that Merton lavishes his attention in the notebook, and it is here that the deepest affinities between these two men emerge, affinities, as I have argued, that may be characterized as at once mystical and pre-postmodern. This is Merton's last extended consideration of Rilke in the notebook, covering about ten manuscript pages (102–11), and, recorded as it probably was sometime in February 1966, some two to three months following his above-discussed comments on Elegies "Nine" and "Eight," it no doubt reflects a deepening empathy resulting quite naturally from this period of sustained contemplation. I think it safe to say that, despite some hedging, stemming mainly from the lingering influence of Guardini's psychological-critical perspective, Merton is essentially able to affirm here in "Duino Elegy One" Rilke's transcendence of the personal or egoic level. He even includes a paraphrase of one of the rare passages in Guardini that reinforce his own deepening spiritual empathy. Here for once Guardini lowers the psychoanalytic lens that blurs everything about Rilke but neurosis and takes the poet's reflections on interpersonal love at face value:

> He [Guardini] goes on to say that 'Openness' for R. is attained not only by respect for other person's freedom, but that the Thou of the other, transcended, gives access to the 'unobstructed path' to freedom—Selfless and 'Thou-less'—love *transcends the personal* into a realm where all being attains to fullness. (107; emphasis Merton's)

Repeated denials elsewhere of Rilke's mystical capacity notwithstanding, Merton reveals here, and throughout these concluding comments on the first Elegy, his continuing fascination with Rilke's notion of "Openness" or spiritual vision, however that experience may be labeled and however it may be come by. He wants to understand precisely Rilke's sense of the conditions necessary for, or at least conducive to, such an opening-up, thus enabling the fulfillment of what Rilke calls our *Auftrag,* the charge or task or challenge imposed on us all by existence. What is required of us that we may enjoy the Pure Experience of the child, the animal, or the lovers, or, as Rilke puts it in "Elegy One,"

> da du vorüberkamst am geöffneten Fenster,
> gab eine Geige sich hin. Das alles war Auftrag.
> Aber bewältigtest du's?
>
> [when you passed by the open window,
> a violin gave itself utterly. All of that was charge.
> But did you master it?] (M; *Werke* I, 442)

Merton's response shows that he sees here, intimately entwined with Rilke's anti- or post-Christian attitudes, a most kindred recognition of a universally sacerdotal gesture of surrender required of all human beings in order to know the experience of oneness with the strains of the violin (i.e., phenomena):

> *Das alles war Auftrag—*
> The violin which gives itself '*hingeben*' (movement from player to hearer)
> Walking past open window you hear a violin giving itself. . . . To hear this giving is *Auftrag,* trust, commission, mandate, message, mission. (prophetic implications—almost a 'calling,' a 'vocation.') (105)

One senses from Merton's emphatic string of translations of *Auftrag* not merely a linguistic but, even more, a spiritual groping toward *rapprochement* with a sensibility intuitively felt to be of a piece with his own.

Merton is impressed by the authentic ring of the voice that cries out the opening lines of the opening Elegy:

> Wer, wenn ich schriee, hörte mich denn aus der Engel
> Ordnungen? und gesetzt selbst, es nähme
> einer mich plötzlich ans Herz: ich verginge von seinem
> stärkeren Dasein. Denn das Schöne ist nichts
> als des Schrecklichen Anfang, den wir noch gerade ertragen,
> und wir bewundern es so, weil es gelassen verschmäht,
> uns zu zerstören. Ein jeder Engel ist schrecklich. (*Werke* I, 441)
>
> [Who, if I cried out, would hear me among the angels'
> hierarchies? and even if one of them pressed me
> suddenly against his heart: I would be consumed
> in that overwhelming existence. For beauty is nothing
> but the beginning of terror, which we still are just able to endure
> and we are so awed because it serenely disdains
> to annihilate us. Every angel is terrifying.] (Mitchell 151)

This is a far cry from the spiritual posturing of the earlier collection, *Das Stundenbuch,* which reminded Merton of the affected piety of the novice monks in his charge:

> First lines—Wer wenn ich schriee—explicit renunciation of the abortive attempt at union with God in Book of Hours I. He accepts complete solitude, renounces prayer & seeks the meaning of his loneliness & his place in the cosmos. . . . The acceptance of loneliness in 1st Elegy is at last a refusal of Narcissistic absorption & an attempt at openness, relatedness, giving. (103)

For Merton the poet has by now given up any attempt to conjure or manipulate a manifestation of Divine Presence; he has matured here to an awareness of the necessity to embrace lonliness as a precondition for connectedness. A wisp of this connectedness Merton sees reflected in line 18 that tells of

> . . . die Nacht, die Nacht, wenn der Wind voller Weltraum
> uns am Angesicht zehrt—
>
> [. . . the night, the night, when a wind full of boundless space
> devours our faces—] (M; *Werke* I, 441)

Merton takes "face" in the sense of ego or individual self that, with the acceptance of one's lonliness over time, is worn away by the powerful gales of spirit: "The wind 'devours' his face in such a way that he is all the more real because of it" (103). This "spiritual" reading of "Wind," no doubt abetted in Merton by the intimate association in Christian tradition between "spirit" and "breath" or "wind," recurs in his later rendering of "das Wehende" [that which gusts or blows] as "the inspiration" (109), this from the famous sequence, "Aber das Wehende höre,/die ununterbrochene Nachricht, die aus Stille sich bildet" [But hear the inspiration,/ the uninterrupted news that grows out of silence] (M; *Werke* I, 443).

But the power of these gales seems at times almost overmatched by that of the force that keeps this face which is really a mask, this sense of individual selfhood, intact: language. The animals, unburdened by language, see right through our uneasy pretentions to knowledge, our doomed logocentric attempts to turn what must forever remain an "interpreted world" [der gedeuteten Welt] into a world of Truth or Meaning:

> und die findigen Tiere merken es schon,
> daß wir nicht sehr verläßlich zu Haus sind
> in der gedeuteten Welt.
>
> [and the crafty animals notice right away
> that we are not very reliably at home
> in the interpreted world.] (M; *Werke* I, 441)

Merton's comment on these lines is an unmistakable anticipation of the current efforts in literary-theoretical circles to come to grips with the question of logocentric versus differential conceptions of language. Does our capacity to manipulate signs reveal or conceal the world's secrets?

> findig—crafty, 'knowing'—not fooled—piercing our disguise. And the disguise is our pretended all embracing knowledge, assurance, base[d] on *explanation,* clarification, analysis, the manipulation of signs, numbers, symbols, our capacity to unlock the world's secrets—yet we are not at home in the world, only in our system of signs. (102; emphasis Merton's)

This sense of all sub-poetic language as fraught with the tension of a gap or separation between word and thing, signifier and signified, gradually came to fruition in Merton from readings in Rilke and Barthes. In one instance in the notebook it causes him to take issue with mentor Guardini, who castigates Rilke for giving psycho-spiritual priority to the world at large over issues of interpersonal love. Merton is quick to take Rilke's side here: the miasma of the I-Thou relationship is itself merely a symptom of the more profound problem of man's estrangement from the world through language: "This [Guardini's criticism] is too strong. For R. the question of the I-Thou relationship is irrelevant as long as man is alienated in a world of symbols and ciphers" (105). "I" and "Thou" are themselves but signs, and the first thing we must do is recognize them as such.

## COURTING THE *COINCIDENTIA*

Seeing through the dualism of language, this hypnotic force that creates such illusions as "I-Thou" or "self-other" or "signifier-signified," is for Rilke one way to get to "das Offene," the heady freedom of Pure Experience. To an appreciative reader such as Merton, himself gifted with mystical insight, it is just in those passages of "Elegy One" where Rilke intimates the Place beyond dualism as a *coincidentia oppositorum,* a meeting point *jenseits* of the agonizing tension of *différance,* that he is pulled most deeply into the poet's orbit.

For pre-postmodern poets such as Rilke and Merton, the gap of dualism or, viewed dynamically, the tension of *différance* is not simply the essential structuring principle of language as a *property* of human consciousness, but of human consciousness *per se.* In other words, to all intents and purposes, language and consciousness are, for the person, coextensive. And since this language/consciousness is experienced on an instinctual level as tension, man is—characteristically—in a state of restlessness or dis-ease, for "we are not very reliably at home in the interpreted world." This perspective, to be sure, also holds for Derrida, who, as Harland says, "expands his theory of language into a philosophy of the world *as* language" (141), but whereas Derrida generally restricts his discussion to linguistic terms, poets feel no such compunction and freely vary the antinomies as the spirit moves them.

Thus, we observe in the notes on "Elegy One" three instances in which Merton responds sensitively to Rilke's staging of a close encounter between fundamental categorical oppositions and, more significantly, to the hint, conjured through poetic language, of some utterly mysterious conflation, some absurd yet inexorable emancipation, behind—indeed, right *within*— the tension of contradiction. I'll take them up in ascending order of Merton's depth of response. First, there is the boundary between inner and outer worlds, already rendered porous by Rilke in the imagery of effacing (read: ego-diluting) spiritual gales. Now the poet exhorts us to "interiorize" the world "out there," literally to take it into ourselves through an emphatic opening of arms:

> . . . Wirf aus den Armen die Leere
> zu den Räumen hinzu, die wir atmen; vielleicht daß die Vögel
> die erweiterte Luft fühlen mit innigerm Flug.
>
> [. . . fling the emptiness from your arms
> out into the spaces that we breathe; so that the birds
> may feel this expanded air with more interiorized flight.]
> (M; *Werke* I, 441-42)

Merton quotes Guardini's slant on these lines to the effect that man must guard against hoarding "inner" spiritual treasures (personal insights, private states of bliss and such) by casting them out into the world and, to the extent he succeeds in this, expanding his sense of self. The flight of the birds is then "inniger" because it has literally become his own. Merton's comment: "Guardini is right about the Elegy being about 'confrontation of inner & outer' & the two spheres 'have a duty to each other'" (103). The sort of duty Merton is suggesting here is that incumbent upon the partners in any marriage (the marriage here being mystical), which is to hold the relationship itself dearer than the terms of relationship. The mysterious "inniger" quality of the birds' flight is not in any way set over against the "outer" world but rather effortlessly contains within itself both inner and outer worlds, in the paradoxical sense of Rilke's notion of *Weltinnenraum,* perhaps also in the subtle sense of the arche-writing that Derrida extols in Plato, an unrealized but somehow still quickening inscription in the soul that bodies forth as both speech (from the "inside") and conventional writing (from the "outside") (Coward 57–58).

The second close encounter of opposites in "Elegy One" occurs in lines 69–85 in which the poet speaks in prophetic tones about the mode of existence of the dead: the total shuffling-off of all earthly concern with limits such as codes of behavior, time zones, personal identity, etc., in short: "alles, was sich bezog, so lose im Raume/flattern zu sehen" [to see everything that was important here fluttering limply in space] (M; *Werke* I, 444). But of course all such losses or negations are now seen as trivial—indeed, illusory—because, by virtue of an inscrutable Affirmation that absorbs negation, even loss itself is experienced as gain. The angels themselves, truth to tell, are not clear on the difference between life and death, not because they are ignorant of it but because it is irrelevant:

. . . Aber Lebendige machen
alle den Fehler, daß sie zu stark unterscheiden.
Engel (sagt man) wüßten oft nicht, ob sie unter
Lebenden gehn oder Toten. Die ewige Strömung
reißt durch beide Bereiche alle Alter
immer mit sich und übertönt sie in beiden.

[. . . But the living all make
the same mistake: they distinguish too sharply.
Angels (they say) often do not know whether they are
moving among the living or the dead. The eternal current
flows through both realms, sweeping all ages along
with it forever, drowning out the voices of all in both.]
(M; *Werke* I, 444)

Merton summarizes, "finding the Unity behind the distinction of dead, alive etc." (111), and then adds parenthetically and perceptively, in a note on Rilke's closing allusion to Linus, a youthful figure in Greek myth cut down in his prime: "(song for Linos = hint of the Orpheus-solution. Myth of pure becoming)" (111). To Rilke's "ewige Strömung," that ineffable current that quickens both the living and the dead, indeed, that flows through, and thereby deconstructs, *all* polarities, not excluding the supposedly irreducible identity-versus-differance, Merton deftly gives the name of Rilke's true God, "Orpheus," the poetic consciousness forever poised on the cusp, open to all possibilites and impossibilites alike. Through his song for Linus Orpheus gets life and death to lie down with one another. What can we say of Linus? We can say of him what one monk, in a Zen legend surely known to Merton, is supposed to have said of his recently deceased master, who had been brutally murdered on the road by brigands. Taking the master's violent death and his own traumatic reaction to it as a koan for meditation, he exclaimed joyfully in the moment of insight: "Ah! Alive and well!"

Rilke's third close encounter of opposites shifts the focus to being and becoming. This is perhaps the most abstractly metaphysical way of formulating the fundamental contradiction that is Reality in the Elegies, so the poet concretizes it, "humanizes" it, by allusion to "jenen jungen Toten" [those young dead] as the mysterious alchemy that fuses the categories:

. . . Aber das Wehende höre,
die ununterbrochene Nachricht, die aus Stille sich bildet.
Es rauscht jetzt von jenen jungen Toten zu dir. . . .

> Was sie mir wollen? leise soll ich des Unrechts
> Anschein abtun, der ihrer Geister
> reine Bewegung manchmal ein wenig behindert.
>
> [. . . But hear the gusting (i.e., Merton's "inspiration"),
> the uninterrupted news that grows out of silence.
> It rushes over to you now from those young dead. . . .
> What they want of me? softly I am to remove
> the appearance of injustice, which on occasion hinders
> a bit the fluid movement of their spirits.] (M; *Werke* I, 443)

Again in his response, a mix of snippets from Guardini (in single quotation marks) and his own thoughts, Merton shows the mystic's simultaneous awareness of difference or distinction and of something primordial that renders difference transparent:

> When R. listens to—*Das Wehende*—the inspiration "the uninterrupted news that grows out of silence"
>
> a) in general—'probably the summons that comes from the realm of Being'.
> 'The silence of things'
> 'The silence which lies behind the things themselves—that of original Being'.
>
> b) in particular—'The voices of the youthfully dead'.
>
> c) He has felt their proximity in churches.
>
> d) He has an *Auftrag* in relation to them—
> They were *apparently* unjustly deprived of a full life.
> He must remove this appearance—show praise in them too. (109; emphasis Merton's)

The deprivation of a natural lifespan, that is, of an opportunity to experience becoming or growth (or: *différance,* the endless process of "othering") to the full, is only an *apparent* cosmic injustice since even the most fragmentary of phenomena, even the flickering camera click of a thought, manifests the fullness of Being itself. Merton goes well beyond Guardini here in recognizing Rilke's identification of both poles, the general (Being or logos) and the particular or fragmentary (death-bound youth or flowering *différance*), with "das Wehende," the irreducible force or "ewige Strömung" that pervades all. From this vantage point, there is no such thing as deprivation: since each is all and all is each, what is there to be deprived of? The *Auftrag* of the poet is to reveal just this, the mystery of the *coincidentia oppositorum,* thereby puncturing all illusion of deprivation. (Contrast Guardini, who characterizes the poet's charge in rather vague emotional terms as "taking the fate of the early deceased up into his heart" [M; Guardini 62].) Such revelation is celebration, which Merton calls "praise" ("show praise in them too") and Rilke, elsewhere, calls *rühmen* ("Oh sage, Dichter, was du tust? —Ich rühme." [Oh tell me, poet, what you do?—I celebrate.]).

There is no doubt that Merton's sudden move here beyond Guardini into direct consonance with Rilke's vision is the spontaneous result of a flash of mystical insight occasioned by sustained contemplation of "Elegy One." That said, we must remember not to minimize the importance of preparatory reading and study to the contemplation that eventually ripens into insight. Weeks, perhaps even days, before taking up the Elegy, Merton made an in-depth study of Nishida Kitaro's late essay, "The Unity of Opposites." Some ten pages of manuscript notes attest to this (85–95). In this essay Nishida, whose grounding in Zen practice, as previously mentioned, attracted Merton, investigates the relationship between self and world, and concludes that the world is "the self-identity of absolute contradiction," or, more simply, the unity of opposites. Over and over again Nishida drives his point home, coming at it from various angles and arguments. Many of these are recorded by Merton in the notebook, such that it is fair to say that he was carrying on a kind of meditation on the mystery of the *coincidentia oppositorum* for days or weeks before taking up the first Elegy in depth. Two entries in the notes, one a quotation from Nishida, the other a brief comment by Merton himself, show that Nishida's ultimate principle reminded Merton of Rilke and that Merton was primed, as it were, by his study of this relentlessly dense philosophical essay to "combust" into a dramatic and immediate apprehension of the first Elegy's poetic mysticism:

> Everything that is given to us in the world of unity of opposites is given to us as a 'task'. Our task in this world is to form. In this we have our life. That which is given . . . is given to be 'completed'. (89)

Nishida's "task," to "form," that is, to live poetically or creatively, would come up again for Merton days or weeks later in Rilke's Orphic *Auftrag,* to celebrate the mystery embodied in the uninterrupted life of "the young dead." A few pages earlier in the notes, Merton scribbles with reference to Nishida's essay:

> unity of opposites—from formed to forming—*'essentially a world of poiesis'.* [This is Rilke exactly!]

Formed/forming, being/becoming, death/life, inner world/outer world—Nishida and Orpheus, German lyric poetry and Japanese metaphysics. All these pairs and many others, it seems, were able to come together and share a moment in a scruffy college notebook, a hand-written text produced by another (?), intensely alive, "text" known as "Thomas Merton." But then, it seems we can just as validly say, as we did at the outset, that a text named "Rilke" has here written a text named "Merton."

## EPIPHANY

On October 15, 1968, some two-and-a-half years after closing the notebook under consideration here, Thomas Merton embarked on a fateful and, as it would turn out, fatal journey to the East. After twenty-seven years of relative immobility at the Trappist Abbey of Gethsemani in Kentucky, Merton was finally free to pursue his heart's desire of deepening ecumenical ties with various Asian monastic orders. He was to address a conference on this theme in Bangkok and, between other scheduled meetings, including three with the Dalai Lama, to tour a number of important Buddhist and Hindu religious sites in Thailand, India, and Ceylon.

The first entry in his *Asian Journal* describes his ebullient mood on take-off from San Francisco Airport:

> Joy. We left the ground—I with Christian mantras and a great sense of destiny, of being at last on my true way after years of waiting and wondering and fooling around.
>
> May I not come back without having settled the great affair. And found also the great compassion, mahakaruna. (4)

The "great affair," of course, is Enlightenment, emancipation from the pairs of opposites. Merton's description of spiritual illumination as an affair to be "settled" hints at perhaps a lifetime of what we shall call fertilizing existential conflict, the experience of long, and at times anguished, struggle with fundamental questions essential to tilling the psycho-spiritual soil of consciousness. We have been viewing Merton's "Rilke-period," the roughly four months covered by the notebook (November through February 1996), as a kind of crucible for this struggle. We have read the notebook as an intimate record of one particular phase of Merton's spiritual struggle, a phase evoked by his ambivalent, at times anxious and at times rapt, confrontation with the provocative "anti-Christian" spirituality of Rainer Maria Rilke. Personal and cultural issues of intense significance for Merton—poetry versus religion, poetic versus mystical insight, rationalist or logocentric versus dialectical or differential world views, language and thought as revealing versus concealing "pure experience" or God—are brought into sharp relief through this fruitful friction of two highly evolved sensibilities.

Certainly the notebook gives us a deep glimpse into the mind and heart of this man for whom the Great Affair, though vivid and vibrant and consumingly passionate, remained as yet "unsettled" at bottom. The pressure of something momentous pending, something undecided and seemingly undecidable, becomes palpable, I think, in the above-quoted bad mistranslation by Merton of the last line of the fifth "Sonnet to Orpheus," which should read: "And he [Orpheus] obeys by transgressing." Perhaps Merton erred here because he had still not quite exhausted his resistance to this literally shattering Orphic truth of the absolute identity of all the pairs of opposites. But the encounter with Rilke must have helped bring his state of undecidability to a fever pitch, to an intensity of spiritual pressure that drove him inward in the direction of previously untapped psychological and spiritual resources. For Merton as for most seekers, only the kind of total pressure that hermetically seals off all escape routes, all calculated "solutions" to be lived with, is able finally to break through to the Solution that can only be lived *from*.

Six weeks into his Eastern tour, on a visit to the massive stone Buddhas hewn out of mountain rock at Polonnaruwa, Ceylon, Merton came to the end of his long, winding path of spiritual gestation. In the twinkling of an eye, the mystical "death before death," a phrase of especially poignant tragic irony in this case in view of Merton's untimely death by accidental electrocution only nine days later, transformed a lifetime of questioning and doubt into a timeless moment of freedom and clarity. In his own words:

> Looking at these figures I was suddenly, almost forcibly, jerked clean out of the habitual, half-tied vision of things, and an inner clearness, clarity, as if exploding from the rocks themselves, became evident and obvious. . . . The thing about all this is that there is no puzzle, no problem, and really no "mystery." All problems are resolved and everything is clear, simply because what matters is clear. The rock, all matter, all life, is charged with dharmakaya [i.e., Buddha-mind] . . . everything is emptiness and everything is compassion. I don't know when in my life I have ever had such a sense of beauty and spiritual validity running together in one aesthetic illumination. . . . I mean, I know and have seen what I was obscurely looking for. I don't know what else remains but I have now seen and have pierced through the surface and have got beyond the shadow and the disguise. (*Asian Journal* 233–36)

Rainer Maria Rilke was, in effect, a critical rite of passage for Thomas Merton on the way to this, his final Orphic "transgression" of shadow and disguise. But such a conclusion calls to mind a variation on a current deconstructionist koan: "How can you tell the passenger from the passage?"

3

# Killing Kafka Koans: West Meets East

Everyone has access to God, but each a different access.

—Martin Buber

Notions of the *coincidentia oppositorum* from many different quarters converged in the fecund imagination of that unstable force of literary genius that was Franz Kafka. Early on there were the miraculous tales of the old Hasidic holy men whose powers enabled them to traverse the boundary between life and death with ease, tales forming part of Kafka's religious-cultural background as an Eastern European Jew. Later there was the dialectical thought of German Romanticism and Idealist philosophy in which he was steeped in the *Gymnasium* and again at the German University of Prague, like his near-contemporary Rilke. His favorite Romantic author was the kindred troubled soul, Heinrich von Kleist, whose brilliant essay, "On the Marionette Theater," had cast the *coincidentia* in lapsarian-mythic terms of Paradise Regained. (Kafka's twist on this was the obscure pronouncement that we would not reenter Paradise until the day *after* the Second Coming.) A further academic influence was the honors course in philosophical psychology that Kafka took in his senior year at the *Gymnasium*. Here he was introduced to some of the new cognitive research of the Leipzig experimental psychologist Wilhelm Wundt (Heidsieck 4–5), which led in turn to his preoccupation with the thought of Wundt's colleague, Gustav Theodor Fechner. Fechner's mystically tinged psychological solution to the age-old mind-body conundrum, the famous "identity hypothesis," intrigued Kafka, such that he soon found himself reading Fechner together with perhaps the West's most profound exponent of the *coincidentia,* Meister Eckhart (Kafka, *Briefe* 20)! Finally, there was Kafka's lifelong friendship with the Prague jurist and moral philosopher, Felix Weltsch, who, in several books well known to Kafka (one of which he even edited), framed the *coincidentia* in terms of a kind of creative *via media* (cf., e.g., *Die Wagnis der Mitte,* 1936) in his search for a solution to the nature-versus-spirit or instinct-versus-free will dichotomy (Schillemeit 168–69).

Yet, fascinating though this creative mingling of influences be, it surely was for Kafka no more than a gratifying corroboration of what was already quite clear to him from his own inner experience. For Kafka writing was from the beginning an almost instinctive kind of spiritual practice, a way of breaking through what he called "the frozen sea" of incessant self-absorption to a "total opening of body and soul" (qtd. in Sokel, "Frozen Sea" 71, 75). On at least one occasion, in his jotting-down of the story, "The Judgment," in a single nightlong trance-like sitting, Kafka felt he had fully experienced this elusive condition of pure writing; it was "as though the tale had written itself through him using him only as its medium" (Sokel, "Frozen Sea" 75). Writing was Kafka's way of touching the *coincidentia,* which for him took the form of the experience of a perfect congruence between his personal will as writer and the autonomous thrust of the process. But not only did the *coincidentia* "write" Kafka, he also wrote (about) *It*—one is almost tempted to say *only* (about) It—and did so in a style astonishingly reminiscent of the anecdotal koans of the ancient Zen masters. If one were asked by a Westerner for an explanation of Zen in Western terms, one could do much worse than to direct him to the short fiction of Franz Kafka.

## KAFKA'S INTUITIVE ZEN

The renowned eighteenth-century Zen master Hakuin once remarked that we must come to regard all of existence as one great koan. This, it seems to me, is what Franz Kafka did. Anyone with even a passing interest in Zen Buddhism will recognize the koan as one of the principal meditation exercises of the Rinzai sect. Kapleau defines it as "a formulation, in baffling language, pointing to ultimate truth. Koans cannot be solved by recourse to logical reasoning but only by awakening a deeper level of the mind beyond the discursive intellect" (369). The "ultimate truth" to which Kapleau refers is what we have been calling the *coincidentia oppositorum,* the no-man's land of spiritual freedom beyond all conceivable dualisms, which a good koan, through its subversion of logic, can disclose to the devoted student.

Typically, the Zen master assigns his student a koan in the form of an absurd question to be worked on during *zazen* (sitting meditation). Examples of koans well known to Westerners include: "What is the sound of one hand clapping?" and "What is your original face before your parents were born?" Every day, often twice a day, the student appears before the master in a private interview called *dokusan* to present his solution to the koan. Almost always the solution is based on reason, is therefore bogus and is gruffly rejected by the master. The student returns to his meditation cushion to continue the work. If all goes "well," he will eventually reach an impasse, a point of crisis at which all his strategies are exhausted and he finds himself pressed, indeed crushed, by this relentless question that, for his very life, demands an answer but for which he has none. He is empty, naked, paralyzed, plunged in darkness, utterly lost. Here is the fertile moment, the creative void. The mind, confronted with its own fundamental inadequacy to the task, surrenders to Mind, the Buddha Nature, which does not so much provide the answer as reveal itself to *be* the answer in ontological fact, the sole, complete, and perfect answer to this koan and every koan. The student is enlightened; in a flash he has grasped directly the nature of existence. At his next interview he presents his solution with the supreme confidence of an initiate and is joyously acknowledged as such by the master.

All of Kafka's fictions are remarkably koan-like in their style and spirit, but it is above all the short parables that show the deepest affinity to the Zen form. This affinity is most likely intuitive, since there is no evidence Kafka had any acquaintance with Zen. Joo-Dong Lee and James Whitlark have, however, pointed out his long-standing preoccupation with Taoism, one of the vital religio-cultural roots of Zen, from which the latter has inherited much of its delight in the pithy paradox as a catalyst of spiritual insight.[1] Of course, in any discussion of Kafka and mysticism in terms of historical influence, there is also the matter of his links to the folk literature of Hasidism, the mystical strain of his own religious culture. For this the reader is referred to Jean Jofen's book, *The Jewish Mystic in Kafka,* the first thorough treatment of the subject. Even here, however, where one would expect, say, explicit echoings in Kafka of themes and images from the Baal Shem tales, one is disappointed. This is so, Jofen argues, because of Kafka's elaborate efforts "to hide all traces of these [Hasidic] sources, in order to identify himself as a German writer" (xii). Nevertheless, as Jofen shows, his works are steeped in veiled allusion to the

Kabbalah and the Baal Shem tales, the latter as known to him through the collections of Buber and Peretz, among others (30–31, 42). Kafka's open enthusiasm for Taoism may have been a "safe" way of expressing affection for the perennial mystical wisdom from which, in its Hasidic garb, he found it necessary to distance himself as a "German writer."

However that may be, my aim in these pages is to examine the distinctly koan-like aspects of Kafka's short fiction and to show how these aspects poise the attentive reader (as they surely did the author) for sudden insight into the *coincidentia oppositorum,* for Kafka the summit of mystical wisdom. In a broader context I also offer this essay in support of the case for Kafka as a religious artist per se, for the question whether Kafka's vision *is* religious remains moot despite (or is it because of?) the sea of critical opinion as to his ultimate concerns. Moreover, like the *coincidentia* itself, it is a more fundamental question than that of particular religious influences and the effort to answer it takes us more deeply into his world than any amassing of historical evidence alone can do. Thus, I proceed here largely by way of analogy and propose to demonstrate an intimate inner congruence between Kafka's parabolic vision and that inspired by the meditative practice of a religion of which he presumably had no immediate knowledge. Indeed, I would suggest that the very foreignness of the Zen koan to Kafka's religious experience makes it an especially contamination-free gauge of that experience. As Max Brod, Kafka's closest friend, has emphasized, Kafka's religiosity is, in the final analysis, very much his own and his mysticism deeply personal (153). It should become evident in my review of several of Kafka's parables that this personal mysticism vouchsafed the artist a deep penetration into the painful contradiction that is human nature and an accompanying intuition of the conditions conducive to the healing of this contradiction.

## THE KOANS

Many of the parables are variations on the basic situation of impasse or entrapment, which, as noted, is precisely the internal condition a good koan is intended to induce in the student of Zen. Either the protagonist cannot move, or can do so only minimally, or, if he can move "freely," it is of no avail. Any action he may take merely tends to thicken the general atmosphere of oppression. Perhaps this is why Sussman, in his fascinating deconstructionist study of Kafka, observes that "air was for Kafka a genuine literary problem" (153).

"The Cell,"[2] "Robinson Crusoe," and "Alexander the Great" are good examples of parables featuring entrapment as critical moment. The first of these, "The Cell," parallels very closely the dynamic inner structure of the koan as it gradually confronts the meditator with the untenably dualistic nature of his own mind. The first-person narrator finds himself imprisoned in a moderately large hall lit by electric light. The hall's several doors open onto a dark, entombing rock-face only inches away: "Here was no way out" (117). Only one door is not an obvious dead-end, leading as it does to an adjoining room rich in color and decorated with several ceiling-high mirrors and a large glass chandelier. The narrator concludes his description with the perplexing remark, "But that was not all" (117), perplexing precisely because it *is* the conclusion, or perhaps, an interruption: we are not told what the something extra is, implied by the remark. On the contrary, a second paragraph is immediately introduced in which the narrator proclaims his liberation: "I do not have to go back again, the cell is burst open, I move, I feel my body" (117).

What has happened? How did the narrator escape the cell? Wisely he does not attempt to say, for to do so would amount to blasphemy: Enlightenment, or God, or Ultimate Reality, transcends all speech. This is implied by the silence that forms the mysterious seam between the paragraph of entrapment and the epilog paragraph proclaiming liberation. Within this silence all conceivable dualities, that is, the "traps" or "cells" that the mind in its ignorance creates for itself, are perfectly harmonized: for example, that of conscious (first room with bland electric light) and unconscious (richly colored inner room), ego (narrator) and self (archetypal glass chandelier), or subject (narrator) and object (cell). The narrator sees in a flash, not that he is *in* a trap, but that he is *himself* the trap, that he is nothing but "trap," that there is, therefore, no "one" to be trapped. Once clearly seen, there is no turning back on this insight. The narrator can only let go of the delusion of ego as a discrete and separate entity and become fully the cell he has always resisted. But what is this cell, this trap, if not perfect freedom itself? In becoming the trap he already ontologically is, the narrator gains his freedom. The opposites have coalesced: freedom and entrapment are realized to be one and the same. The freedom that, not being different from entrapment, can flourish right within the heart of entrapment—indeed, *only* there—is true freedom indeed.

Of course, all of this strikes ordinary intelligence as absurd, since it is, quite literally, inconceivable. But that is precisely Kafka's—and Zen's—point. Ultimate truth, lying beyond all conception, *is* absurd, but it is an infinitely fertile Absurdity that provides the matrix within which all concepts arise. Unless the mind is forced into unequivocal awareness of the limits of its own point of view, it has no chance of bursting through those limits. All formal koans and, as I maintain, all of Kafka's short parables, are calculated to trap the mind, to drive it back into itself until a certain optimal pitch of tension is reached at which point the explosive flash of Enlightenment may occur: "the cell is burst open, I move, I feel my body."

Many Zen koans recall stern teaching methods of the ancient masters the aim of which was to back their students into a desperate corner, much like the one in which the narrator of "The Cell" finds himself. D. T. Suzuki, the premier interpreter of Zen to the West, cites several of these:

> Ummon expressed the same idea with his staff, which he held up, saying: "What is this? If you say it is a staff, you go right to hell; but if it is not a staff, what is it?" Hima's (Pi-mo's) way somewhat deviated from this. He used to carry a forked stick and whenever a monk came up to him and made a bow, he applied the stick on the neck of the monk, and said: "What devil taught you to be a homeless monk? What devil taught you to go round? Whether you can say something, or whether you cannot say anything, all the same you are to die under my fork: speak, speak, be quick!" Tokusan (Tê-shan) was another master who flourished a stick to the same effect; for he used to say, "No matter what you say, or what you say not, just the same thirty blows for you!" (276)

In each case the student's opting for *this* position vis-à-vis *that* is blocked; the logical dualism of the conscious mind is mercilessly frustrated. In the same vein, having tried the various apparent exit-doors of the electrically lit hall without success, the narrator of "The Cell" is reduced to the stark realization: "Here was no way out." Only by giving up all hope of escape and plunging more deeply into his cell does he have any chance, as Suzuki puts it, "of affirming the truth transcending the dualism of 'to be' *(sat)* and 'not to be' *(asat)*" (277).

By virtue of the fact that koans stymie the mind's natural tendency to see things in either/or terms (true/false, good/evil, beautiful/ugly, pleasurable/painful, etc.), they cause suffering, at times intense suffering. Zen practice soon reveals to the student that, protestations to the contrary notwithstanding, deep down he does not want to heal the fissure within his own mind because he senses that such healing will require him to surrender the delusion that is the most fundamental expression of that fissure, that of subject versus object, or ego versus world. He will do anything to hold onto his belief in himself as an independent entity standing apart from the rest of the universe. Yet it is precisely this belief that must go in order that his True Nature, the Buddha Nature (the term for the fundamental interdependence of all things), may become manifest. The symbolic equivalent in Christianity for the suffering inextricably linked to koan work is the crucifixion. In order for the true Oneness of things to emerge, the apparent split between them, represented by the cruci-form, must be willingly endured until it is overcome.[3] In koan meditation one's entire personal psychology, the suture of contradictions, shallow and deep, that make up one's individual identity, is gradually evoked and crystallized by the formal koan, such that in penetrating the koan one is penetrating oneself. In effect, through the koan one nails oneself to the cross of one's own fissured nature, becoming fully conscious of it in order thereby to go beyond it. This going-beyond is a death, but the death of the old man is, at once, the birth of the new in absolute freedom.

This hard lesson taught by koans, that the way out of suffering leads *through* suffering, that the way out of the trap of one's own mind leads more deeply into, and not away from, the trap, is cogently demonstrated in Kafka's parable, "Robinson Crusoe," a virtual companion piece to "The Cell":

> Had Robinson Crusoe never left the highest, or more correctly the most visible point of his island, from desire for comfort, or timidity, or fear, or ignorance, or longing, he would soon have perished; but since without paying any attention to passing ships and their feeble telescopes he started to explore the whole island and take pleasure in it, he managed to keep himself alive and finally was found after all, by a chain of causality that was, of course, logically inevitable. (185)

Here again we have the suffering of entrapment as starting point, in this case agoraphobic rather than claustrophobic, but they are, of course, two sides of a coin: either way, the conscious mind is imagined as a place of solipsistic pain. (Often in Kafka opposite situations or strategies are shown to be symmetrically futile, e.g., actively trying to gain entrance to the Law and passively waiting for the Emperor's message, Kafka's "metamessage" being that there is nothing you can do, no attitude you can take.) Here the conscious mind is represented as the "highest . . . most visible point" of an island the base of which is shrouded in mystery, much as Jung was fond of depicting the mind as an archipelago the most superficial contours of which alone were visible.

Robinson as metaphor for the meditative mind, the mind attempting to explore itself, commune with itself, represents a rather deep stage of meditation, for the typical panoply of passions that bind the conscious mind ("desire for comfort, or timidity, or fear, or ignorance, or longing") and that can be summed up in the second of the Buddha's Four Noble Truths: "The cause of suffering is desire," has already been virtually surrendered. Concomitantly, the a priori categories of mind by which human desire is structured and ordered, time and space, are also fast dissolving: in giving up hope of rescue, that is, his own sense of expectancy, Robinson renounces the future and simultaneously lets go of the distancing space between himself and the hoped-for rescue ship created by desire. But every letting-go of ego boundaries (time, space, and desire) is also, and necessarily, a letting-in, an embrace of the here and now, not the *hic et nunc fluens* of the ordinary alert mind, but the *hic et nunc stans* of the meditative mind, the mind in the state of samadhi that takes utter delight in everything that arises within it. Thus, Robinson began "to explore the whole island and take pleasure in it," playfully plumbing his own depths, as it were, and finding therein a great treasure, namely, his perfect adequacy to all circumstances, just as the narrator of "The Cell" gains freedom by completely penetrating the room within.

Both parables end with a tantalizing allusion to spiritual Enlightenment *(satori),* the breakthrough to absolute freedom for which koan work prepares the ground. But the dramatic and unequivocal first-person exclamation of "The Cell" ("I move, I feel my body") yields here to a rather enigmatic reference to the logical inevitability of Robinson's rescue: "he . . . finally was found after all, by a chain of causality that was, of course, logically inevitable." The characterization of Robinson's rescue as logically inevitable, when it would seem anything but, cues us to look beyond the superficial dualistic logic of the rational mind, which sees no intimate connection between abandonment and rescue, to the deeper dialectical logic of the transpersonal or cosmic Mind, which beholds the eternal interplay of the opposites: at that indeterminate moment when Robinson gives himself up totally to his isolation, thus dying to desire, he is rescued—by his Self, the Buddha Nature, which, by virtue of its absolute nondiscrimination between abandonment and rescue, constitutes the only true rescue. Here again the Christian equivalent would be contained in Christ's paradoxical utterance, "whoever loses his life for my sake will gain it" (Matt. 10.39).

While both "The Cell" and "Robinson Crusoe" end on the triumphant note of the Great Awakening, the protagonist's emancipating realization of his seamless solidarity with all existence, "Alexander the Great" stops short of this triumph, focusing on the object of Kafka's deepest fascination: the mind as its own trap. (The perfect emblem of this trap of the deluded consciousness is also a creation of the author's: his stick-figure etching of the man hemmed in by a three-sided fence who fails to see the exit right behind him.) This is, of course, the far more typical—and familiar—"Kafkaesque" scenario of the protagonist who is immobilized by the lethal insight that there is nothing he can do, that any move he might make would be binding. To be sure, Alexander is bound whether he knows it or not; but his dawning *awareness* that he is bound leaves him no choice but to confront this already intact condition of entrapment. It is this very awareness of the totality of the trap that is rife with spiritual possibilities. Thus, the hero enters the Dark Night of the soul and approaches the Great Death of which all mystical traditions speak. He sees that the only conquest that really matters is that of his own mind. Can he die to his own ego and thus subdue the inner world as successfully as he has the outer?

> It is conceivable that Alexander the Great, in spite of the martial successes of his early days, in spite of the excellent army that he had trained, in spite of the power he felt within him to change the world, might have remained standing on the bank of the Hellespont and never have crossed it, and not out of fear, not out of indecision, not out of infirmity of will, but because of the mere weight of his own body. (95)

The narrative of "Alexander the Great" parallels the koan meditative process up to the point of the deep despair that accompanies ego death, ending with that despair. The only term in Kafka's text that alludes to the human agony of self-surrender is, aptly, that on which it ends: "Erdenschwere" [the mere weight of his own body]. This wonderfully dense and, in this context, enigmatic word suggests a key principle of koan work in particular and Buddhist psychology in general: the principle of the Middle Way.

The Middle Way is the pathless path between any given (dis)position of mind and its opposite, thus inferring a transcendent consciousness that envelops the pairs of opposites, indeed, that gives birth to them. Christmas Humphreys puts it well:

> The doctrine of causation applied to the individual character is expressed in the Four Noble Truths; the omnipresence of suffering; its cause, selfish desire; its cure, the elimination of that separative desire; and the way to this removal. This way is the Middle Way between extremes. For if manifestation is based on the 'pairs of opposites', the way to the Unity from which they sprang must be between them and above them and beyond. (21–22)

Thus, human consciousness is by nature partial, ever at odds with its own unconscious correspondent. The Middle Way is the neutral, but in no sense uninvolved, cusp, the lean, taut non-position between dynamically opposed mental configurations, the s-shaped curve connecting yin and yang in the well-known Taoist symbol. And that is precisely the point: it is the *connection* between "things" rather than any "thing" in particular; it is, when fully realized, the spirit of relationship itself, seen to be prior to the terms of relationship. Since it is not a thing but that by which things are connected, it is not "bedingt" and as such enjoys Absolute Freedom. A man who realizes the Middle Way realizes the *coincidentia oppositorum* and thus his potential for Divinity, for this is what the neutrality of the Middle Way implies and points to. But, of course, to do so man must die as man. All positions must be relinquished, all intentions surrendered, all values abandoned. Manifestations of partiality as they all are, they bring suffering, for all parts can but crave their counterparts.

Kafka's sense of the unfathomable (to the human mind) wisdom of the Middle Way is expressed through the utter strangeness of his Alexander's "Erdenschwere." How could such a titan find himself rooted to the spot, stuck on the bank of the Hellespont? How could this very embodiment of worldly power suddenly become impotent? It is precisely because his conquests have shown him the limits of even the grandest of human enterprises that he begins to become aware of the weight of his own body. The energy that had been flowing out centrifugally into his various campaigns is now drawing back centripetally into itself, its mounting density a measure of the despair of his insight that there is nothing he can do. If there is nothing he can do, then certainly he will do nothing. But truly to do nothing, to die to one's own intentionality, is to die. Alexander's own life has become his koan, just as all formal koans, seriously pursued, are eventually seen to be one with the meditator's life. The Hellespont is Alexander's personal impasse, the mid or crosspoint from which emanate the many potential directions for action all of which the hero now sees to be futile. His weight, compressing him like a good koan ever more tightly into his own center of gravity, portends implosion, the implosion of Enlightenment.

One sees by Alexander's "Erdenschwere" that Zen koans comprise no monopoly on the wisdom of the Middle Way. Indeed, Western expressions of this wisdom are legion and by no means exclusively, or even predominantly, ancient. From the late medieval mystic Nicolaus Cusanus's notion of God as the *coincidentia oppositorum* [4] through the dialectical visions of Goethe, Hegel, and Jung to Jacques Derrida's currently powerful deconstruction with its ironic delight in unearthing the *aporiai* by which texts (expressions of mental sets) cancel out their own positions, the sense that ultimate truth is more likely to be found *between* things than within them, and that even this "within," if examined closely enough, must turn out to be but a subtle form of "between," has always run as a countercurrent to mainstream Western rationalism. Like the Zen koan, this countercurrent validates Alexander's experience of "Erdenschwere" as a dreadful prelude to an irreversible move beyond the familiar dualistic contours of his own mind, prelude to a lethal leap "beyond the pairs."[5]

A brief look at the most renowned of all Zen koans, "Joshu's 'Mu,'"[6] will further clarify the nature of the Middle Way taken by Alexander, as well as by another of Kafka's victims of "Erdenschwere"—Gregor Samsa. *Mu* is the first of the forty-eight koans that make up the medieval collection entitled *Mumonkan (The Gateless Barrier),* compiled by Zen master Mumon:

> A monk asked Joshu, "Has a dog Buddha Nature?" Joshu answered, "Mu." (Sekida, *Two Zen Classics* 27)

Taken by countless Zen students down through the ages as the focus of *zazen* meditation, this *Mu* (literally "no," "not," "have not," or "nothing") has been a most powerful form of "Erdenschwere." To solve this koan, the student must go beyond *Mu* as signifier (negation vis-à-vis affirmation) and grasp it directly as a *Ding an sich,* or, as Shibayama puts it, as "the Truth that transcends both affirmation and negation, subject and object. . . . the Truth experientially grasped by each individual by casting away all his discriminating consciousness" (348). When *Mu* is grasped, not conceptually but ontologically, the gap between signifier and signified is closed, the rift of language healed, and since, fundamentally, there is from the Zen point of view only one rift, that between "I" and "Not-I," to solve the koan is to resolve the problem of man's *apparent* alienation from nature induced by the "distancing" linguistic consciousness. I stress "apparent" and place "distancing" in quotation marks to emphasize Zen's point of view that alienation is a delusion and that this delusion, with all its attendant suffering, constitutes the human condition: man is not separate from nature, but only *believes* himself to be so, not realizing that even this hypnotic belief is itself part of nature.

To realize *Mu* is to go the Middle Way and die to the belief in a separate self. (To speak of "ego-death" as such, rather than the death of the *belief* in an ego, is an imprecise, even if generally accepted, shorthand, since the ego has in Buddhism no substantial reality.) The months or, more typically, years of work required to solve the koan thus constitute a process of dying, a gradual giving-up of one's sense of individuality invariably entailing agony and despair. This death throes would seem unavoidable since to give up one's sense of oneself as a discrete being is to give up one's most fundamental "position," indeed one's very world. "Erdenschwere" is here experienced in the deepest phase of koan work as a sense of being simultaneously pulled in opposite directions, both backward in fear to the familiar confines of the old ego-identity and forward in longing toward the not-yet-realized Truth of *Mu*. The dread of an absolute claustrophobia mounts as any move is seen to be futile. One has come too far to return to the old "I," and yet any grasping for Ultimate Truth only brings frustration since all grasping is of the "ego." According to Mumon, this total paralysis, this despair over the utter vanity of all human (i.e., one-sided) effort is propitious for Enlightenment. When the student feels thus "stuck" in *Mu, Mu* is doing its proper work:

> It will be just as if you swallow a red-hot iron ball, which you cannot spit out even if you try. All the illusory ideas and delusive thoughts accumulated up to the present will be exterminated, and when the time comes, internal and external will be spontaneously united. You will know this, but for yourself only, like a dumb man who has had a dream. Then all of a sudden an explosive conversion will occur, and you will astonish the heavens and shake the earth. (Sekida, *Two Zen Classics* 28)

"Erdenschwere" is, then, Alexander's *Mu,* the riveting weight that attends the clear awareness of the futility of any further move, whether in advance or retreat. It is, I believe, also Gregor Samsa's *Mu,* as he arrives at a similar impasse after a season of hellish struggle between human and insect identities: "'And now?', Gregor wondered and looked around in the darkness. He soon discovered that he was completely unable to move. This did not surprise him, rather it seemed to him unnatural that he had ever been able to get around on these spindly little legs at all" (M; *Erzählungen* 88). Hours later, shortly after the allusive "third hour of morning," Gregor dies, but his biological death has been preceded by the far more significant death to the self or self-will. From the vantage point of the razor's edge, that is, the painful interface of indecision between human and insect identities, Gregor clearly sees the futility of trying to resolve his identity crisis in terms of one side or the other.[7] He sees that he can never be "human," never be an "insect," never be any one thing to the exclusion of any other. The insight that all moves to fix positions of identity are futile is the psycho-spiritual death that makes of his biological death an anticlimax. Gregor's surrender of his own will, with its welter of conflicting urges, conscious and unconscious, toward and away from either "human" or "insect," is, in effect, the total surrender to *Mu,* the fiery iron ball stuck in the throat that "melt[s] down your illusions . . . [t]he opinions you hold and your worldly knowledge . . . [i]n short, all conceivable ideas."[8] Having arrived finally at that inner emptiness prized by Zen—"in this state of empty and peaceful reflection" (M; *Erzählungen* 89)—Gregor suddenly experiences rebirth in freedom on the very threshold of biological death, and the compassion for others that had heretofore been blocked by self-absorption flows out in unalloyed profusion: "He thought back on his family with affection and love" (M; *Erzählungen* 89). He fulfills that paradoxical jingle of the mystics, "If you die before you die, then when you die, you won't die" (qtd. in Wilber 135), living on perhaps in the quasi-divine dimension of the narrator, whose intimate proximity to Gregor throughout the tale Kafka has taken great pains to establish.[9]

Reading Kafka through the ignescent lens of the Zen koan helps us to grasp his essentially Buddhist perspective on the individual ego, a perspective that is subtly and incontrovertibly anatmic. To miss Kafka's anatmic or no-self insight is fundamentally to misread him, however deeply one may penetrate him on other fronts. This is why I was at pains above to distinguish between ego-death, so-called, and death to the *belief* in an ego, for it is, according to Zen—and Kafka—only a belief or erroneous point of view that "dies," not a substance. It is also why I support Sussman's important critique of Sokel, a critique issuing from Sussman's fruitful deconstructionist approach with its unnerving claims of having unmasked the fictitious nature of the self or ego:

> Sokel would not experience the impossibility of an integrated or unified self in Kafka's fiction as such a loss if he gave the priority in his analysis to the question of fictive language. The self would then appear as a construct applied retrospectively [presumably by both critic without and character within] to a dynamic which operates primarily according to linguistic principles [Zen would say rather: the dualistic principle of the deluded mind], and not as a preexisting spiritual entity.[10] (12)

In other words, Sussman is saying that Kafka-critics with a depth-psychological orientation are themselves mesmerized by the very egoic phantom that Kafka's art attempts to expose, much as Lacan holds the ego-analysts responsible for perpetuating the pain-inducing assumption of the reality of an ego (Harland 37–38).

There is a chilling passage in Sussman's discussion of "The Burrow" from which we can clearly glean the basic anatmic point of view shared by Kafka, Zen, and deconstruction:

> It is, then, with some skepticism that we must observe the animal "embrace" its work. The creature issues a voice to publicize the construction and preserve it for posterity. But the voice is already the house organ of the construction. The animal "self" which is the master of the voice is likewise already in the employ of this work. The creator finds itself circumscribed by its own creation, by the reality for which the construction serves as limit. The author embraces its work, but the labor . . . hugs back, its grasp not constrained and certainly not so loving. The author may suffocate, loved to death by its own work. (153)

"The Burrow" can be read as a stunning metaphor for the kind of claustrophobic dread entailed by koan work. In embracing (deconstructing) the koan (construction, mind), the meditator is embracing death. Death hugs him in the form of the smothering realization that there is no meditator, only meditating; or, as that perennial Buddhist paradox has it: "Suffering there is, but none who suffer; deeds there are, but none who perform them; the way there is, but none who travel it." But, in the leap of the opposites to identity, the killing blow turns out to be the liberating stroke: if one does not exist as this or that, one is free. Once released from being anything in particular, one is free to be everything without exception: "the cell is burst open, I move, I feel my body," "body" having now become the self-realized Body of the World.

But it is precisely this freedom, hinted at by Kafka, which is not the opposite of anything, even of entrapment, being therefore absolute, that the deconstructionist approach seems, if not wholly to miss, at least not fully to appreciate, whereas from the Zen point of view it is the heart of the matter. Take, for example, Sussman's concluding flourish in which he links Kafka to the painter Bosch: "Like Kafka, Bosch summons a world fragmented by a priori deconstruction. Also like Kafka, however, for Bosch there is the possibility of moving two ways, of assimilating the pristine into the sweep toward fragmentation" (181). But we saw how Kafka's Alexander became rooted to the spot as he realized the futility of *any* move inasmuch as that move, by its partial, exclusionary quality, would of necessity reestablish the illusory "I" over against the equally illusory "Not-I" and land him back in dualism. Hence the Hellespont as an apt image of the fundamental impasse of the dualistic mind: the hero can neither advance nor retreat from it. Sussman notwithstanding, for Kafka there is *no* possibility of movement. Indeed, if there were, suffering would be endless, since all moves create the confining illusion of "someone" moving, or, to speak with Sussman, of "someone" "assimilating the pristine," whereas freedom is movement without a mover, assimilation without an assimilator, and is what it is *because* there is seen to be no mover/assimilator.[11] Kafka glimpsed what Zen never loses sight of: that the ecstatic flow of consciousness released by seeing through the egoic mover *is* the True Self. The "I" in "I move" is strictly a concession of Kafka's to language. By insisting on retaining directionality, in the sense of options for purposeful movement, at all, Sussman falls victim to the very illusion of self or subject he is otherwise at pains as a deconstructionist to debunk, and to show Kafka as debunking.

"Alexander the Great" casts the human dilemma onto an external space and portrays it as the futility of movement; "The Spring" may be seen as its internal correlative, presenting the dilemma in more recognizably Buddhist terms as the unquenchability of desire. These two parables complement each other somewhat in the manner of the various sets of koans that make up

Hakuin's elaborate modern system,[12] coming at the same fundamental problem from different angles or "spaces." For Kafka, both desire and movement are manifestations of what he elsewhere calls man's "primal sin: impatience. Because of impatience they [i.e., men] have been driven [from Paradise], and because of it they do not return" (M; *Hochzeitsvorbereitungen* 39). Impatience is thus man's self-will, his relentless itch to "get somewhere," which prevents him from seeing that the only destination worth reaching is always already arrived at.

"The Spring" beautifully concretizes the problem as one of thirst:

> He is thirsty, and is cut off from a spring by a mere clump of bushes. But he is divided against himself: one part overlooks the whole, sees that he is standing here and that the spring is just beside him; but another part notices nothing, has at most a divination that the first part sees all. But as he notices nothing he cannot drink. (185)

Taken as a koan, "The Spring" aims, through the example of the persona, to awaken the reader to the fact that he already has everything he needs, the only problem being his *belief* that he lacks something. Thus the problem of desire is itself shown by Kafka to be a problem of false consciousness or unconsciousness. This parable has a close counterpart in case 10 of the *Mumonkan,* entitled "Seizei Is Utterly Destitute":

> Seizei [a monk] said to Sozan [a master], "Seizei [referring to himself] is utterly destitute. Will you give him support?" Sozan called out, "Seizei!" Seizei responded, "Yes, sir!" Sozan said, "You have finished three cups of the finest wine in China, and still you say you have not yet moistened your lips!" (Sekida, *Two Zen Classics* 49)

To thirst for anything is to believe, falsely, that that thing is outside us. It is the implicit (unconscious) sense of separation that is the root problem, not the putative lack of the desired object. To solve the koan-parable is to realize this fully and undergo a transformation of one's entire being in which all "objects" are seen to be always already inside one. In Kafka's picture, it is for consciousness to make the leap from the part to the Whole, or from ignorance ("but another part notices nothing") to Enlightenment or the True Self which comprehends—and is therefore master of—all things, not excluding the antinomy, thirst versus satiation or desire versus fulfillment ("one part overlooks the whole, sees that he is standing here and that the spring is just beside him").[13]

Though desire is fundamental ignorance, yet the wisdom that would in any way remain aloof from ignorance is not True Wisdom. Rather, True Wisdom is that which is perfectly at home with ignorance, never leaving it for an instant. This twist of the paradox, pointing again to the identity of opposites, is ingeniously adumbrated by Kafka in "The Truth about Sancho Panza":

> Without making any boast of it Sancho Panza succeeded in the course of years, by devouring a great number of romances of chivalry and adventure in the evening and night hours, in so diverting from him his demon, whom he later called Don Quixote, that his demon thereupon set out in perfect freedom on the maddest exploits, which, however, for the lack of a preordained object, which should have been Sancho Panza himself, harmed nobody. A free man, Sancho Panza philosophically followed Don Quixote on his crusades, perhaps out of a sense of responsibility, and had of them a great and edifying entertainment to the end of his days. (179)

Just as "Alexander the Great" and "The Spring" pair off differentially as outside (movement) and inside (desire) approaches to the human predicament, so too do "The Spring" and "Sancho Panza," but in this case as approaches from the respective viewpoints of ignorance and Wisdom (or Enlightenment). "The Spring" shows the suffering inevitably generated by the delusion of separateness; "Sancho Panza" shows the joy and freedom (True Wisdom) flowing from the awareness of the symbiotic relationship of ignorance (Don Quixote) and wisdom (Sancho Panza),[14] and, in so doing, hints at that which man must do in order to solve the basic koan of his own life. One could say that Wisdom issues here, as in all koans, from an ownerless voice, or from the writing/reading/comprehension itself (there being, à la deconstruction, no writer/reader/comprehender), or from the True Self that Sancho has finally found himself to be. (Kafka would doubtless assert that for us to identify the source of Wisdom in a reflex gesture as himself would merely be to give a name to the Nameless, relieving ourselves thereby of our anxiety over confronting an authorless text.)

However one may phrase it, it is clear that Wisdom is here alluded to as the combustive act of the koan-parable's grasping itself, that is, "one" solves the koan-parable in the instant the koan-parable solves itself. As a narrative, "Sancho Panza" may be said to be *about* this combustive flash of the opposites (the Don and Sancho) into identity, but the object of this narrative referentiality or "aboutness" (what Zen calls "the finger pointing at the moon") is nothing other than the narrative itself. The text is poised to close the gap between one set of putative opposites, signifier and signified, by narratively playing on the symbiotic unity of the members of another set, ignorance and wisdom. Thus, Sancho is initially characterized as a quasi meditator or koan-student (an avid reader of romances) who has emancipated himself from the demon of ego (the proud but deluded "adventurer" Quixote) by resolving a series of koans: "by devouring a great number of romances of chivalry and adventure." In studying a koan, one studies oneself. Sancho has looked into the mirror, so to speak, the mirror of romances that, like powerful koans, have confronted him again and again with his own egoic delusion (the Don). At last seeing through delusion, realizing its essential emptiness, he is "a free man," even as he continues to live in the very midst of it. He is like a man in a dream who suddenly realizes he is dreaming, the realization freeing him to enjoy to the utmost whatever the dream may conjure up, good or bad: "A free man, Sancho Panza philosophically followed Don Quixote on his crusades . . . and had of them a great and edifying entertainment to the end of his days." In a similar spirit, Rinzai describes the Enlightened Man as one who has "nothing to do" for the rest of his life.

As a description tantamount to a demonstration of the joyfully protean interplay of the opposites, "Sancho Panza" is evidence of the penetration of Kafka's spiritual insight far beyond the orthodox boundaries of the religions of his own culture which tend to keep the opposites apart. Wisdom and ignorance, salvation and bondage, self and ego, signifier and signified—"Sancho Panza" shows True Wisdom, True Salvation, True Self, True Text to lie in the perfect, and necessary, coexistence of each of these with its partner. There is no separate, idealized God or Reality here; the Divine is as intimate with human foolishness as is the liberated Sancho with the Don, or the latter with his horse, as intimate, to cite a frequent Zen image, as is the lily with the mud from which it sprouts.

If Don Quixote, "accompanied" as he is by Sancho, is Wisdom qua illuminated ignorance, the man from the country in "Before the Law" is ignorance unregenerate. In failing to pass through the gate to the Law, he fails to solve his "koan," that is, the problem of existence. That it is not only existence as such, but also *his* existence in all its particularity with which he fails to come to terms, indeed, that he fails to see the absolute congruence of these two, which insight would constitute one possible solution to his "koan," is made clear at the end by the doorkeeper's icy revelation: "No one but you could gain admittance through this door, since this door was intended only for you" (65).

The Law is Kafka's version of the Dharma or Tao, "the Way things are," with which the man is "out of synch."[15] But again, as always in Kafka, the idea of disparity is itself problematic. Since the Law comprehends all things, not excluding disparity, then disparity is also part of it, and the man's problem becomes, again, one of viewpoint rather than substance, that is to say, he takes disparity or separation to be a "problem," rather than an aspect of the Solution. The man is caught in delusion; he sees a barrier to the Law that is, in Reality, no barrier at all. Viewing separation as a problem, he resists it through his striving to close the *perceived* gap between himself and the Law. He does not see that all attempts to do something—"He makes many attempts to be allowed in" (61)—to overcome the "space" between himself and the Law are actually creating that distancing space with all its malevolent denizens: a doorkeeper, nay, several doorkeepers, an endless succession of doorkeepers positioned "between" the man and his goal. These can only be an image of the obsessive samsaric mind, the mind inflamed with desire, whose every move toward fulfillment merely empowers the barriers to fulfillment: "From hall to hall keepers stand at every door, one more powerful than the other" (61). There can no more be an end to the receding column of doorkeepers (sequential time) than there can be an end to the problem of desire, even desire for God, from within the blinding confines (time and space) of desire. Desire that does not know itself to be its own barrier is endless.

Putting it in terms of deconstruction, this infinite series of doorkeepers is the never-ending interpretive text, the human mind's self-perpetuating compulsion to understand ("reach and come to rest in") an illusory originary text (idealized God or Truth), which, precisely because it is an illusion/elusion, the mind can never quite "get right" and must interpret and interpret and interpret again. Each successive interpretive act, by its very intent (desire) to close in on its imagined object, ends up a more potent "doorkeeper" than the last. The doorkeeper(s), then, is an image of man's own projected illusion of separation from what he *thinks* he lacks.

Right here, in this irony of the impasse, Kafka catches precisely, brilliantly, the spirit of the *Mumonkan,* the premiere Zen koan collection. As Sekida tells us, the title "is usually translated as 'gateless gate' or 'gateless barrier' (*mu,* nothing, no; *mon,* gate; *kan,* barrier)." He goes on to explain that the title contains, on closer inspection, an ambiguity, inferring thereby its allusion to the ambiguous nature of all koans: "['gateless barrier'] would suggest a barrier with no passage through it. However, the ideograph *kan* may also refer to a checkpoint on national or prefectural boundaries where travelers' credentials are examined by police, so that a possible interpretation of *Mumonkan* is 'a checkpoint that is not blocked in any way.' Hence, the title might also be translated as 'open checkpoint'" (*Two Zen Classics* 27). Koans, then, are barriers that are no-barriers, problems that *are* their own solutions. When the problem, be it called desire, text, or man, is seen to be its own solution, it becomes obvious that there *is* no problem, and never has been one. The man from the country always already *is* the Tao. Had he only recognized the fact!

## WRITING AS KOAN PRACTICE

It is clear that Kafka's deepest moments of spiritual insight revealed to him the truth of the *coincidentia oppositorum,*[16] the elusive interface binding the pairs where, according to Zen, the Divine is at home. But only here and there, in this and that short piece, and perhaps at the end of *The Metamorphosis,* does Kafka give evidence of so much as a fleeting glimpse of the solution to his own literary koans in a Divinity felt to be so total, so enveloping, as to embrace even the undiluted pain of contradiction, absurdity, madness—indeed, death itself—without blinking. Most of the time he is absorbed in elaborating that madness unto death in the guise of metaphors, not only of writing, as Sussman correctly but narrowly argues, but of the mind of ignorance in any of its infinite permutations. The burrow with its endless passageways, the maze-like castle complex, the ceaseless textualizing of the court bureaucracy—all nightmarish evocations of the deluded mind hopelessly entangled in its own karmic activity, each "new" cavern, path, or document merely serving to tighten the straitjacket of delusion another notch. (Let the irony not be lost on us that at any moment any one of these metaphors of anguish can flash out into the dimension of the symbolic, revealing itself to *be* what it means. In such moments of the *coincidentia* of word and thing, *Bild* and *Vorbild,* Kafka's free Zen spirit is revealed. To ask *who* reveals it or to *whom* it is revealed would be to pose a koan Kafka would doubtless have relished. In the spirit of such a koan all nouns and pronouns referring to "Kafka" from here to the end, quotations aside, are placed in quotation marks.)

With time and patience, the Zen student learns that only by sustained mental focus on the koan as it comes to embody his personal madness in all its Byzantine complexity can he hope to penetrate that madness to the very bottom and, from there, see it as only part of the story, only one of the gestures of the Spirit that freely "moveth as it listeth." "Kafka's" writing activity was, I think, a courageous, self-styled kind of koan practice that occasionally penetrated deeply enough to reveal to "him" some sense, however dim, of this blissfully integral swim of things known in Zen as Enlightenment or satori.[17] Doubtless "Kafka's" entire literary career, which is to say, in effect, "his" life, was a sustained effort to grasp clearly the essential freedom of things as vouchsafed by the very unfixity of their nature. It seems that early on "he" had an intuition of the blithe dance of Truth between even those ultimate poles of being and non-being, *samsara* and *nirvana*. The rational mind balks at this concluding diary entry in which the "author" recalls a solitary hour of stock-taking in youth:

> Once, many years ago, I was sitting on the slope of Mount St. Lawrence, sad enough to be sure. I was reviewing the wishes I had for my life. The most important or beguiling one turned out to be this: to gain a view of life (and, as a necessary corollary, to convince others of this view through my writings) in which life would still have its natural palpable ups and downs but, at the same time, with no less clarity be recognizable as a cipher, as a dream, as a floating. Perhaps a beautiful wish, if I had really wished it. The wish, say, to be able to hammer a table together with meticulous workmanship while, at the same time, to be doing nothing, but not in such a way that one could say: "That hammering is nothing to him," but rather, "To him that hammering is a real hammering and, at the same time, also a nothing," whereby the hammering would've become even bolder, more decisive, more real and, if you will, more insane. (M; qtd. in Wagenbach 44)

"Perhaps a beautiful wish, if I had really wished it." This strikes me as the regret of a "man" intuitively in search of the koan as a royal road to the *coincidentia oppositorum*.

4

# *Interface:* Identity/Difference/Prestidigitation

When the two disappear into the one, where does the one go?

—Zen mondo

Let us pause here in the middle of our study, poised between Figure and Ground, to reflect on the Interface, the seamless seam between them, as indeed between any pair of opposites. But to do this is perhaps recklessly to hazard the impossible, to lift the eyes in fear and trembling to the Face of God, for it is to reflect directly on the *coincidentia oppositorum* itself, no longer shielded from its subtle brilliance by the muting refracted colors of Rilke's poetry or Kafka's parables. How does one adumbrate what is not meant for human vision, outer or inner? One feels rather like poor Borges in "The Aleph" who likewise arrives "at the ineffable center of my story. And here begins my despair as a writer. All language is an alphabet of symbols whose use presupposes a past shared by all the other interlocuters. How, then, transmit to others the infinite Aleph, which my fearful mind scarcely encompasses[,] . . . a sphere whose center is everywhere and whose circumference is nowhere?" (149).

The Aleph, a radiant globe miraculously suspended in the dark, dank air of a cellar somewhere in Buenos Aires, is one of many images of the coincidence of opposites studding the works of the great Argentinian writer. For, when first beheld, it is experienced as the center of the universe, but then very quickly comes to *comprehend* the universe. Is it then figure or ground, center or circumference—or both, or neither? Such imponderables, bubbling up as they do from the volcanic heat of Borges's prose, virtually induce in the reader's consciousness a confrontation between the antagonists that make up the most fundamental antinomy of all: identity and difference. Are things basically the same or different, one or many? As William James put it with respect to the mind-expanding proclivities of alcohol, experience of the Aleph would seem to bring this issue from the "chill periphery" of abstraction to the "radiant core" of lived mystical experience; for if identity and difference are each themselves yet somehow also one, then all the other eternally warring pairs of opposites (truth/falsity, good/evil, beauty/ugliness, etc.), subsumed as it were under this template, come into ineffable harmony even as they *appear* to carry on the ancient struggle. It is as if real-life conflict had suddenly been transformed into the tragedy of grand opera, full of sound and fury signifying nothing but aesthetic enjoyment.

Let us see in the following pages what a very old Eastern and a contemporary Western discipline, Zen and deconstruction, can help us to "say" about the *coincidentia oppositorum* in this, its most fundamental and spiritually compelling form. The issue is momentous, for suspended from it is the question whether man is condemned to confinement within his own quotidian rationality. Or might there be some magical gesture, some act of prestidigitation, that can get him out?

## THE CASE OF MRS. K.

It is one thing to hack one's anguished intellectual way through the thickets and brambles of Derrida's differential *Urwald,* only to wonder at the end whether one need have bothered, and quite another to read one of the autobiographical accounts of moments of spiritual illumination included in Philip Kapleau's *Three Pillars of Zen*. It turns out, however, that the latter experience validates the former! In a single gesture of majesterial authority, Zen cuts through all the neurotic perseveration of deconstruction to lay bare the solution to the problem whether things are, at bottom, the same or different. What is more, it does so without disturbing so much as a single leaf in deconstruction's overgrown forest; indeed, it reveals that forest of theoretical language, with all its smothering density, to be the very soul of order itself.

We begin, therefore, with Zen, relying on its unflinching vigilance to lead us safely past the snares of compounded discursive subtlety—even as we observe some of these along the way—to an awareness of the awesome freedom concealed in the seemingly insoluble contradiction between identity and difference. Kapleau climaxes his series of autobiographical vignettes with the testimony of a Canadian housewife, a Mrs. D. K., age thirty-five, who came to Enlightenment toward the end of the rigorous *rohatsu sesshin* (eight-day retreat in December commemorating the Buddha's own Enlightenment) at a Soto temple near Tokyo. This woman's report of her experience reveals the intensely human and personal side of an issue that may seem to many, including many academics, to be just another ideological skirmish in the current academic-generational culture wars between the older logocentric humanists entrenched beneath the banner of Truth and the younger differentialist guerrillas taking pot shots at same. For Mrs. D. K. the question whether things were fundamentally the same or different, one or many, became a matter of spiritual life and death.

Nagged by a sense of futility, of not "getting anywhere" after some six days of intense concentration on *mu,* the koan assigned her by the *roshi* (Zen master), she reports going for a walk and venting her frustration with an irritated and cynical self-interrogation:

> What is this Mu, anyway? I asked. What in the name of heaven can it be? It's rediculous! I'm sure there is no such thing as Mu. Mu isn't anything! I exclaimed in irritation. (276)

Something in this anger that has mounted slowly but steadily over six days causes a sudden shift to clarity, as the woman goes on to say:

> As soon as I said it was nothing, I suddenly remembered about the identity of opposites. Of course—*Mu is also everything!* While bathing I thought: If Mu is everything, so is it the bath water, so is it the soap, so is it the bathers. This insight gave fresh impetus to my sitting when I resumed it. (276)

This is a foretaste of *satori* (Enlightenment), which would come to her soon enough. When it did, after another day of unbroken concentration, it would take the form of the astonished words:

> "Mu is me!" I stopped short—even my breathing stopped. Could that be so? Yes, that's it! *Mu is me and me is Mu!* A veritable tidal wave of joy and relief surged through me. . . . and I exclaimed "It's all so simple!" (277–78)

Of course, what is so simple in that brilliant moment beggars description, though it contain the answer to all questions of Truth and Meaning that have ever bedeviled the human mind. Let us put it very plainly here: three basic pronouncements issue from this woman with the ring of utter conviction:

1. *Mu* is nothing.
2. *Mu* is everything.
3. *Mu* is me.

It must seem—to the subject at least—that all questions of identity and difference are "covered," as it were, by these three permutations of Zen insight: there is something—call it "*Mu*"—that *is being* everything even while somehow remaining itself. Therefore identity is forever *being* difference. And these two that are forever *being* each other constitute the *being* that "I" am. The quasi-syllogistic style in which Mrs. K. conveys such blatantly self-contradictory insight has the strange effect of turning logic in on itself and, in effect, deconstructing it. The very contradiction in her expression between form and content may begin to suggest the thunderous astonishment of this discovery for this woman in this moment. As if by contagion, we too feel acutely alerted to the mortal insufficiency of a purely intellectual consideration of the matter. Clearly, something more than intellect is at work in insights of such stunning absurdity. Similarly, one senses that the sheer intellectual gymnastics marking most poststructuralist discourse is screaming the inadequacy of intellect and its instrument, language, to make any conclusive point about identity and difference, or more simply, "the way things (and language too is a [systemic] thing) are." I would even say Derrida would agree that it is precisely this "never quite making the point" that is what *différance,* for want of a better word, "is."

Some six years later, Mrs. K. would have another experience, this one "a bolt from the blue" in the midst of everyday life, that would take her even more deeply into the mystery of identity and difference. The sudden, dramatic obliteration of the delusion of ego-identity ("as though . . . struck by a bolt of lightning" [279]) first sets the scene for the perception of truths never conceived nor dreamt of:

> Slowly my focus changed: "*I*"m dead! There's nothing to call *me!* There never was a *me!* It's an allegory, a mental image, a pattern upon which nothing was ever modeled." I grew dizzy with delight. Solid objects appeared as shadows. and everything my eyes fell upon was radiantly beautiful. (279)

Thereupon she reports being intoxicated by wave upon wave of revelation, extending over a period of days. Some time later, during an hour of insight "recollected in tranquility," she would jot down some of the most salient aspects of her vision. Two comments in particular evidence a maturing of her initial Enlightenment experience of six years earlier:

> When I am in solitude I can hear a "song" coming forth from everything. Each and every thing has its own song; even moods, thoughts, and feelings have their finer songs. Yet beneath this variety they intermingle in one inexpressibly vast unity. (280)

The "identity" of identity and difference is again recognized, but here the earlier delight in standing logic on its head has deepened into a kind of appreciative "beholding" of the identity of opposites wherever she casts her "inner" eye. In this moment the world is for her a ubiquitous play of the *coincidentia oppositorum*. The universality of the principle and omnipresence of its manifestation (she speaks of a "vast 'geometry of existence'" and "an indescribably vast complex of dynamic force" [279]) may be accounted for by thinking of identity/difference as a polarity of polarities or metapolarity comprehending all other—and ontologically lesser—polarities: the very existence of "truth" and "falsehood," "good" and "evil," "beautiful" and "ugly" depends on whether the members of these pairs are, in each instance, the "same" or "different." Mrs. K's Enlightenment is a rising-up onto a high inner bluff from which she can clearly see that the world around her is literally a dynamic ongoing *Gestalt* of her own consciousness. She has stepped into the very workshop of Nature, the *sanctum sanctorum* where the a priori categories are seen to be whirring away like so many precision tools, and discovered that the whole enterprise is being run by none other than *herself.*

This accompanying realization, that "I am the Source of all," had also occurred in her earlier experience *("Mu is me and me is Mu!")* and may again be viewed as an instance of the lightning flash of Enlightenment "looking-glass logic": if one thing truly *is* another, then I, being "one thing" among many others, must be those others as well! In her later experience Mrs. K. puts this insight in typically paradoxical terms that, again, indicate a deepening and subtilizing of Enlightened perception:

> I feel a consciousness which is neither myself nor not myself, which is protecting or leading me into directions helpful to my proper growth and maturity. . . . It is like a stream into which I have flowed and, joyously, is carrying me beyond myself. (280)

## THE END OF INTELLECTUAL INQUIRY

There is a brilliant bit of analysis done in the eighth century by Chandrakirti, eminent Indian commentator on the Madhyamika philosophy of Nagarjuna (whose fourfold negation Zen monks are fond of quoting), showing clearly that the identity/difference issue is one intrinsic to language, in other words, to the very means by which the issue itself is conceived and formulated, and that therefore language can never suffice to resolve it. Taking as his example the statement, "The human soul is eternal," Chandrakirti inquires into the relationship between the subject, "the human soul," and the predication, "is eternal," and asks, with deceptive simplicity, whether the two terms are identical or different: "If the two terms are identical, we are left with a tautology: the eternal human soul is eternal. If they are different and distinct, what could possibly justify the claim that they are related?" (qtd. in Coward 186).

Let this, along with the experience of Mrs. D. K. related above, suffice to reinforce the point that no amount of intellectual muscle will ever settle the question of "the way things are." A muscle, after all, cannot subdue itself. The linguistic categorizing of aspects of the world as "identical" and "different" is a perpetual psychosomatic process as unconscious and as binary as breathing, as Chomsky's apt term for it, "deep structure," implies. And yet the humility that overcomes one by this very realization *can* settle the matter, or at least serve as a prelude to settlement. Which means that the utmost exertion of intellectual muscle can indeed be a very useful psychological and spiritual exercise, not as a means to "the answer," but as a force for creating the conditions for an inevitable dead end to inquiry (precisely the function of a good koan), at which point one might in one's anguish instinctively reach for resources one never knew one had. Such resources might be characterized as a subtly concentrated, quasi-meditative state of consciousness capable of making one directly aware even of normally unconscious linguistic processes. It is in this spirit of the quest for the intellectual dead end, and for the unmapped territory stretching beyond, that the following exercise is undertaken.

For the past thirty years poststructuralism has cast itself in the role of a sort of therapeutic devil's advocate, poking and prodding the Western intellectual community out of what might be termed the sleep of logocentric or foundationalist or unitive thinking. That things have essences, that man's noblest instincts drive him to seek a meaning to life; that the self as a discrete, autonomous, conscious entity exists; that history (biological, human, cosmic) is evolving away from an innocent alpha and, most likely, toward a beatific omega point—these more or less commonsense notions of our culture are all symptoms of a mass cognitive hypnosis that has afflicted it from the "beginning." Insofar as this condition *is* hypnotic, and hence not—or at least no longer—freely chosen, it must, so goes the poststructuralist perspective, be regarded as ideologically driven and maintained; that is, the few who have power use it, largely unconsciously,[1] as a litany of Svengali-like mantras to keep the many who do not content with their lot. Thus we have a most curious kind of sociopolitical *folie á deux* in which the blind, as it were, lead the blinder: "Surface appearances are deceiving. Keep digging and eventually you'll get to the truth." "Suffering in this life is a necessary preparation for happiness in the next." "America is the land of the rugged individualist."

It seems one must grant that poststructuralism has clearly recognized the fundamentally dialectical organization of human consciousness: anything valued is so only by being framed or set off by what is not valued; every position has a counterposition; every self an other; every right hand a (sinister) left. The more socially engaged of the poststructuralist thinkers (Foucault, Althusser, Lyotard, Baudrillard) would awaken us to the dark side of our cultural moon, to the side we have turned our back on. And this perhaps to some extent necessarily: as Émile Durkheim, often cited by poststructuralists as an early contributor to the cause for his anthropological attacks on what he argues is the historically recent concept of the individual self, has pointed out with reference to primitive totemistic societies: any human group *needs* "outsiders" in order to know who belongs to it and therefore whom to value. In order for self-recognition to be there, someone must be excluded.

Though known by many names, this collective cultural Shadow has probably been best captured in recent times in the poststructuralist shibboleth "difference." The word verily brims with the suggestiveness of suspicious alterity: odd, apart, out of place, unusual, anomalous, alien; then on to: deformed, freakish, grotesque, etc. "Difference" is embodied in just about anything that puts us ill at ease or makes us feel out of sorts. It arouses a restlessness in us that impels us to "set things right," to "smooth out the creases." In its cultural aspect it is the vagrant itch on the body cultural, equatable with racism, sexism, etc. (in a word, "otherism") in their endless permutations, that constantly irritates, now here now there, and must incessantly be scratched.

But the scope of "difference" for poststructuralist thought far exceeds the domain of culture, in the sense of cultural studies, per se. Indeed, there would seem to be few artistic or intellectual disciplines that have not recently come under the sway of one or another of the facets of its explanatory power. (Poststructuralists might well warn us of the danger of the concept's reification by academic epigones into some perverse, "backdoor" version of "truth" or "logos.") Even fields such as musicology that have so far managed to remain relatively immune to its intellectual charisma are struggling these days to avoid being left behind by the poststructuralist bandwagon. (Check the reviews of recent "breakthrough" books on Beethoven and Schubert, for example, appearing in the *New York Review of Books* over the past seven years or so, books questioning the legitimacy of the classical canon or detailing the social and artistic "marginalization" of the gay composer.)[2]

But let us, in sketching the current intellectual-historical contours of "difference," confine observation to those few seminal areas in which creative spadework of the first order has been done. In the area of philosophy of history

*(Geschichtsphilosophie)* Michel Foucault has profoundly challenged our modern conception of history as development or evolution from a presumed point of origin—in other words, the idea of history as monolithic "genealogy." Such genealogy, whether construed as the panoramic tracing of an entire society's generations over centuries or of the branches of a private family tree, is always at bottom an attempt, deceptive of self and others, to cosmeticize one's own "messy" origins. It is the self-interested projection of the genealogist. If Durkheim is a forerunner of poststructuralist socioanthropology, Nietzsche is the early prophet of Foucault's championed decentered or differential historiography, which presumes the true genealogy to be, if not precisely objective, at least to some extent anegoically alert to its own cultural rootedness and, in consequence, always revelatory of a self-constituting fragmentation:

> Why does Nietzsche challenge the pursuit of the origin *(Ursprung),* at least on those occasions when he is truly a genealogist? First, because it is an attempt to capture the exact essence of things, their purest possibilities, and their carefully protected identities, because this search assumes the existence of immobile forms that precede the external world of accident and succession. This search is directed to "that which was already there," the image of a primordial truth fully adequate to its nature, and it necessitates the removal of every mask to ultimately disclose an original identity. . . . What is found at the historical beginning of things [however] is not the inviolable identity of their origin; it is the dissension of other things. It is disparity. *(Language* 142)[3]

It is, however, in Jacques Derrida's philosophy of language that "difference," as *différance,* has truly come into its own. While this is not the place for a comprehensive discussion of this notoriously elusive and multivalent term,[4] I would emphasize here that aspect of it that insists on maintaining the gap between any signifier and its presumed signified. I mean Derrida's refusal to indulge our need for language to deliver, as it were, a virtual identity with the world, inner and outer, we commonly believe it to reflect. This refusal may be regarded as the brunt of his radical critique of the Western philosophical tradition from Plato to Heidegger. What the historical genealogy is for Foucault, the signified—in the sense of a meaning or ground or source or logos outside language—is for Derrida: a delusive and ultimately self-interested construct of the Western mind-set. What is real or fundamental for Derrida is certainly not the signified (a metaphysical fiction), nor even so much the signifier (which is never quite "here"), but the incessantly sensed pressure of the latter to reach the ever receding former. This pressurized, and hence dynamic, gap is *différance.* Which means that *différance* is, strictly speaking, nothing, but a nothing that, as we shall see, is everything!

The same insistence on difference as irreducible gap or separation is the stuff and substance of Paul de Man's "anti-aesthetic." Whether ranting against what he considers the sentimental ideology of the Romantics in their exalting of the unitive symbol over the dualistic allegory, or doting on the fundamental rhetorical ambiguity of literary language ("A literary text [is one which] simultaneously asserts and denies the authority of its own rhetorical mode" [*Allegories of Reading* 17]), de Man takes endless delight in the paradox of a world (de)constructed on the principle of linguistic undecidability: "How can we know the dancer from the dance?", the person from the act, substance from process, description from described? As Frank Kermode so concisely puts it, de Man "was always looking for the point where necessity encountered impossibility, or intention its fated undoing. He is the great impresario of the rhetorical impasse. . . . Some such aporia—another favorite word—is the goal of de Manian meditation, a kind of substitute for the obsolete satisfactions of closure, now known to be impossible because of the very nature of texts" ("Paul de Man's Abyss" 6–7). One can only wonder whether it ever dawned on de Man how close his koan-like obsession with rhetoric brought him to a realization of the *coincidentia oppositorum,* to insight into the inconceivable identity of identity and difference. Was he ever able to train what must have been formidable contemplative faculties, in Zen-like fashion, on that rhetorical seam long enough and deeply enough to behold it as the matrix of all the paradoxes and contradictions by which we are both charmed and tortured? Finally, was he ever struck by the irony of the closeness of many of his views to those of the "sentimental" Jena Romantics he abhorred? In particular, could he see Friedrich Schlegel smiling over his shoulder as he wrote, "Poetic writing is the most advanced and refined mode of deconstruction" (*Allegories of Reading* 17)?

Literature is terribly important to poststructuralists, not only because it displays the intrinsically differential, and hence ambiguous, nature of language at its most transparent, but because its finest creators, sensitively attuned to this ambiguity as they are, have developed masterly devices of style and figure that have the vertiginous effect of alluding to their own ambiguity, so that poststructuralists can point to an impressive array of earlier imaginative writers who have intuitively anticipated their own radical critique of language. Thus, just as Freud had hailed Dostoyevsky and C. F. Meyer as "natural" psychologists whose fictive intuitions about repression and Oedipal family dynamics had taught him a great deal, more recently we have had

Barthes citing Proust for his ingenious creation of characters whose lives are dominated by the culturally conditioned "signs" of things such as love or nobility, or Camus for deflating in *The Stranger* the illusion of the significance of literary style *(écriture blanche)*.

On the German—or more precisely German-language—scene, there is Kafka, extolled by Deleuze and Guattari for his "Prague German . . . a deterritorialized language, appropriate for strange and minor uses" (17), political uses in particular: "to oppose the oppressed quality of this [major literary] language to its oppressive quality, to find points of nonculture or underdevelopment, linguistic Third World zones by which a language can escape" (27). The irony here is that it is this very impossibility of escape, escape from "difference" on any level, linguistic or otherwise, that is perhaps Kafka's most obsessive theme and trope. Imagery of inescapability abounds in Kafka, but there are two images in particular that suggest that the human trap is, at its core, a relentlessly nagging sense of difference or gap that we long to but, despite our best efforts, cannot eradicate. One of these is the scenario of Gregor Samsa's superhuman (because *sub*human!) effort to get out of bed and open his bedroom door in part one of *The Metamorphosis;* the other is the vain lifelong attempt of the man from the country to gain admittance to the Law in the parable "Before the Law." The first of these two images is implicit, that is, more seamlessly and less noticeably embedded in the narrative and all the more powerful for that; the second is explicit, that is, it is about—and *only* about—that which cannot be reached, and gains its power from its sheer denuded explicitness. What the images have in common is the nightmarish suggestion of a series of obstacles that can never be overcome because it is literally infinite. If Gregor can only roll his hideous insect body out of bed and onto the solid floor! And then, if he can only stand up on two legs "like a man"; and then, if he can only walk (not crawl) to the door and open it; and then, have his breakfast; and then, catch the late train; and then . . . . Here each successive move gives the illusion of a bit of progress in overcoming difference (between Gregor and his father, Gregor and his family, Gregor and his boss, Gregor's loathesome self-image and his ego-ideal), just enough to keep Gregor going. But long before Gregor, it dawns on the reader with horror that each modest and sorely-won expansion of Gregor's world (bed to floor to door, etc.) is only an opening-up to a slightly roomier cell, as if he were forever emerging from within an infinite set of Chinese boxes, and that however far he may manage to push back the bars, the cell itself will remain.

"Before the Law" is an abstraction with variation on *The Metamorphosis,* the Victorian domesticity (and hence partially repressed anxiety) of the latter distilled down to the pure panic, overlaid with the thinnest veneer of numbness, of an expressionist house of mirrors. Here the dynamic of difference is personified by an endless series of doorkeepers, "each more powerful than the last," that stand between the man from the country and his goal, the Law. The Law, of course, like all law, represents Freedom (here synonymous with Identity or Unity) since it is the one thing that is not subject to itself. But in conceiving of this freedom as somehow existing outside himself, that is, separated from himself in space ("over there") and time ("not yet"), in a word, as *different* from himself, the man from the country unconsciously creates difference; and since he is unconscious of his creation, difference must be endless. However many doorkeepers he succeeds in getting past, there will always be the next one.

But this man does not have Gregor's ambition; he is quite content to wait for an invitation to enter the Law, and wait he does, till his eyes close in death. Waiting for an end to difference is for Kafka just a passive-aggressive form of the perennial human struggle to subdue it. Whether one "attacks" or waits, the fundamental itch to breach the gap, an itch described elsewhere by Kafka as man's Original Sin of "impatience," still dominates the moment.

In both scenarios Kafka suggests a solution to the insoluble dilemma of difference that goes beyond the putative purview of deconstruction, coming as it does out of the author's deepest spiritual experience. As it turns out, this experience puts him in close company with the masters of the koan tradition of Rinzai Zen. The only solution to the problem of difference is death, death in the sense of a moving beyond the confines of a human consciousness that is differentially structured to begin with. (In order for man to be aware of any *thing* in particular, he must differ-entiate it, tear it asunder, from all else.) Thus, Gregor becomes the narrator, the creator of this world teeming with difference; and the man from the country dies a merely allegorical death which is at once an awakening to himself as the very source of the Law's radiance. If difference is all there is, and we are that difference, is there any difference?

To be sure, Kafka has no interest in facile leaps to some Enlightened panacea, not least because he knew that such leaps were anything but facile. Not unlike a good Bodhisattva in the Zen tradition who postpones his own *parinirvana* to help others, he largely confines himself to an endless parabolic mapping of the territory of difference. Kafka's situations are tropes of *fundamental differentiality,* for him the *conditio humana*. They are soulscapes lined with what deconstruction currently calls "signifiers," which are really perennial psychospiritual red herrings, that is, promising waystations of "Meaning" where one can rest (like Gregor whose exhausted leaning against the armchair upright on two feet "means," for a moment at least, that he *is* human after all), but only tentatively and only for a while before once again succumbing to the infernal push-pull of what is forever "over there" and "not yet." In the end, on the level of self-reflection, we are faced with the paradox that it is, strictly speaking, impossible to say what Kafka's differential tropes are about, for it is this very "aboutness," this very prepositional bridge to meaning, that they demolish through the implicit infinity of their sequencing. Might one then venture that the steady stream of books "about" Kafka that shows no sign of abating is what Kafka is really all "about?"

French poststructuralism conveys a strong sense that the attachment to identity and aversion to difference is a fundamental mindset peculiar to Western Eurocentric culture: a philosophical tradition grounded in Platonic idealism; a general cultural sense of history as telic, if not eschatological, process; along with the welter of assumptions generated by these, assumptions buried in sciences hard and soft no less than in "common sense." There is, however, at least one French critic who argues that logocentrism has always been just as ingrained in the Eastern mind, one possible implication being that it is a perverse feature, if not indeed of the very essence, of human cognition per se. We are *built,* then, to desire unity and abhor division. In brilliant Foucauldian style Bernard Faure conceives of the entire Indo-, Sino-, and Japanese Zen Buddhist tradition, not as the phylogenetic unfolding of the Buddha's original Enlightenment experience under the bo tree that the tradition itself promulgates, but rather as the history of that very promulgation. In other words Zen history is the history of a certain *Rhetoric of Immediacy* (Faure's title), of a certain revered and even covetous way of viewing "spiritual experience," whatever the latter may actually "be." "Immediacy" alludes to Zen's renowned insistence on a direct grasping of one's Self-nature or True Nature, in other words, Enlightenment, and implies therefore an experience that is culturally unmediated. In poststructuralist terms immediacy is, for Zen, Identity Realized or Pure Presence, which is Enlightenment, the existential metacondition in which everything *is* everything else, or, to put it again in terms of the present discussion, in which identity *is* difference or presence *is* absence. Since the Buddha's awakening under the bo tree is presumed to have been pristine, the spiritual culture that has derived from it is to be regarded as the genetic unfolding of a primordial seed or source or origin. For Faure such notions constitute religious-cultural rhetoric, Oriental style. Thus, in his opening chapter he sets himself the following project:

> Instead of the "monotheism" of the One practice . . . in the orthodox tradition . . ., I will attempt to make the "polytheism" of

> values and practices reappear and to show that neither the "purist" vision of unitarian Zen, nor even the dualism of the "blind windows" found in theories such as the "convergence of Chan and the teachings," faithfully reflects the experience of Chan adepts. The differentiation produces a dissemination, a setting in motion of various paradigmatic pairs [e.g., sudden versus gradual Enlightenment, Northern versus Southern schools] that can no longer be assigned to precise and unchanging sectarian positions. Once again, it is important to consider these various examples of "differential Chan" merely as ideal types and to avoid reifying the divisions into groups. Chan is, and always was, an "imagined community." The notions of *distinction* on the social level and of *différance* on the philosophical level may help us to account for this constant production of gaps (*écarts*). As in the Saussurian conception of *langue,* there are no "substantial" entities, only differential *écarts.* (31)

If one takes "difference" in this sense of Faure's as an irreducible "agonistic tension" (316) constituting any antinomy, then certainly one would have to agree with him in his harsh concluding assessment of Zen as a religion that delusively claims for itself a metareligious status:

> Even if Zen can be characterized as what exceeds or subverts the [binary] structure, it remains an effect of this structure and cannot exist apart from it, just as ultimate truth cannot exist apart from conventional truth. It is perceived through it and framed by it. When such a metaphysical, antistructural claim is made, it falls back into the structure and turns into ideological discourse. . . . [I]t's *hybris* led Chan to deny its hybridity in the name of pristine purity and to leave the solid ground of practice for the icy sphere of antinomian metaphysics. (308)

But the whole debate between traditional religio-metaphysical *Weltanschauungen* and the current culturalist critique leveled by poststructuralism hinges precisely on this question of the reducibility or irreducibility of the agonistic tension constituting difference. Assuming this tension to be the conative and probably even physiological component of a differentially structured human consciousness, a consciousness that categorically divides things by its very nature and then "suffers" the consequences of that division, the question then becomes: is human experience bedrock? Is the tension that is built into all human experience, be it high or low, eu-stress or "bad" stress, agony or ecstasy or anything in between, fundamental? Is this tension and its subjective correlative, differential consciousness, "the way things are?"

If so, then we can only label as sado-masochistic the mystic's claim to an inner alchemy enabling him to walk through scenes of horror as though strolling through the Garden of Eden: Blake's devils who are very much at home in Hell; the (doubtless apocryphal) Zen monk who offered his own body as food for some starving wolves; or the poet Walt Whitman who had what one might call an existential encounter with "difference" when he toured the Brooklyn field hospitals during the Civil War and could only exclaim amidst a sea of mutilated bodies, "Perfect!"

But the religious sensibility asserts there is something more fundamental than difference, taken in the poststructuralist sense of irreducible agonistic tension. It claims to see in the very jaggedness of difference—indeed *only* there—something utterly conciliatory, something that assures us that Whitman's exclamation is not the ranting of a misanthrope. Simple logic compels the insight that whatever it is, it cannot be any "thing" in particular, since thingness or particularity by definition (or should I say "differentiation") leads us right back to the tension of difference. Therefore this mysterious "non-thing" can only be: *nothing!* It can only be what the Romantic mystic Novalis was punning about when he lamented that "[w]ir suchen überall das Unbedingte und finden immer nur Dinge" [Everywhere we seek the unconditional (lit.: un-be-thing-ed) and forever find mere conditions (things)] (M; *Werke* 325). And it is precisely this nothing that is bedrock, that is more fundamental than human consciousness, that is "the way things are."

Having arrived finally at this new and, at first blush, admittedly unsettling first principle, we can use it to begin to disentangle the strands of confusion making up the current discussion of "difference." In the first place, this principle of nothing enables us to raise the very relevant question as to whether the Magus of *différance* himself, Jacques Derrida, is "a good Derridean," for if he is not, with how much greater caution must we regard disciples like Faure who insist on difference as a *conditio sine qua non* of human affairs? There are commentators who, having examined Derrida against a background of religious-contemplative traditions, Oriental ones in particular, read certain passages in him as indications that even he views *différance* as ultimately involving more than simple irreducible agonistic tension between the members of linguistic antinomies; in other words that he sees the possibility of some significant "alchemical" change in, if not outright dissolution of, the tension between signifier and signified. Harland, for example, quoting from the essays, *Positions* and *Speech and Phenomena,* emphasizes Derrida's meditative disposition (149–51) from which supposedly arise such paradoxical distinctions as that between sameness and identity:

> "*différance* is . . . the element of the *same* (to be distinguished from the identical) in which these [static simultaneous] oppositions are

> announced." Or, in another description, "The *same,* which is not the identical . . . is precisely [*différance*], as the diverted and equivocal passage from one difference to another, one term of the opposition to the other." In 'différance', alternative meanings are not the same to the extent of being identified in a single meaning; they are the same to the extent that a single force passes through them, crosses the boundary between them. (138)

Harland's Derrida strikes me as someone in quest of the *coincidentia oppositorum,* that Nothing we arrived at above that, in not being any particular thing, bodies forth as everything, or, better still, that is forever dancing in and out of the pairs of things it creates (by *being* them) and discreates (by *un*being them). This Nothing is, then, in no way to be understood as blankness, vacuity, or privation; quite the contrary, it is pregnant, dynamic, and infinitely creative. And while it may also function differentially in the manifesting flux of its creativity, it is also that which blends the very differences it creates by *being* each of them in turn. If we accept Harland's Derrida, then it seems to me we must read *différance* as, ultimately, *Différance,* a spiritual principle that, when realized, transforms the world from the valley of tears of common experience into the Garden of Paradise, for what else but the bliss of freedom can arise from the realization that One *is* every one of those mutilited bodies in the Civil War field hospital, that they are all, even in their abject misery, signifiers of Oneself, or, as Whitman put it, "the Other" that "I am."

This latent, though perhaps not so latent, super-differential dimension in Derrida, which it seems to me proper to call "spiritual," is even more emphatic in Harold Coward's study, *Derrida and Indian Philosophy,* a collection of essays comparing Derridean differentialism to the linguistic philosophy of some of the great Hindu and Buddhist sages. In the essay on "Derrida and Sankara," Coward comes extremely close to reading *Of Grammatology* as a manifesto of the mystical *coincidentia oppositorum,* seen here as the principle of liberation from the "prisonhouse of language," a prison we build around ourselves by "privileging" (deconstruction's version of Hindu-Buddhist "desire") one side of a linguistic antinomy, say, the Signified or Identity, over the other:

> The functional parallel for *avidya* (Sankara's notion of the obstruction of the real) is, for Derrida, the privileging of one of the opposites of language over the other, and thereby destroying the dynamic tension between the opposites. . . . The tension between the opposites is, for Derrida, the hallmark of the real. . . . Identifying oneself with either of the terms that make up these oppositions (e.g., *identity* for Sankara; *difference* for Derrida) is the trap of language that must be overcome. . . . Derrida thinks this trap may be

> escaped by staying within language but on the middle path between the pairs of opposites. When the opposites of language are maintained in dynamic tension, through a continual deconstruction of first one opposite and then the other, the real is experienced. For the moment the real is spoken it is tending to swing the pendulum of language toward either one or the other of the opposites. Only by a continual deconstructing and reversing of each pendulum swing *may we experience the real as the middle point*—where the tension between the pairs is momentarily in balance. (87–89; final emphasis mine)

For Coward's Derrida then, the soil of consciousness is, as it were, tilled for the seed of the *coincidentia oppositorum* through the sustaining of an austere attitude of nonattachment to any linguistic terminus: signifier, signified, terms lateral to either, speaker, listener, author, reader, etc. This seems not very different from the Madhyamika or Middle Path philosophy of Nagarjuna and Buddhism generally, which views attachment to all metaphysical positions, be they logocentric or differential, as victimization, witting or unwitting, by imaginary constructions of language *(vikalpa)* that "play over the surface of the real without giving us access to it" (Coward 135). At first glance one might be tempted to invalidate comparisons between Nagarjuna and Derrida on this issue of language vis-à-vis accessibility (to the real): for the former language prevents it, for the latter it provides it. But I think this difference is more semantic than substantive. Ultimately, does it matter whether one "gets to" the real by "abandoning" language or by using it as a vehicle? If abandonment is the way, then certainly what is abandoned is the vehicle.

The important question is whether Derrida's spiritual instincts get him off the treadmill of *différance* narrowly conceived. Do they take him beyond the perpetually self-deconstructing pendulum swings of the vigilant linguistic consciousness, which in the end can only be a meditative consciousness, or do they, for now at least, leave him poised there? Is he able to keep the balance of this middle point long enough for it to expand into the infinite Nothing of what is called in Buddhism *sunyata,* the "no-thing" that underlies and supports all things by *being* them and that the reader will recognize as our first principle announced above, or does that middle point remain for Derrida the phenomenal nothing of tension between the opposites, the phenomenal nothing of *différance?*

If I read him accurately, Robert Magliola answers the question of the reducibility for Derrida of *différance* to *Différance,* of the phenomenal pressure between linguistic terms to the fundamental matrix of language known as *sunyata,* in the affirmative. I couch my judgment in caution here because

Magliola's study, *Derrida on the Mend,* though a tour de force of erudition and insight, is devilishly dense in style and seems bent on matching its subject in intellectual opacity. Nevertheless, Magliola is brilliant and knows the Eastern traditions and languages better than most, and so is better positioned than most to use these traditions to attempt to locate Derrida on the phenomenal-noumenal spectrum of experience.

Essentially, Magliola's assertion of the functional equivalence of Derrida's *différance* with the Buddhist *sunyata* rests on his analysis of Derrida's notion of definition as functioning always and only by negative reference:

> If we recall conventionally a "self-identical element" such as a sign is understood to be temporally and spatially "present to itself," then a Saussurean critique of this notion (at least as adapted by Derrida) argues that "each element that is said to be 'present' . . . is called the present by this very relation to what it is not, to what it absolutely is not . . . " (the essay "Differance," in *Speech and Phenomena*). (21)

The key apparently lies in what is "going on" during the blink of an eye it takes for consciousness to make this reference to the realm of the "is-not." Certainly what is going on is some kind of inner movement, a movement too lightning-quick for consciousness itself to pick up on. According to Magliola, Derrida regards this unconscious movement of negative reference as "one devoted to 'the movement of signification,' to the 'trace,' and 'differance,'—all provisional names for what somehow 'constitutes' *that which survives* absolute negative reference" (21; emphasis Magliola's). That which survives is itself defined negatively as not involving "an 'origin'; nor does *that which survives* operate in the mode of signifier/signified or even existence/non-existence" (21). Clearly, Magliola reads Derrida as gesturing here toward that which transcends all conceivable dualisms. What "survives," what endures before the pairs of opposites have arrived on the scene or after they have left it? What can we *provisionally* call it?

While still not quite ready to pronounce Derrida a "universal Buddhist," Magliola gingerly approaches this position with a turn of phrase recalling my earlier distinction between *différance* and *Différance,* or phenomenal nothing and absolute Nothing: "To follow this thread [i.e., Derrida's idea of negative reference], we must undertake a preliminary reconnaissance of *différance,* though not yet of *différance* as the 'constituting' of *that which survives*" (22). It is only some two chapters later that Magliola is finally able to state outright: "I shall argue that Nagarjuna's *sunyata* ("devoidness") is Derrida's *différance,* and is the absolute negation which absolutely deconstitutes but which constitutes directional trace" (89). (The somewhat awkward relative clause I take to be Magliola's attempt to make language do precisely what it cannot do [and to make sure we notice this]: comprehend the *coincidentia oppositorum.* What I believe he is trying to say is that the absolute principle, call it *sunyata* or *différance,* liberates one from, even as it reinstates, phenomenal trace or difference. Difference returns, though the person living in *sunyata* is no longer bound by it. This corresponds to certain oft-heard paradoxical assertions in Zen, such as: the Enlightened man moves about freely within his own karma, or: with Enlightenment everything is radically transformed, though remaining just as it was.)[5]

If one may speculate, one possible, and very interesting, implication to be drawn from the "spiritual (which is not to say 'metaphysical') Derrida" I have teased out of Harland, Coward, and Magliola has to do with the endlessly subtle distinction often made in the Zen tradition between the so-called ignorant and Enlightened mind. Zen is fond of insisting, to the utter consternation of Western students especially, that there is absolutely no difference between the two: Ignorance is Enlightenment, Enlightenment Is Ignorance:

> STUDENT: What am I lacking? You are enlightened and I am not. What is the difference between your touching fire and mine?
>
> ROSHI: No difference at all, absolutely none! A verse in the *Mumonkan* reads: "When the sun shines, its rays spread throughout the earth,/ When there is rain the earth becomes wet." In this there is neither beauty nor ugliness, neither virtue nor evil, nothing absolute, nothing limited. (Kapleau 122)

The *Mumonkan* uses sunshine and rain as metaphors, while Derrida uses *différance* or trace or "the element of the *same* (to be distinguished from the identical) in which these . . . oppositions are announced." What is this mysterious element of the Same that courses through all the pairs, including the pair we are accustomed to regarding as ignorance and enlightenment? Let's say it is Nothing, Nothing at all. But it is none other than this Nothing, this *différance as* "the *same,*" or *Différance,* that the master is beholding when he tells his uncomprehending student that there is absolutely no difference between enlightenment and ignorance. Awareness of this Nothing, which is to say Its self-awareness (for *who* is there to be aware of it?), liberates the dialectic, allowing the pairs of opposites to flow into and out of each other like the empty, airy, playful forms they fundamentally are; ignorance of it, the "cloud of unknowing" brought on by Buddhism's "desire" or Nietzsche's "valuation" or deconstruction's "privileging," condemns the dialectic to contradiction and conflict, giving the pairs a ghostly substantiality, leaving us in the never-never land between signifiers, or between signifier and signified, the unconscious never-never land of phenomenal *différance.*

There are, to be sure, Oriental religionists who fail to see in Derrida anything remotely resembling notions of transcendence, Oriental or otherwise, and in this they are aligned with the general view. David Loy, for example, again comparing Derrida and Nagarjuna, sees the former as deconstructing only identity, whereas the latter makes the ultimate move to deconstruct both poles as equally delusive metaphysical positions. Consequently, for Loy Derrida remains bound by the endless chain of signification he calls *différance:*

> Derrida's single-deconstruction leads to the "temporary" reversal . . . and/or to a discontinuous, irruptive "liberation" from reference grounded in the search for unattainable origins, into the dissemina-tion of a free-floating meaning beyond any conceptual *clôture.* For Nagarjuna, this would only be the illusion of liberation, while remaining trapped in a textual "bad infinity" which tends to become increasingly playful. ("Clôture" 60)

Anne Klein regards it as self-evident that Eastern Buddhists and Western poststructuralists live in different philosophical universes:

> Virtually no contemporary Western thinker would take seriously, much less agree with, the notion that conditioned persons can have an experience outside of historical, cultural, psychosocial, and other sets of conditionings. Neither Derrida, Foucault, Lacan, nor those following Kant, for example, would postulate or even seek a resolution between their own positions and the Buddhist claim that there are states of mind unaffected either by personal or cultural histories or by epistemic limitations. (298)

Needless to say, this essay is intended as, among other things, a brief for the other side and as a gesture toward theo-philosophical *rapprochement* between East and West.

The issue of Enlightenment and cultural mediation, or perhaps simply Enlightenment versus culture or even sacred versus secular, which Klein sees as bedrock to the East-West disjunction, is certainly not one that is ignored or glossed over by the Eastern traditions. Quite the contrary, Zen for one feeds on such culturalist critiques, particularly critiques leveled against its own validity, in the form of *mondos* or challenging spiritual questions pitched by masters to students without warning to test the maturity of the latters' insight. Thus, a master, perhaps having in mind the second case of the *Mumonkan,* "The Wild Fox," which takes up this very issue of causes and conditions, cultural and otherwise, vis-à-vis liberation, may suddenly shout out: "Is the Enlightened man subject to cause and effect?!" and expect from his mature student an answer the validity of which has nothing whatever to do with the referential sense of either "yes" or "no." To the Zen mind most poststructuralist thought is just as one-sided, and hence deluded, at its own differentialist end of the spectrum as is the logocentrism it inveighs against. Klein puts this point very well:

> For Buddhists, the unconditioned is epistemologically meta to the conditioned—not the other way around. For them, the emphasis that Foucault and Lacan put on cultural and linguistic constructions of experience is like theorizing the existence of dependent-arising without positing the emptiness that is its inseparable counterpart. (298)

We, of course, have been arguing that Derrida is an exception to this, that *différance* may indeed contain glimmerings of a conciliatory Emptiness. Westerners who would rescue Derrida from such "pirating" by Eastern transcendentalists usually cite passages such as the following from *Speech and Phenomena* in which he explicitly rejects any conflation of *différance* with a theological or ontological absolute, positive or negative:

> [D]ifferance is not theological, not even in the most negative order of negative theology. . . . Not only is differance irreducible to every ontological or theological—onto-theological—reappropriation, but it opens up the very space in which onto-theology—philosophy—produces its system and its history. It thus encompasses and irrevocably surpasses onto-theology or philosophy. (134–35)

My response to this is that the *différance* that Derrida is here protecting from a kind of spiritual emasculation by the "cutting edge" of disciplinary thought is *Différance,* which in truth cannot be subject to any form of thought, however subtle or lofty. Any attempt to capture *sunyata* by thought alone inverts it into the very nucleus or logos that both Zen and Derrida warn against. To put it plainly, the tail cannot wag the dog. Zen masters never tire of alerting their "*Mu*-ers" (students working on the koan *Mu*) to the dangers of allowing a conception, that is, a signifier, of *Mu* to substitute for *Mu* itself. Consider, for example, the ancient counsel of Master Mumon:

> Do not construe Mu as nothingness and do not conceive it in terms of existence or non-existence. . . . When you have cast away all illusory thoughts and discriminations, and inside and outside

> are as one, you will be like a mute who has had a dream [but is unable to talk about it]. . . .
>
> How then, do you achieve this? Devote yourself to Mu energetically and wholeheartedly. If you continue this way without intermission, your mind will, like a light flashed on in the dark, suddenly become bright. Wonderful indeed! (Kapleau 76–77)

## THE CASE OF GUTEI'S ATTENDANT

From the *Mumonkan,* case 3: "Gutei Raises a Finger":

> Whenever Gutei Osho was asked about Zen, he simply raised his finger. Once a visitor asked Gutei's boy attendant, "What does your master teach?" The boy too raised his finger. Hearing of this, Gutei cut off the boy's finger with a knife. The boy, screaming with pain, began to run away. Gutei called to him, and when he turned around, Gutei raised his finger. The boy suddenly became enlightened.
>
> When Gutei was about to pass away, he said to his assembled monks, "I obtained one-finger Zen from Tenryu and used it all my life but still did not exhaust it." When he had finished saying this, he entered into eternal Nirvana.
>
> *Mumon's Comment:* The enlightenment of Gutei and of the boy does not depend on the finger. If you understand this, Tenryu, Gutei, the boy, and you yourself are all run through with one skewer. (Sekida, *Two Zen Classics* 34–35)

*Author's Comment:* Leaving aside here the epilog paragraph on Gutei's demise, we note that the koan proper has a transparent tripartite division: 1) Gutei raises his finger; 2) the boy raises his finger; 3) the master shocks the boy into Enlightenment. This corresponds to the tripartite Christian, but indeed universal, myth of the Fall: Eden/Fall/Redemption; and both represent the quintessential spiritual response to this most human issue of identity vis-à-vis difference. Enlightenment, embodied in the master, is Identity: all things are One, but this is not a One that can be spoken; hence the finger upraised in silence. Ignorance, exemplified in the boy, is difference. The boy merely imitates the master's signature gesture, delusively taking the signifier, the upraised finger, for the Signified, Enlightenment. Ten thousand perfect enactments of the gesture will still leave the putative gap between master and student, originality and imitation, Signified and signifier, intact. Indeed, the boy's aping behavior will harden over time into habit, making spontaneous, creative action less and less likely. So the master, in a gesture of compassionate (and most likely apocryphal) cruelty, severs, at it were, the boy's ties to this unconscious habit. But there is more, much more, to his intention. Aware that the boy is ripe for Enlightenment, the master also uses the trauma to "catch his fertile attention" so that the final teaching can be driven home, this in the form of the master's climactic upraised finger.

What is the significance of this paradoxically climactic anticlimactic upraised finger that triggers the boy's Enlightenment? It can only be the master's deft tactic for utterly disabusing the boy of the very terms of the contradiction, for plucking him like a ripe fruit from the tree of propositional, either-or knowledge with respect to identity and difference. Cutting off the boy's finger may have cured him of one particular habit of imitation, but not of the far more deeply ingrained longing for identity, delusively conceived as something absolutely discontinuous with difference. The boy's delusion of demonstrating Enlightenment through his digital gesture has the unilaterally differential mindset built right into it: the very thought, "*This* (finger) is *that* (illumination)," is already the Zen-proverbial "hair's breadth that separates heaven and earth." The final upraised finger of the master is, then, the removal of that first and final hair's breadth of difference that keeps the boy in ignorance. In thunderous silence it pronounces: "Continue to think and desire in terms of identity and difference, 'Enlightened me' over against 'ignorant you,' 'this' versus 'that,' and so will your reality be. But look, this infamous finger of mine is nothing, nothing at all. It has no more substance than the space formerly occupied by your missing one. Your absent finger is just as good as my present one!" Thus, while the knife surgically clears the boy's field of consciousness of confused dualistic thinking, it is the upraised finger that, as Mumon puts it, "skewers" him (and the diligent koan meditator) for Enlightenment.

Taken as an emblem of the third, redemptive phase of the universal lapsarian myth, the master's final upraised finger both points to and *is,* that is, both re-presents and presents, the resolution of the contradiction between phases one and two, blending in a miracle of seamlessness the conciliatory compassion of identity with the discriminatory wisdom of difference. For the boy this is true prestidigitation. Once again in the words of Mumon, "Wonderful indeed!"

5

# East Meets West: Zen and Rilke in Salinger's *Catcher*

> Nothing is so profound as the pose, nor so shallow as depth.
>
> —Oscar Wilde

Like his American contemporary, Thomas Merton, J. D. Salinger developed an affinity for the mystery of the *coincidentia oppositorum* primarily from the synergistic East-West mix of Zen and Rilke. But whereas Merton left New York City behind in the late thirties to carry on his exploration of the Eastern wisdom traditions from within the contemplative walls of Gethsemani in Kentucky, Salinger stayed in the metropolis and imbibed the heady atmosphere of the New York City postwar Beat culture with its spiritual turn to the East. With respect to Rilke, Merton was, as we have seen, mainly interested in the lofty spiritual cycles of the *Elegies* and *Sonnets,* while Salinger was more drawn to the vivid, concrete imagery of the earlier *Dinggedichte,* poetic apotheoses of intensely observed people, animals, and objects. For both men the German Romantic sensibility as filtered through Rilke was a vital source for the rather elitist notions they entertained regarding the calling to poetry and the nature of the true literary artist, though in Salinger's case the Rilkean influence met with far less resistance. In a fascinating manifestation of literary-creative alchemy during the writing of his masterpiece, *The Catcher in the Rye,* Salinger, upon noticing a subtle but powerful image of the *coincidentia* in Rilke's celebrated lyric, "Das Karussell" (one that probably escaped Merton), linked in his text a reference to this image with a series of oblique allusions to perennial Zen koans and situations. The result was the classic American *Bildungsroman* we know, but a novel, it turns out, that delivers its hero through the most exotically non-American precincts of Zen and Rilke to a close—indeed a shattering—encounter with the *coincidentia.*

## BACKGROUND

As we have seen, Zen koans are supra-logical spiritual projects meant to be worked on full-time. Even when the monk is not formally meditating, the koan continues to resonate from the hinterlands of consciousness, suffusing every thought, word, and deed with its impenetrable mystery. So, as Holden Caulfield dutifully attends to the wisdom dispensed to him by his history teacher Mr. Spencer upon his dismissal from Pency Prep, in the back of his mind an odd question lingers and asserts itself: "I was thinking about the lagoon in Central Park . . . wondering where the ducks went when the lagoon got all icy and frozen over."[1] Holden, of course, knows nothing of Zen, but Salinger wants the *reader* to think of him as working on a koan. The matter of the Central Park ducks, silly though it be on the surface, is to bedevil Holden throughout his lost Christmas weekend in New York City and, like a good koan, will not leave him alone until he comes to terms with the central problem of his life, that is, with his so-called *life* koan, which the ducks symbolize.

Although the topic of Zen in Salinger's writings has often been addressed, coverage has been limited primarily to the fiction collected and published subsequent to *The Catcher in the Rye,* that is, to fiction in which the Zen theme is explicit.[2] Among those few commentators who have searched for traces of Zen in *Catcher* in particular,[3] one finds interesting speculation as well as enlightening discussion of Buddhism in the broad generic sense, but not a single unequivocal reference to the unique Sino-Japanese form of Buddhism known as Zen. This is especially mystifying in the case of Rosen, ninety percent of whose monograph is devoted to the topic. Alsen, perhaps the most authoritative voice on the subject of Salinger's interest in Eastern religion (123–64), takes the fictive Buddy Glass's self-characterization as reflective of the author, insisting that Zen is far less important in Salinger's work than "the New and Old Testaments, Advaita Vedanta, and classical Taoism" (134).

This is an odd state of affairs. Since Zen figures so prominently in *Nine Stories,*[4] the compositional chronology of which overlaps that of *Catcher,* and so explicitly in the conversational fabric of "Zooey," one would expect to find at least some evidence of it in *Catcher,* the more so since, according to Skow (84–90) and Lundquist (70–71), Salinger had been immersed in Zen studies at least since the mid-1940s. Yet *Catcher* is apparently Zen-less. I propose by way of explanation that there are indeed traces of Zen in *Catcher*, at least two traces, but that they are quite subtle, seamlessly woven as they are into character and narrative, hence easily overlooked, but nevertheless unequivocal once they are linked to their proper sources in Zen lore. The remainder of this chapter purports to establish this linkage and, in so doing, to evoke our appreciation of the way the scenes in question symbolically enrich Holden's characterization, lending it the subtle mythic, and at times mock-mythic, aura of the Hero's journey toward final emancipation in the *coincidentia*. All of this, in turn, should significantly modify and deepen our understanding of the shifting circumstances of Salinger's interest in Zen.

Symbolic echoes of other literature in the work of a great writer are usually a matter of deliberate encoding. This, however, does not preclude a significant degree of spontaneity from the process, as such echoes often tend, as it were *on their own,* to insinuate themselves in clusters, or even to coalesce, in the writer's imagination, much in the way of what Freud called the "overdetermined" or condensed imagery of dreams. Analogous to the dreamer, who has his entire personal history to draw upon in shaping his unconscious narrative, the well-read writer in the throes of creation has a vast "inner library" of texts at his disposal, and the particular focus of that writer's interest in any given moment will tend to draw ("check out") certain of these stored texts to itself metonymically and virtually without effort. As a more or less automatic process, then, literary allusions in texts often freely intermingle, paying no heed to a future interpreter's need for discrete thematic taxonomies or stylistic levels.

Such is the case with Salinger's novel, for it turns out that we cannot fully appreciate the symbolic significance of Zen for Holden Caulfield's final cathartic opening-up to the *coincidentia* without noting its fusion in the penultimate chapter with an allusion to the above-mentioned key image from Rilke's "Karussell." Though intuitively Zen-like in many ways as we have seen, Rilke, like Kafka, most likely had no formal acquaintance with that religion. Thus, it is fair to say that in Salinger's *Catcher in the Rye* sources East and West not only meet but, in the crucible of Salinger's genius, become mutually determining.

## HYAKUJO'S GEESE

The first trace of Zen in Salinger's novel takes us back to the above-mentioned ducks, which appear four times in the narrative, in each instance as a seemingly superfluous preoccupation of Holden's. After their introduction as a "quirky mental distraction" during his farewell talk with Mr. Spencer, they recur as a "spontaneous question" put by Holden to the first cabby in chapter 9, then again in conversation with the second cabby in chapter 12, and finally in chapter 20 as the object of a desperate nocturnal search. Viewed together the four instances form a kind of *leitmotif* structured by a sense of increasing urgency, very much like the build-up of tension that leads to the sudden breakthrough to solution in koan meditation practice.

It is likely this odd blend of emotional urgency on Holden's part with a seeming irrelevance of the ducks to the narrative in any logical or figurative sense that initially calls one's attention to them. If the attending reader should happen to be familiar with Zen folklore, he might suddenly recognize the ducks' symbolic derivation therein, at which point it would become quite obvious that these "extraneous" fowl lay right at the heart of Holden's identity crisis. Salinger's source for the motif is an anecdote contained in D. T. Suzuki's *Essays in Zen Buddhism (First Series),* which initially appeared in New York in August 1949 while the author was hard at work on the first draft of *Catcher* (Hamilton 113).[5] In Essay V, entitled "On Satori—The Revelation of a New Truth in Zen Buddhism," Suzuki relates the following:

> Hyakujo (Pai-chang Huai-hai, 724–814) one day went out attending his master Baso (Ma-tsu). A flock of wild geese was seen flying and Baso asked:
>
> "What are they?"
>
> "They are wild geese, sir."
>
> "Whither are they flying?"
>
> "They have flown away, sir."
>
> Baso, abruptly taking hold of Hyakujo's nose, gave it a twist. Overcome with pain, Hyakujo cried aloud: "Oh! Oh!"
>
> "You say they have flown away," Baso said, "but all the same they have been here from the very beginning."
>
> This made Hyakujo's back wet with cold perspiration. He had satori. (240)

Here the master is testing his student's insight by means of a *mondo,* that is, a sudden question meant to evoke the latter's delusive view on some significant spiritual matter—in this case, the relationship between change and permanence. Hyakujo's conventionally one-sided view of the issue, which sees only change (geese coming and going), is thrown up to him through Baso's carefully timed nasal shock tactic. The master senses that his mature student needs only a little jolt, some deft act of "compassionate cruelty," to precipitate in him that final *salto mortale* from ignorance to Wisdom. As Hyakujo cries out in pain, the master suddenly calls his attention to the other side of the issue ("all the same they have been here from the very beginning"):

change and permanence, the transitory and the abiding, are one and the same, an inseparable identity of opposites. From the Zen point of view, to resolve one contradiction is to resolve them all (since the distinction between the one and the many is itself a delusion). This instantaneous coalescence in his consciousness of all that has heretofore been separate is Hyakujo's *satori* or Enlightenment. Having propelled the monk from his long-suffering state of separative dualism into the rarefied atmosphere of Enlightened monism, Master Baso's *mondo* has served its purpose.

Holden's preoccupation with the ducks is clearly a symbolic extension of this traditional Zen anecdote as recounted in Suzuki's *Essays*. Hyakujo's *mondo* becomes Holden's koan, a koan that embodies the core conflict of his life: how can he hang onto the innocence of childhood while moving, inexorably, into the phony world of adulthood, or, how can he discover that changeless, inviolate innocence that never flies away but "all the same has been here from the very beginning." His brother Allie had found a way to preserve it (as Holden sees it): he died. To the living that is, of course, a one-sided solution: a loved one who dies has made himself inaccessible to change in the minds and hearts of the survivors. Such a denouement falls short of the absolutist standards of Zen, in particular of the koan, which demands a solution that somehow includes both terms of the contradiction: both change and permanence, corruption and innocence, in a seamless *coincidentia oppositorum*. In a word, Holden is trying to do the impossible. It will indeed take nothing less than a death to accomplish this, not biological death, but that much more difficult death of the ego, the mystics' "death before death," a conscious and voluntary surrender that is prelude to Enlightenment, the spiritual condition in which all conflicts and contradictions are resolved "suddenly," and forever.[6]

With the ducks' first appearance—in Holden's consciousness during that farewell chat with Mr. Spencer—Salinger makes allusion to an interesting aspect of koan psychology: even when the aspirant allows the koan to move from the center to the periphery of his attention so that he can take up other tasks, the koan continues to exert its influence. Though the monk has stopped working on it, it continues to work on him. Kapleau says of this subliminal dimension of koan work: "[O]nce the koan grips the heart and mind . . . the inquiry goes on ceaselessly in the subconscious. While the mind is occupied with a particular task, the question fades from consciousness, surfacing naturally as soon as the action is over, not unlike a moving stream which now and again disappears underground only to reappear and resume its open course without interrupting its onward flow" (12). Thus, as Holden tells us:

> The funny thing is, though, I was sort of thinking of something else while I shot the bull [with Mr. Spencer]. . . . I was wondering where the [Central Park] ducks went when the lagoon got all icy and frozen over. I wondered if some guy came in a truck and took them away to a zoo or something. Or if they just flew away.
>
> I'm lucky, though. I mean I could shoot the old bull to old Spencer and think about those ducks at the same time. It's funny. You don't have to think too hard when you talk to a teacher. (13)

Since Holden is only half-listening to Mr. Spencer's sage counsel, the thing that is really on his mind is able to surface in consciousness.

In the three subsequent duck-episodes there is, as noted, a pattern of growing tension as the issue takes on for Holden the tightening grip of an obsession. As one Rinzai master put it in terms of *Mu,* the fundamental Zen koan: "[You must reach the point where you feel] as though you had swallowed a red-hot iron ball that you cannot disgorge despite your every effort."[7] This sense of entrapment by the issue, of feeling utterly unable either to advance or retreat from it, while at the same time compelled to do *something,* is fertile ground for the lightning flash of insight. During his first cab ride through Central Park in chapter 9, Holden puts the question to the surly cabby: "You know those ducks in that lagoon right near Central Park South? That little lake? By any chance, do you happen to know where they go, the ducks, when it gets all frozen over? Do you happen to know, by any chance?" (60). In verbalizing his concern Holden begins to experience the unsettling ubiquity of the koan as it spreads from the private inner to the outer social domain. At the same time he is becoming aware of its frustrating imponderability. For a koan to be effective, the meditator must at some point come up against its diamond-hard resistance to reason, otherwise he will not be driven to arouse his own latent supra-rational resources: "I realized [in asking the cabby] it was only one chance in a million" (60).

Later on, this time in Horwitz's cab, Holden presses the issue further: "Hey, Horwitz. . . . You ever pass by the lagoon in Central Park? . . . Well, you know the ducks that swim around in it? In the springtime and all? Do you happen to know where they go in the wintertime, by any chance?" (81). Unlike his predecessor who dismissed Holden's question with contempt, this cabby engages him in a mock-comic round of what is known in Zen as "dharma dueling," defined by Kapleau as "a verbal joust or battle of 'wit' as respects the dharma, usually between two enlightened persons" (363). Here Horwitz takes the role of Holden's/Hyakujo's enlightened master whose task it is to pry his student loose from a one-sided view of things: whereas Holden continues to brood obsessively on the ephemeral (the vanished ducks, with their unconscious associations to his brother's death and to the impending "death" of his own innocence), Horwitz aggressively calls his attention to the fish frozen in the lagoon, which embody constancy:

> "The *fish* don't go no place. They stay right where they are, the fish. Right in the goddam lake."
>
> "The fish—that's different. The fish is different. I'm talking about the *ducks,*" I said.
>
> "What's *dif* ferent about it? Nothin's *dif* ferent about it," Horwitz said. . . . "Use your head, for Chrissake." (82)

Unlike the mature Hyakujo who teeters on the brink of insight, needing only a sharp tweak of the nose to transcend the logical boundaries of his own mind, Holden stays mired in his "Dark Night," continuing to struggle and resist the master's Truth: "'You don't think them fish just *die* when it gets to be winter, do ya?' 'No, but—'" (83).

The fourth and final duck-episode, occurring several hours (and drinks) later, finds Holden wandering around Central Park in half-drunken confusion as he presses on with the quest: "I figured I'd go by that little lake and see what the hell the ducks were doing, see if they were around or not" (153). After much fruitless groping and stumbling, "Then, finally, I found it. What it was, it was partly frozen and partly not frozen. But I didn't see any ducks around. I walked all around the whole damn lake—I damn near fell *in* once, in fact—but I didn't see a single duck" (154).

There are in this sequence several allusions to the traditional ordeal of the spiritual path, allusions that are subtle yet unmistakable when viewed in a Zen context. For example, just as the masters warn of sorely testing periods of melancholy, so Holden complains, "I was feeling so damn depressed and lonesome. . . . I wasn't tired or anything. I just felt blue as hell" (153–54). Also, as one would expect, the motif of darkness is emphasized: "Boy, was it dark. . . . I kept walking and walking, and it kept getting darker and darker and spookier and spookier" (154). Kapleau points out that "[i]n Zen it is said that 'the grand round mirror of wisdom is as black as pitch,'" and quotes his teacher Yasutani Roshi's version of St. John's "Dark Night of the Soul": "To renounce such conceptions [i.e., what one presumes to know of the way the world works] is to stand in 'darkness.' Now, satori comes out of this 'darkness,' not out of the 'light' of reason and worldly knowledge" (118).

In its subjective aspect, the darkness motif embodies the anguish of being utterly lost. As another master, Shibayama, has it: "the koan will mercilessly take away all our intellect and knowledge. In short, the role of the koan is not to lead us to satori easily, but on the contrary to make us lose our way and drive us to despair" (qtd. in Kapleau 71). Thus Holden, even in the park's familiar surroundings: "I had the most terrific trouble finding that lagoon that night. I *knew* right where it was—it was right near Central Park South and all—but I still couldn't find it" (154).

Finally, there is Holden's eventual discovery of the duckless lagoon, "partly frozen and partly not frozen." The qualities of frozenness and fluidity echo Holden's life koan, that is, the painful contradiction between permanence and change, symbolically played out earlier in Holden's duck/fish "dharma duel" with Horwitz. The half-and-half or neither/nor aspect of the lagoon's state alludes to the prickly razor's-edge nature of koan work which prevents the meditator from lapsing into either (or, for that matter, *any*) logical position suggested by the koan. Only the Middle Way, a central tenet of Buddhism, leads by its very a-positional "narrowness" to the promised land of Enlightenment, to the ineffable *coincidentia oppositorum* in which all dualities are transcended, all contradictions resolved. Holden has not yet arrived at the promised land ("But I couldn't find any [ducks]" [154]), but he is at this point well along the path.

Although Salinger nowhere mentions Suzuki's *Essays* by name as his source for the ducks, the circumstantial evidence for his having worked with this well-known introductory text during the writing of *Catcher* is compelling. As Hamilton tells us, "From summer 1949 to summer 1950 he seems to have worked flat out on the novel" (113). The British Rider edition of the *Essays in Zen Buddhism* came out in both London and New York in August 1949. The first American edition of the book appeared in New York City on May 10, 1950, published by HarperCollins (then called "Harper Brothers").[8] The publication of *Catcher* by Little, Brown and Co. just over a year later, on July 16, 1951, means that Suzuki's book was available to Salinger in its earlier British edition during his writing of the novel's first draft and, in its American edition, during his completion of the draft in Spring and Summer 1950. This is not to mention the all-important months of revision extending through Winter and Spring 1951 preceding publication in July.

I say "all-important months of revision" because it was Salinger's working style not simply to revise and edit his stories but virtually to rewrite them again and again, often incorporating in the rewriting, as suggested earlier, new elements culled from various interesting books that came his way (Hamilton 167–68). When one considers that Salinger fancied himself a Zen bibliophile,[9] that he makes several references to D. T. Suzuki in the Glass stories, revealing his affinity for this renowned transmitter of Zen culture, and that he can be definitely linked to at least *one* other early 1950s book of Suzuki's,[10] it seems virtually certain that a copy of the *Essays* lay not far from the typewriter during his completion of the first draft and revisions of *Catcher*.

## AMBAN'S DOUGHNUTS

The second reference in *Catcher* to a specific Zen source occurs only once, in chapter 25, as Holden walks uptown from Grand Central Station the next morning looking for a place to have breakfast. In the wake of his tearful reunion with Phoebe and traumatic encounter with Mr. Antolini, Holden's spirits have reached their lowest ebb ("I think I was more depressed than I ever was in my whole life" [194]). Beset by morbid hypochondriacal thoughts ("So I figured I was getting cancer" [196]), he thinks he might feel better with something in his stomach:

> So I went in this very cheap-looking restaurant and had doughnuts and coffee. Only, I didn't eat the doughnuts. I couldn't swallow them too well. The thing is, if you get very depressed about something, it's hard as hell to swallow. The waiter was very nice, though. He took them back without charging me. I just drank the coffee. (196)

Holden's gagging on the doughnuts is an allusion to the fourty-ninth and final koan contained in the *Mumonkan* (Ch., *Wu-men-kuan: The Gateless Gate*), the renowned medieval Chinese collection assembled in 1228 by Master Mumon Eikai (Wu-men Hui-k'ai). The koan is entitled "Amban's Addition" because a lay student, so-named, later attached it to Mumon's original edition of forty-eight. In it, Amban gives a mock portrayal of himself as seeking revenge on old Master Mumon for foisting those forty-eight undigestible koans on any passerby willing to swallow them. The added koan is Amban's "priceless opportunity" to give Mumon a taste of his own medicine:

> Mu-mon has just published forty-eight koans and called the book *Gateless Gate*. He criticizes the old patriarchs' words and actions. I think he is very mischievous. He is like an old doughnut seller trying to catch a passerby to force his doughnuts down his mouth. The customer can neither swallow nor spit out the doughnuts, and this causes suffering. Mu-mon has annoyed everyone enough, so I think I shall add one more as a bargain. I wonder if he himself can eat this bargain. If he can, and digest it well, it will be fine, but if not, we will have to put it back into the frying pan with his forty-eight also and cook them again. Mu-mon, you eat first, before someone else does:
>
> Buddha, according to a sutra, once said: "Stop, stop. Do not speak. The ultimate truth is not even to think." (Reps 128)

Indigestible doughnuts are an apt comic image for the psycho-spiritual impasse that koans are designed to produce. Unaided reason does not equip man to comprehend ("swallow") the freedom from, indeed *within,* contradiction (permanence/change, innocence/corruption, childhood/adulthood) promised by Enlightenment. He simply cannot "take it in." Unless he be driven by an intolerable suffocation to summon up from the abyss of consciousness a power equal to this Truth, he will choke on it. Perhaps instinctively sensing this, Holden backs away from the doughnuts before getting completely "stuck." But stuck he is and, at least for a while longer, stuck he will remain between child and grownup.

Holden's doughnuts echo Amban's doughnuts, and both echo *Mu,* mentioned earlier as the koan of koans or meta-koan. As the signature koan of Rinzai Zen, *Mu* is placed first in the *Mumonkan.* Its wording is as follows:

> A monk asked Joshu [a master], "Has a dog Buddha nature?" Joshu answered, "Mu." (Sekida, *Two Zen Classics* 27)

This *Mu,* variously "nothing, not, nothingness, un-, is not, has not, not any" (*Shambhala* 147), is assigned by the *roshi* (master) to most Zen novices as an object of meditation *(zazen).* Like any koan, it is not an intellectual exercise, nor does it have any "correct" answer or interpretation. Any answer, verbal or non-verbal, presented by student to master is correct that demonstrates the former's clear intuitive grasp of the main issue: nothing (no thing) is real, all is emptiness; and hence, by virtue of the *coincidentia oppositorum* portended by the Middle Way of the koan, everything is real, all is fullness. Net result: *Mu* is absolute Freedom, ineffable Mystery, ground zero Truth. Hence its traditional representation in Japanese ink-brush calligraphy as a thick doughnut-shaped cipher. (We noted above *Mu's* similar characterization by Hakuun Yasutani as a half-swallowed "red-hot iron ball that you cannot disgorge despite your every effort.") Doughnut or iron ball, *Mu* is what nearly chokes Holden.

Salinger's most likely source for the doughnut interlude is Nyogen Senzaki and Paul Reps's 1934 edition of *The Gateless Gate,* published by John Murray in Los Angeles. This liklihood is increased by the fact of the compilers' inclusion of Amban's "49th koan," whereas the "purist" editors of most other English translations leave it out. Salinger is also linked to Reps by Alsen (160, n. 21–22), who cites another Reps collection, *101 Zen Stories* (1939), as a probable source for the Zen motifs in *Nine Stories* and "Raise High the Roof Beam, Carpenters." The point of emphasis here, of course, is that Salinger was already interpolating specific elements of Zen lore into the creative process as early as *Catcher.*

## RILKE'S CAROUSEL AND HOLDEN'S ENLIGHTENMENT

It has been shown that the aim of a koan is, by dint of its logical absurdity, to frustrate the binary either/or structure of ordinary consciousness; in Western terms, to straitjacket the conventional rationalist Aristotelian viewpoint so that something akin to the mystical Platonic can break through. This is why so many koans and anecdotes in the ancient collections feature the imagery of impasse: a monk hanging from a lofty branch by his teeth, or facing the master's bamboo stick no matter what he says or does, or being challenged to take one step forward from atop a 100-foot flagpole. The more oppressive the dilemma, the more favorable the conditions for inner revolution. Clearly the damned-either-way gallows humor of Zen appealed strongly to Salinger's sense of irony. The missing ducks, the half-frozen pond, and the gagging doughnuts are intended, as symbolic echoes of classical Zen situations, to lend an aura of both gravity and, in Balzac's sense, comedy to the situation of a youth mired deep in crisis. The novel is all about Holden's weekend at the crossroads. As the reader approaches the climactic scene at the carousel, the question verily burns: what will Holden *do?* Similarly, the old Zen masters often put this nakedly terrifying question to their spiritual charges for whom they had just devised some intolerable bind.

What Holden does in fact "do" at the carousel is resolve his life koan. His subsequent "illness" and therapeutic confinement in no way cast doubt on this. Zen literature is replete with accounts of Enlightenment experiences *(kensho* or *satori)* that are so shattering to the individual's conditioned world view that the rush of emancipation they bring is initially experienced as a kind of nervous breakdown. Kapleau reports the case of one Zen student, a Japanese business executive, who, in his own words, one night

> abruptly awakened. At first my mind was foggy, . . . Then all at once I was struck as though by lightning, and the next instant heaven and earth crumbled and disappeared. Instantaneously, like surging waves, a tremendous delight welled up in me, a veritable hurricane of delight, as I laughed loudly and wildly: "Ha, ha, ha, ha, ha, ha! . . . "
>
> . . . . . . . . . . . . . . . . . . . . . . . . . .
>
> My son told me later he thought I had gone mad. (216)

What one might call Holden's Divine Madness commences with his sudden announcement of his decision to "go home" (212), made to Phoebe at the carousel: "'Yeah,' I said. I meant it too. I wasn't lying to her. I really did go home afterwards" (212). Perhaps here too Salinger had in mind Suzuki who describes Enlightenment in lapsarian-mythical terms as the return of conscious will to its "own original abode where there was yet no dualism, and therefore peace prevailed. This longing for the home, however, cannot be satisfied without a long, hard, trying experience. For the thing [consciousness] once divided in two cannot be restored to its former unity until some struggle is gone through with" (*Essays* 131).

However that may be, there can be little doubt of the Zen reference contained in the rain that then begins to fall, as Holden says, "[i]n *buckets*" (212; Salinger's emphasis). Holden's cliche is an "inside" Zen allusion to this shattering or explosive quality that often ushers in an Enlightenment experience. The bucket or pail or barrel that has its bottom smashed through, thus releasing the flow of water heretofore "confined," is a traditional Rinzai metaphor for the aspirant's longed-for breakthrough to spiritual freedom. The image may have its origins in the biography of the medieval Japanese master Bassui by his student Myodo who describes the moment of the former's Enlightenment as a feeling of having "lost his life root, like a barrel whose bottom had been smashed open" (qtd. in Kapleau 166). However, Salinger's source for the image is more likely to have been an anecdote in Senzaki and Reps's *101 Zen Stories* recounting the sudden awakening of the nun Chiyono who "one moonlit night . . . was carrying water in an old pail bound with bamboo. The bamboo broke and the bottom fell out of the pail, and at that moment Chiyono was set free!" (*Zen Flesh* 31). Of course, in narrating the climactic event of Holden's spiritual breakthrough, Salinger works some deft displacements on the image to avoid obviousness: the water does not rush out through bottomless buckets, rather it is the buckets (of rain) themselves that come pouring down. Similarly, the analogous onrush of tears expressive of the aspirant's emancipation that usually accompanies the bucket image (Myodo says of Bassui that the tears overflowed, "pouring down his face like rain" [qtd. in Kapleau 166]) is truncated in Holden's case to: "I was damn near bawling, I felt so damn happy, if you want to know the truth" (213).

However, what is truly arresting about Salinger's rendering of *Catcher's* denouement is the particular way he uses the German poet Rilke's *Dinggedicht,* "Das Karussell" (1908), to say the unsayable, that is, to convey through oblique symbolic allusion the sudden breakthrough within Holden of awareness of the *coincidentia oppositorum,* the essence of the solution to his life koan. Salinger's veneration of Rilke is well known (Hamilton 108; Stone 521). Rilke is one of very few poets mentioned by name in the fiction.[11] Also, some preliminary scholarship has been done showing influence,[12] but no one has as yet nearly done justice to the profound connection between Rilke's and Salinger's carousels.

Both poem and novel are about the loss of innocence marking the passage from childhood to maturity. This, as noted above, is precisely the issue (koan) at the root of Holden's crisis: "How can I possibly move on to a world teeming with phonies [change] without becoming one myself [permanence]?", as it were. The reference to "Das Karussell" as a reflection of the miraculous solution now suddenly at long last welling up in Holden is contained in the blue coat worn by Phoebe as she rides the carousel. Giddy with delight, Holden exclaims, "I felt so damn happy, . . . I don't know why. It was just that she looked so damn *nice,* the way she kept going around and around, in her blue coat and all" (213). Blue-clad Phoebe alludes to the "little girl in blue" (M; Rilke, "Rainer" 228) who rides the stag in Rilke's lyric and stands for innocence, that is, the child's capacity for complete absorption in the moment of play. In counterpoint, the older girls in "Karussell" riding nearby already have, like Holden, one foot in adulthood and thus are afflicted, as is he, with that relentless self-consciousness that breeds phoniness, the bane of Holden's existence: "girls, so fair, having all but outgrown such play; in mid-ride they look up, at something, over this way—" (M; Rilke, "Rainer" 228). These girls on Rilke's carousel, one a child, the others no longer quite, dramatized for Salinger the collision of world views that bedevils Holden.

The solution to any koan is some realization of a dialectical synthesis that shifts the aspirant to a phase of consciousness deeper and more comprehensive than the logico-rational, one that can effortlessly accommodate both terms of the conflict. This realization must be more than intellectual (in fact, intellect need hardly be involved at all); it must have the immediacy of an insight grounded in experience and must take one well beyond the pairs of opposites that are forever dogging the human mind. In Rilke's poem this is subtly indicated in the line, "And now and then a wide grin turned this way" (M; Rilke, "Rainer" 228).[13] The wide grin is that of some child on the carousel; it is "turned this way" [hergewendet], that is, toward the poet-persona. Poet and child, for a flickering instant locked in each other's gaze. What else can this be but the realization of the *coincidentia oppositorum?* The poet is the one who is somehow able to grow up while yet remaining a child. As Rilke says elsewhere, in response to an imaginary interlocuter, the poet is gifted with the ability to behold all things, good and bad, genuine and phony, with the celebratory eyes of a newborn: "So tell me, poet . . . /Wherefore thy right to be in any mask, in any costume true?/—I celebrate" (M; Rilke, "Rainer" 230). Indeed, just like a newborn, the poet beholds things by *becoming* them. As Keats has it: "The poet has no self; he is forever filling some other body." This I take to be Salinger's understanding of Rilke's "Das Karussell," and it is this understanding, rather viscerally than intellectually experienced, that now overcomes Holden like an ancient dream fulfilled, releasing him from his long bondage to a worn-out world view.

To be sure, Holden is no poet in the conventional sense, but I believe Salinger takes "poet" in this deeper archetypal sense shaped by the German-Romantic tradition to which Rilke was heir and which he in fact fulfilled: the poet represents the cutting edge of human spiritual evolution, one who has, at least once, been struck by lightning, one who has made, however tentatively, the quantum leap from human to cosmic consciousness. This notion of the poet as spiritual archetype also seems to be what Franny is trying to convey to her boyfriend as she struggles to justify her dislike of the self-styled poets in the English Department:

> I mean they're not *real* poets. They're just people that write poems that get published and anthologized all over the place, but they're not *poets*. (*Franny and Zooey* 18)[14]

The archetype of the poet as (wo)man-child, as a seamless sacerdotal identity of opposites, and therefore as the solution to Holden's koan, is also hinted at in Holden's repeated references at the carousel to "old Phoebe," the child who incarnates the wisdom of the ages.

In Salinger's multiveiled allusion to this Rilkean meeting of eyes, this interlocking glance, it is not only man and child, or experience and innocence, that fuse in Holden's at last emancipated spirit, but also, as it were in miniature, the great Wisdom traditions of East and West, for Holden's character, suddenly becoming in this apocalyptic moment more than itself, is a syncretic expression of their mutual recognition of the universal mystical truth of the *coincidentia oppositorum*. In Zen the recognition of this truth lies at the heart of any koan; in Rilke its expression reflects a perennial German spiritual insight the lineage of which can be traced back at least as far as Meister Eckhart's "Single Eye" by which man and God view each other.[15] It is Salinger's particular genius in this climactic scene to have brought these great mystical traditions together in the simple, homey tableau of an older brother happily watching his kid sister as she takes a turn on the local merry-go-round. One need hardly point out that all of this is punctuated, so to speak, by the image of the carousel itself as a mandala-symbol of the dynamic Eye of Wisdom to which the path of Holden Everyyouth inevitably leads.

A final question suggests itself. The Zen masters tell us that to have solved one koan is, at least for a time, to have solved them all, since every koan, upon solution, vouchsafes a glimpse of the "same" Absolute. If, as is argued here, Holden has accomplished this, if, for the duration of his cheerful repose on that park bench (and doubtless well beyond), he basks in the glow of Enlightenment, then why does Salinger have him end his story on a note of lack or deficit, as if he were still ensnared by what Buddhists call *avidya,* that is, the primal Ignorance that gives rise to desire: "About all I know is, I sort of *miss* everybody I told about. Even old Stradlater and Ackley, for instance. I think I even miss that goddam Maurice. It's funny. Don't ever tell anybody anything. If you do, you start missing everybody" (214)?

Oddly, the question answers itself when taken paradoxically, that is, when one reads "missing" in the paradoxical context of Enlightenment, wherein all contradictions are resolved, as *itself* a form, even the supreme form, of "having." C. S. Lewis, no mean adept in spiritual matters, makes this point most eloquently in his description of the state of "Joy," that is, Enlightenment considered in its affective aspect. Recalling his experience of a walk during which this sense of Joy had been especially acute, he reflects

> [W]hat I had felt on the walk had also been desire, and only possession in so far as that kind of desire is itself desirable, is the fullest possession we can know on earth; or rather, because the very nature of Joy makes nonsense of our common distinction between having and wanting. There, to have is to want and to want is to have. (*Surprised by Joy* 166)

For Holden here and now, in the flush of the *coincidentia,* to miss is to have—fully. As for his missing "even . . . that goddam Maurice" (214), it is another curious fact of Enlightenment that, viewed through Its eyes, all things assume an aura of infinite value, however noble or base they may rank on the valuative scales of ordinary consciousness. Suzuki goes so far as to say:

> But with the realization of Enlightenment, the whole affair [i.e., life] changes its aspect, and the order instituted by Ignorance is reversed from top to bottom. What was negative is now positive, and what was positive now negative. Buddhist scholars ought not to forget this revaluation of ideas that comes along with Enlightenment. (*Essays* 139)

To all appearances, Holden Caulfield is neither a poet nor a Buddhist scholar. Yet he is, by novel's end, an intimate of the Truth both stammer to convey.

## CALCIFICATION OF THE *COINCIDENTIA*

Indications are that Salinger's interest in Zen slowly waned in the course of the 1950s as he turned to other Eastern religions and to Christianity for inspiration. In fact, the gradient of this waning interest can be traced in terms of the kind of narrative treatment given the Zen motif from *Catcher* (1950) through *Nine Stories* (1953) to "Zooey" (1957) and "Seymour: An Introduction" (1959). Generally speaking, the movement is from implicit to explicit, or from subtext to text. In *Catcher* Zen has a clear but strictly covert presence. It is there as symbolic echo and oblique allusion, imbuing the "banal" tale of a modern adolescent's identity crisis with the power and gravity of ancient legend. Its use is, in a word, aesthetic, the more so in view of its subtle but profound resonance, as we have seen, with a spiritually akin yet culturally remote literary echo, this from the German poet Rilke. In *Nine Stories* Zen still serves a quasi aesthetic function (e.g., Seymour's semi-implicit banana-fish koan, or Teddy's eccentric "emptying-out" theory of education, a transparent reference to the Buddhist concept of *sunyata*), but the one-hand-clapping koan that prefixes the book signals the emergence of Zen as more an intellectual than a creative issue for Salinger. This is precisely its status in "Zooey," where it is lavishly entertained in the probing religious dialog of brother and sister, and in "Seymour: An Introduction," which features a longish peroration on Zen given by Buddy near its end. As the author's religious enthusiasms shift away from Zen, Zen becomes in the fiction something that has always been anathema to the masters—a subject of discussion.[16]

Of course, Salinger is not to be faulted for this. Passions wax and wane, interests come and go, for artists no less than mere mortals. An artist's only duty is to follow his daimon wherever it may lead. The matter of waning interest is raised here only as an attempt to account for the peculiar failure of previous critics to identify specific elements of Zen in *Catcher,* elements, as we have seen, that disclose the *coincidentia oppositorum* as the shaping principle of the novel. The announced presence of Zen in the later fiction seems to have lulled most critics into the assumption that it has little or no presence in *Catcher*. Ironically, just the opposite is the case: the presence of the East in *Catcher* is all the stronger precisely for its being unannounced, not to mention covertly commingled with the strains of the poet from the West. Salinger himself recognized this gradual slackening of his ability to make creative use, not only of Zen, but of religion generally, in his work. He fretted over the question whether he really was following his daimon. Hamilton tells us that Salinger, in an unpublished letter to his friend and confidant, Learned Hand, written in the late 1950s, "admits he is well aware that his new [post-Zen] religious preoccupations might turn out to be harmful to his writing, and that he sometimes wishes he could go back to his old methods. But it seemed to him that there was little he could do about controlling the direction of his work" (154). In contrast to Holden who arrives at Enlightenment at the end of a painful inner struggle, Holden's author seems to have been blessed with a touch of Enlightenment at the beginning, only to have it calcify with the passing years into something not unlike those glass-encased exhibits in his masterly novel.

# 6

# Without an Object, without a Subject: The Consciousness of Franklin Merrell-Wolff

> The perceiver in fact has arrived at a point in his investigation at which he is looking at what he is himself; he has reached a dead-end in his analysis and finds himself face to face with his own nature, but, instead of recognizing it as such and realizing that his void is what an eye sees when it looks at itself, he goes on trying to objectify what he does not see, what he can never see, by turning it into an objective concept, like the good and well-trained philosopher he usually is.
>
> —Wei Wu Wei

As we have seen, both Thomas Merton and J. D. Salinger came to the *coincidentia oppositorum* through Eastern religion and German Neoromanticism. A third, somewhat older, American contemporary, Franklin Merrell-Wolff, followed a similar course, only in his case the Eastern tradition was not Zen but Vedanta, an Indian ancestor of Zen, and the Romanticism was not the latter-day reincarnation of Rilke but the original philosophical arc of German idealism including Fichte, Schelling, and, above all, their mentor, Immanuel Kant. Nevertheless, of Merrell-Wolff it must be said, as of Kafka, that his own inner experience was key, which in this case took the form of a sequence of two profound mystical "Recognitions." All of Merrell-Wolff's significant writings in the philosophy of religion grew—indeed burst—directly and immediately out of these Recognitions, the latter and deeper of which was a direct apprehension of the *coincidentia,* or, in Merrell-Wolff's term, "the High Indifference."

Franklin Merrell-Wolff was a true American original, a native Californian who went East early in the twentieth century to train in philosophy and mathematics at Harvard, only to return to the "Wild West" at the end of his studies and hole up in semi-seclusion in the California mountains. He combined intellectual mastery of the most abstruse Hindu and German religio-philosophical thought with an American pragmatic sense of what worked and what did not work in bringing about realization of the deeper mystical states. He elaborated a systematic philosophy of mind, basing it, not on airy rationalist speculation, but on what he called "introception," that is, the rigorous empirical observation of his own expanded states of consciousness. He is, as of this writing, an undiscovered American master but, one suspects, not for long.

## BACKGROUND, INFLUENCES, BREAKTHROUGH

Is the West finally yielding to the East's age-old insistence that the intellect has no significant role to play in leading us to ultimate Truth or Reality? And in so yielding, are we in the West perhaps playing away our trump card? Unquestionably, in modern times the human intellect has come into bad repute in certain religious, philosophical, and psychological circles. Perhaps unconsciously swayed by cultural myths of the "Fall" into reflective consciousness, perhaps revulsed by the ubiquitous materialism spawned of scientific reasoning, many prominent voices in what has become our global guru culture have thundered against the intellect, reviling it as the "bastard child" of the mind, a willful impediment to any final reckoning with "Ultimate Reality." Poststructuralism, with its putative exposure of our delusive logocentric pursuit of the chimeras of "essence," "truth," or "meaning," is only the most recent wave of what one might term "the thinking man's anti-intellectualism." Dedicated advanced students of Zen Buddhism, East and West, forgetting that many of the masters hold doctorates and "moonlight" as professors, rail against the slightest hint of any tendency on the novice's part to—God forbid!—"think" his way to Enlightenment. (The hoary old anecdote of the sage who overfills the visiting professor's teacup to shock him into awareness of the lack of room for Truth in his overstuffed mind has rendered yeoman service here.) Less establishmentarian modern gurus from Gurdjieff to Krishnamurti ("Thought is always old") and Rajneesh ("Sooner would one of my limos pass through the eye of a needle than an accountant get Enlightenment") have warned us tirelessly of reason's utter impotence in the face of the Mystery.

On the less cosmic, more modest front of merely personal integration, depth psychology has branded thought a "defense mechanism" and unmasked reason as "rationalization." Jung was wont to allude to the intellect's basically tricksteresque nature: "The intellect is undeniably useful in its own field, but is a great cheat and illusionist outside of it whenever it tries to manipulate [psychic] values" (*Psyche and Symbol* 32); and Gestalt therapist Fritz Perls loved to tickle his rapt groupies at Esalen with such outrageous pronouncements as "The intellect is the whore of the mind!" Professors of literature reflexively cite Romanticism's emotionalist manifesto against the excesses of Enlightenment (in the eighteenth-century sense) rationalism as cultural-historical precedent for all of this, overlooking, as one instance among many, the mystic Novalis's insistence, through the mouth of his fictional poet-sage Klingsohr, on the absolute necessity of highly developed faculties of reason and observation in the making of a poet.[1] This oversight—let's call it a failure-by-neglect to correct the record—has had the unintended ironic effect of giving a kind of academic sanction to this intellectual anti-intellectualism.

Franklin Merrell-Wolff is that rare modern man, a guru or spiritual teacher whose mission in life it was to show how intellect, and its objective correlative, language, could, when used in a certain way by a certain type of person, be a most dependable and efficient raft to that "other shore" of the land beyond the pairs of opposites. He was as keenly aware as any of the great mystics, oriental or occidental, of the dangers of overintellectualizing, and thereby withering, the spiritual quest, but, as a philosopher weaned on Kant and German idealism, he was also more sensitive than most to the intellect's subtle capacity to point the thinker beyond its own limits to a realm of consciousness of far superior noetic value. If thought, in dichotomizing the world, had been the culprit in our banishment from the Garden, Merrell-Wolff knew well how to use that very forked-tongued serpent to get us back in. And the Garden of our return should be envisioned as an infinitely richer place than the one of our departure since, equipped with thought as we then would be, we would, in Eliot's deathless phrase, "know the place for the first time."

Franklin Merrell-Wolff was born in Pasadena, California, in 1887, the son of a Methodist minister. A precocious child, he began serious reading and reflection on "ultimate" religious and philosophical questions in early adolescence, soon concluding that the orthodox church was "utterly barren, so far as cognitive values were concerned, and puny in what it offered for feeling" (*Pathways* 104). Turning in college at Stanford to mathematics "for what religion usually gives to men" (*Pathways* 104), he soon felt the need to supplement this rarefied study with philosophy for "its reflecting and focussing power" and eventually psychology, in particular the new analytic psychology of Carl Jung, no doubt sensing a nascent need to develop "his skill to perform

. . . the clear introspection and articulation of experience" (Leonard 18).[2] Almost unawares, the young student was equipping himself with utmost care for spiritual epiphanies that still lay decades off in the future.

A scholarship sent Merrell-Wolff from Stanford to Harvard for graduate study in philosophy for the academic year 1912–1913. It was at Harvard that he "became convinced of the probable existence of a transcendent mode of consciousness that could not be comprehended within the limits of our ordinary forms of knowledge" (*Consciousness* 19), a consciousness, in other words, essentially beyond the reach of epistemological or psychological inquiry. Once clear on this, Merrell-Wolff saw his future laid out before him: he would make it the business of his life to realize this consciousness, which he sensed both instinctively and intellectually to be of inestimable value, and would relegate every other aspect of his life to a role strictly instrumental to this realization.

This meant the abandonment of plans for a promising academic career at Stanford, where he briefly taught mathematics upon leaving Harvard, for Merrell-Wolff was wary of the scholar's tendency to lose the forest of his vision for the trees and shrubs of painstaking argument and documentation. He wanted to use the methodological rigor of scholarship while dispensing with its formal protocol. Embarking on a course of private study and experimentation with his own consciousness that would introduce him to a vast spectrum of Western and Eastern esoteric thought, Merrell-Wolff was to endure for some twenty-four years before his search finally came to fruition with his breakthrough Recognition in August of 1936. During the long years of spiritual groping, involving many setbacks and periods of self-doubt, he supported himself and his wife Sherifa, who was also his spiritual partner and aide, with odd jobs that included beekeeping (learned from his father), group instruction (in Yoga and theosophical wisdom), and even prospecting for gold (a subterranean activity he credits, as did the Romantic mystic-minerologist Novalis before him, with profound archetypal-preparatory significance in his final breakthrough).[3]

It is important to note that, contrary to the conventional spiritual wisdom, Merrell-Wolff found his way to Enlightenment substantially on his own, without the help of a personal teacher or guru. His teachers existed solely between the covers of the books he read, and of these there were many, as he gratefully acknowledges. (More about the important ones below.) Clearly, a powerful synergy developed over the years between his intense study of mystical and philosophical literature and his experimenting on himself with various techniques of meditation. All this culminated in the above-mentioned breakthrough or "Recognition" in August 1936, in which Merrell-Wolff felt he had profoundly penetrated the subjective or "Nirvanic" pole of consciousness. However, he tells how some three weeks later he was taken completely by surprise by an even deeper penetration to an absolute or nonderivative stratum of consciousness which he terms "the High Indifference," a state in which he experienced the complete and utter reconciliation of all the pairs of opposites inasmuch as "the logical principle of contradiction simply had no relevancy. It would not be correct to say that this principle was violated, but rather, that it had no application" (*Consciousness* 69–70).

On these two fundamental Recognitions, the latter clearly a direct apprehension of the *coincidentia oppositorum,* Merrell-Wolff based his two important religious-philosophical works, *Pathways through to Space* and *The Philosophy of Consciousness without an Object.* The former is part autobiographical account of and part philosophical reflection on the inner events in question, and was substantially written during the weeks of revelation themselves and in the two months that followed, thus conveying the dramatic impact of intense spiritual life as it unfolds. The latter was written immediately thereafter, between November 1936 and March 1937, and represents Wolff's desire to appeal to the academic intelligentia with a more sober, systematic examination of the philosophical implications of his experience.[4]

Following these two books that literally exploded out of the brief period of his epiphanies, Merrell-Wolff wrote very little for the rest of his life. Instead, he turned to the tape recorder, recording by conservative estimate a million words on a variety of philosophical, religious, and psychological topics (Leonard 14, n. 29). He also continued his group work and gave public lectures as he had done earlier, but, according to Leonard, "those who knew him well found that, as a result of his Realizations, his presence carried a force which could induce an altered state of consciousness in his audience" (21). A merely interesting man had become a charismatic one. Content to let the seeking world find its way to him, Merrell-Wolff took up residence in a self-built house nestled on the eastern slope of the Sierra Nevada mountains near Lone Pine, California, in deliberate shouting distance of the majestic Mt. Whitney, a location he felt to be of spiritual significance (Leonard 20–21). Drawn by his books and his reputation for spiritual pluralism, visitors came over the years from as far away as Australia and Nepal. To the sparse local population he became "the wise man of the mountain," a quasi-legendary status he enjoyed, but certainly had not sought, until his death in 1985.

As with all true devotees of the *coincidentia,* Franklin Merrell-Wolff's genius is ultimately synthetic in nature. His Recognitions were literal "re-memberings" of a Consciousness torn asunder, of a world stifling in its multiplicity. He preferred the term *Recognition* to other traditional designations of mystical insight (e.g., awakening, enlightenment, realization) precisely for its implication of the rediscovery of something precious that has long been lost, as well as for its designation of this lost treasure as valuable not merely to the life of feeling or aesthetic sensibility but to the well-being of the cognitive or thinking part of us as well. It is the second of William James's renowned four marks of the mystical experience, the one labeled "noetic quality," that endlessly preoccupied Merrell-Wolff and that received his strongest endorsement:

> Although so similar to states of feeling, mystical states seem to those who experience them to be also states of knowledge. They are states of insight into depths of truth unplumbed by the discursive intellect. They are illuminations, revelations, full of significance and importance, all inarticulate though they remain; and as a rule they carry with them a curious sense of authority for after-time. (293)[5]

This sense of the fundamental wholeness of reality as something appreciable by—indeed *created* by—intellect as well as feeling largely accounts for the three major influences on Merrell-Wolff's development: Pythagoras, Kant, and Shankara (in this particular, overlapping chronological order).[6] In Pythagoras the young mathematician found confirmed his own nascent awareness of the mystical power inherent in numbers and of the mathematically precise ordering of the universe as not merely a rational intuition but a physical fact as well. How marvellous: numbers were not just formal abstractions but also "units, geometrical points and physical atoms" (Leonard 25)! Could the mystical implications of higher mathematics hold a key to the reintegration of mind and body, spirit and matter, spirit and nature? One of Merrell-Wolff's dreams, never more than tentatively enacted, was the development of a "yoga of mathematics" or Western yoga to serve as a sort of intellectual counterpart to the devotional yoga of the East. He believed the Western psyche was grounded in the Apollonian attitude of knowledge for its own sake and that this grounding made mathematics, the concept-oriented discipline par excellence, an ideal candidate for the development of a uniquely Western mystical path.

Merrell-Wolff thought of Pythagoras as a kind of "Western Shankara" and of his mathematical mysticism as an "objective" correlate to Shankara's subjective philosophy of the Self or *atmavidya:*

> Again, pure mathematics is the only real invariant that we have in the ever-changing phantasmagoria of experience. . . . To be sure,

> there is a profound sense in which the pure Self is a similar invariant, but the peculiar psychology of the West is too objective in its orientation to permit this Self to be generally and effectively accessible. It is otherwise in India. (*Consciousness* 173)

To be sure, Merrell-Wolff well understood that mystical paths of *any* cultural stamp or origin were only for the select few who were ready to tread them. However, that said and all other things being equal, "[I]t is," as he put it, "by its power, and not its weakness, that an individual or class attains the best. Thus, I would select the mathematical road as the one of preeminent power so far as western culture is concerned" (*Consciousness* 172).

It was, however, the philosophy of Immanuel Kant that was most integral to Merrell-Wolff's growth as a thinker and seeker. The sober Königsberg professor was for him "the most profound Western philosopher" (*Pathways* 99) and the *Critique of Pure Reason* "the most important work in the whole of western philosophical literature" (*Consciousness* 16). Merrell-Wolff credits Kant's "Copernican revolution" in philosophy for providing him with a rational-intellectual base from which to articulate mystical insights that would otherwise have remained, as it were, "stillborn": "Without him I might have *experienced,* but I could not have understood nearly so well the Meaning unfolded through the Transition" (*Pathways* 36). This is to say, Kant's lowering of the lens of cognition from the formless metaphysical heavens, in the endless scanning of which it had dissipated itself in the systems of Enlightenment rationalism, to the earthbound precincts of the scanner, thus making knowledge of the knower a precondition for knowledge of anything else, resulted in the replacement of metaphysics by epistemology in the philosophical pecking order. Because of Kant the knowing subject became the most fascinating object of philosophical interest. According to Merrell-Wolff, this Copernican shift from object to subject brought about by Kant was the decisive factor in preparing the nineteenth-century Western mind to understand and appreciate the transpersonal-ego-psychologies of the East (a *sine qua non* of his own development).

Moreover, Merrell-Wolff took Kant's proof of unaided reason's impotence to wrest metaphysical truth, together with his hints in the *Critique* that there might be some other way to get at that truth, as his own cue to explore a possible "third organ" of cognition (in addition to sensation and conception), the mystical organ, which he came to call the "introceptive faculty." Merrell-Wolff felt strongly that, despite his dry-as-dust style and disparagement of metaphysics, Kant must have had some degree of mystical perception. Leonard telescopes Merrell-Wolff's line of thought thus:

> It may appear odd to place Kant among the mystics, even if his familiarity with apperception [the faculty enabling us to be aware of the a priori functions by which the mind orders experience, such as time, space and causality] strongly hints at adumbrations of mystical consciousness. Nevertheless, even though Wolff characterizes his mind as scientific rather than mystical, he contends that "buried deep in Kant's thought lies the Recognition." Kant stands at the foundation of German Idealism which is the Western philosophical school most consonant with Eastern philosophy and with Wolff's system. (31)

If, as Merrell-Wolff saw it, Kant's shift of focus to the subject prepared the West to appreciate Eastern subjectivism, certainly no Westerner has benefited more profoundly from this than Merrell-Wolff himself. For when he finally came to meditate upon the Vedantist philosopher Shankara's notion of the "pure Self" in Paul Deussen's *System of the Vedanta* (published in English translation in 1912),[7] it was none other than Kant's "pure transcendental apperception" that he discovered in that notion. With the assurance of one who *knew,* he was later to write in *Pathways,* some weeks after his initial breakthrough:

> Recognition of the SELF in its purity is Realization of Identity with absolute Emptiness, Darkness, and Silence, when viewed from the standpoint of relative consciousness. In point of fact this Emptiness is Absolute Fullness but, as such, never can be comprehended from the perspective of egoistic consciousness. In one sense it is the "thing-in-itself" of Kant. Relative consciousness deals with phenomena alone and can never reach beyond phenomena. But the phenomenal world rests upon the Real or Noumenal World. Thus it is that the Consciousness of [i.e., enjoyed by] the SELF or 'pure apperceptive consciousness' sustains the whole universe or cosmos. (12–13)

Establishing this bridge from Kant to Shankara, or West to East, gave great impetus to Merrell-Wolff's spiritual quest. Once into Shankara's Advaita Vedanta, he felt that he had finally found his true intellectual home, and since for him it was intellect and not feeling that lay closest to the mystical faculty, it was the thought of Shankara that was finally to provide the key to his breakthrough. Comparing the great Vedantist to the many other Eastern luminaries he had known, Merrell-Wolff writes: "Of all such Teachers whom I met, either through their living presence or their written word, Shankara, alone, adequately satisfied the intellectual side of my nature" (*Consciousness* 23).

It was two interrelated ideas of Shankara's in particular that stimulated the mystical sense in Merrell-Wolff and began to orient him toward the *coincidentia.* One was the identity of subject and object, or consciousness with its content: one *is* what one is aware of; the other was the primacy, in terms of the real, of the subject over the object, for, although subject and object were mutually conditioning in the polarized structure of ordinary relative consciousness, still the world or "Object" was a projection of the pure Subject and therefore ultimately "resolvable" (or "withdraw-able") into It (*Consciousness* 24). It is important to realize that Merrell-Wolff's response to Shankara's meticulous argumentation in working out these ideas was much more than simple intellectual assent, even enthusiastic assent. Since the Vedantist's thinking was grounded in direct experience of the transcendental and had nothing of airy rationalist speculation about it, Merrell-Wolff immediately sensed its deeper impact on himself as a kind of "direct transmission" to which the particular line of argumentation was, after all, incidental. As he puts it in *Consciousness:*

> When I had reached this point in the unfoldment of my understanding, I really had achieved the positive value of decisive importance that, some years later, was to prove the effective entering wedge for opening the Way to the transcendent level of consciousness. . . . In fact, it may be entirely possible that a sufficiently concentrated meditation upon the inner significance of these principles might prove an efficient means for effecting the transformation without the aid of any other subsidiary factor. However, they were not the sole factors that were operative in my experience, though they occupied the position of first importance. (25)

Clearly, Merrell-Wolff felt that intellectual contemplation alone, in the sense of a taut (not tight) fixation of the attention upon the noetic value of an idea transgressing empiric and rationalist strictures, could lead to Enlightenment. "Subsidiary factors," such as specialized techniques of concentration, might be helpful but were not essential. Still, as he admits, he himself needed a little "something extra" to finally break through; and the little "trick" or technique he improvised for himself, though but a hair's breadth removed from the simple reflection on these ideas, made all the difference in the world: it was simply to *look directly at* what the ideas were pointing to. In making this instinctive shift from reflecting on to direct looking at, he did what has come naturally to mystical seers from time immemorial, what Goethe, for instance, insists must finally "kick in" in the exhaustive analysis of any phenomenon: the *Urphänomen* itself must become manifest and eclipse one's phenomenal image of it, however finely calibrated that image may be. At some point all one's atmospheric calculations must finally give way to the blue of the sky itself. So, somewhere along a wearying trail littered with books and thoughts, Merrell-Wolff cast it all aside and simply began to look directly into the only consciousness he knew firsthand: his own. This isolation of the "I-point" or "subjective factor," as he variously calls it, this turning of the light of consciousness around and in upon itself, now an existential *act* rather than an intellectual exercise, was the instinctive move that finally brought Merrell-Wolff's near quarter-century-long spiritual quest to climax.

In his various reports of the inner events immediately prefacing and accompanying the long-awaited realization of the pure Self of Nirvanic consciousness, two elements stand out. One is his insistence, contrary to the stereotypic view of meditation as a kind of inner Olympics of Herculean concentration, that this focus of attention on the "I" in no sense demands the suppression or "blocking" of the ordinary stream of consciousness concerned with objects. The difference between ignoring something and actively pushing it to the periphery of awareness is the difference between discriminative emphasis, which can be creative (in the way "figures" are created from "grounds": see, for instance, the Table of Contents of this book), and conflict, which is generally antipathetic to discovery: "It was by applying this method of isolation of the essential element in the midst of a complex [i.e., field of consciousness], without trying to restrain the other components, that the Transition was effected during the early part of this month" (*Pathways* 10).

The other element is Merrell-Wolff's ingenious characterization of the ineffable moment itself as a shift in his sense of self from pointal to spatial identity. What a moment before had been merely a point of "location within," literally nothing, had now suddenly shot out in all directions at once and become literally everything:

> It is true that in one sense the "I" is a point, and the first objective of the discriminative practice is the isolation of this point from all the material filling of relative consciousness, and then restricting self-identity to this point. For my own part, I finally applied this technique with success. But, almost immediately, at the moment of success, a very significant change in the meaning of the "I" began to develop. A sort of process of "spreading out" began that culminated in a kind of spatial self-identity. I found that the "I" had come to mean Space instead of a point. It was a Space that extended everywhere that my consciousness might happen to move. I found nowhere anything beyond Me, save that at the highest stage both "I" and Divinity blended in Being. (*Pathways* 217)[8]

The intoxicating fragrance of the *coincidentia* was beginning to caress the sensibility of the seeker. The direct realization that one *was* whatever one might happen to become aware of, that, in the deepest sense, *knowing* was always *being,* brought to Merrell-Wolff, as might well be imagined, priceless noetic and affective values. Most to be savored among the former was, of course, the sense of utter "Liberation" or *moksha* consequent upon the dissolution of all boundaries. Its affective aspect, an all-pervading "Joy," was Divine Nectar and beggared description. He writes of each in turn:

> I knew myself to be *beyond space, time and causality.* As the substantial, spatial, and transcendent "I", I knew that I sustained the whole phenomenal universe, and that time, space, and law are simply the Self-imposed forms whereby I am enabled to apprehend in the relative sense. . . . Closely associated with the foregoing realization there is a feeling of *complete freedom.* . . . This is largely an affective value, but one which, to me, is of the very highest importance. . . . It seems as though but a brief experience of this Joy would be worth any effort and any amount of suffering that could be packed into a lifetime that might prove necessary for its realization. (*Consciousness* 40; 44)

## SPIRITUAL AWAKENING AS LINGUISTIC EVENT

The foregoing account of Franklin Merrell-Wolff's long spiritual struggle and final triumph is tightly telescoped. Of necessity, it omits a welter of fascinating obstacles, detours, and experiments for the perusal of which the reader is referred to the primary sources themselves. One of these, however, is of such interest and importance, not only for understanding that "final turn" of the mystical key but for "catching on" to the subtle power of language to cast a veil over the deeper mystical states including, ultimately, the *coincidentia,* that it is elevated here from footnote to textual "status." I described above the critical move on Merrell-Wolff's part as a shift from *thinking about* to *looking at* the Self, or a shift from reflection to contemplation, the latter understood as a kind of fascinated yet serene beholding. However, my narrative omits a phase occurring between these two, an intermediate phase of misunderstanding that caused him and has always caused sincere seekers a great deal of frustration. For between *reflecting on* the Self via the thought of Shankara and *looking at* the Self in a spontaneous and ultimately successful turn, Merrell-Wolff endured a period of *looking for* the Self that was as doomed to failure as the frantic circling of a dog in pursuit of its own tail. This *looking-for* phase is, of course, the perennial state of the human-all-too-human consciousness, grounded in the unconsciously accepted ego-world paradigm and its concomitant psychology of desire: the Self, being by all accounts a marvelous thing, must be somewhere else, hence something to be looked for. Merrell-Wolff gives the following revealing account of inner events leading to his first Recognition:

> While engaged in this course of reflection [on Shankara's discussion of "Liberation"], it suddenly dawned upon me that a common error in meditation—and one which I had been making right along—lay in the seeking of a subtle object of experience. Now, an object or an experience, no matter how subtle, remains a phenomenal time-space existence and therefore is other than the supersensible substantiality [i.e., the Self]. Thus the consciousness to be sought is the state of pure subjectivity without an object. . . . Further, I realized that pure subjective consciousness without an object must appear to the relative consciousness to have objects. Hence Recognition did not, of itself, imply a new experiential content in consciousness. I saw that genuine Recognition is simply a realization of Nothing, but a Nothing that is absolutely substantial and identical with the SELF. This was the final turn of the Key that opened the Door. (*Consciousness* 36–37)

Here we have a dramatic instance of profound spiritual repercussions resulting from the correction of a simple error in logic (the Self is some "thing"). However, though simple, this error is yet so thoroughly grounded in the "common sense" orientation of relative consciousness as to be virtually impossible to uproot without some such intense, extended meditation on the "correct" reverse view as contained in Shankara. It took long years before Merrell-Wolff was "suddenly" ready to realize that there was no "thing" to find, since anything found would be just another object, and not that which grounds objects.

This is the kind of "Eureka" experience that can "shake the foundations of heaven and earth," once the soil of consciousness has been properly tilled. What proceeded to open up for Merrell-Wolff right then and there was the Abyss, the mysterious Nothing with its depths within fertile depths "that is absolutely substantial and identical with the SELF." In an instant he knew the awesome power of all the negative theologies that typically strike even the highly educated Western mind as perversely nihilistic. In a flash he saw that only that which is not itself an entity, however lofty or noble or beautiful, among other entities can be of lasting value; only that which is in itself Nothing can totally transform everything while yet leaving everything exactly as it is.

Later in *Pathways* Merrell-Wolff would allow his Recognition to crystalize into one of his most fascinating "cosmological hypotheses." One might call it the "less is more" hypothesis: we are to regard the phenomenal universe as a vast network of relative vacuity. This is to say, all things are relative deficits in the only true Substance which is Nothing or Self *(nirvana)*. The more palpable or ponderable the entity (e.g., something material), the emptier; the less (e.g., thoughts), the fuller. Reality value is thus measured by the relative approximation of a phenomenon to absolute Nothingness:

> Most of humanity has fallen into the error [of equating reality with "ponderable matter, or the sensuously perceived world"], and that is the cause of all suffering. But the very agency that caused the fall may be used as a stepping-stone to Recognition. To achieve this, a certain Copernican shift in individual consciousness is necessary. Thus, instead of regarding the sensuously apparent as being substantial, the standpoint should be reversed. Then we would view the seeming emptiness of space, where there is a relative absence of physical matter, as being actually far more substantial than any ponderable matter. We would thus say: "Increase of ponderability implies decrease of substantiality and vice versa." Consequently, in some sense, the laws governing the ponderable become the obverse of the laws governing the substantial. (159–60)

Merrell-Wolff's mistake of seeking, of *looking for,* was, of course, conditioned by the linguistic consciousness, which, in order to carry out its natural discriminating function, must promote the idea of separation, an idea that, in its more invidious subtypes, shades off into notions of absence, hiddenness, and unconsciousness. Language, in its ceaseless bifurcating activity (word from thing, thing from other things, speaker from word from thing), forever leaves us with the nagging sense that something is missing from the moment. The irony is that it seems to remove things precisely so that we can "get at them." The mere fact that words point to things other than themselves means that those things are never "here," at least not in the sense in which we experience our language as being "right here beside/inside us" (though, as indicated above, even this "intimate" proximity is problematic).

This brings us to Derrida's notion of the sign or signifier as a notorious *perpetuum mobile* and to Merrell-Wolff's answer to its putative irreducibility. If language in general, and the signifier in particular, is, as deconstruction variously puts it, endlessly "restless," "pregnant," "in dynamic tension," "moving beyond itself," Merrell-Wolff would say that is because of this delusion of reference conjured by language itself. Referring is only conceivable in terms of space and time, which, though they be the great organizers of experience, as both Kant and Merrell-Wolff affirm, are also its separators. The "not here" and "not yet" mistiness that forever keeps meaning just beyond our grasp, like Kafka's Law that is always ensconced just behind the next gatekeeper, is being generated, *together with the very sense of meaning itself,* by that ultimate fog-machine of language. As Kafka's parable implies, it is the man from the country who renders *himself* impotent by delusively (read: linguistically) projecting the Law outside himself, to some future time and place when It *may,* he hopes (the delusion of futurity), deign to admit him to its presence.

Like Kafka, Merrell-Wolff sees the endless movement of the signifier as the human hypnosis par excellence, but, also like Kafka, insists that, as with any ordinary trance, it can be awakened from. Nor is this awakening to be imagined as in any sense a "protective" estrangement or divorce from the snares of language but rather as its infinite enrichment—indeed, as the true birth of poetry. Spiritual awakening as, among other things, a vivid *linguistic* event is one of the most fascinating features of Merrell-Wolff's account of his second Recognition. In the following he describes what, in deconstructionist terms, can never happen: the collapse of the (delusive) gap between signifier and signified and the recovery of their primordial *coincidentia.* This is the *Ursprache* or Language of Presence pined after by Heidegger and the German Romantics before him:

> The Event came after retiring. I became aware of a deepening effect in consciousness that presently acquired or manifested a dominant affective quality. It was a state of utter Satisfaction. But here there enters a strange and almost weird feature. Language, considered as standing in a representative relationship to something other than the terms of language, ceased to have any validity at this level of consciousness. In a sense, the words and that which they mean are interblended in a kind of identity. Abstract ideas cease to be artificial derivatives from a particularized experience, but are transformed into a sort of universal substantiality. The relative theories of knowledge simply do not apply at this level. So "Satisfaction" and the *state* of satisfaction possess a substantial and largely inexpressible identity. Further, this "Satisfaction", along with its substantiality, possesses a universal character. It is the value of all possible satisfactions at once and yet like a "thick" substance interpenetrating everywhere. (*Consciousness* 62)

This would be Merrell-Wolff's response to Derrida's assertion as to the irreducibility of the sign, the latter summed up by Coward as follows:

> Although "sign" is "irreducible," it cannot be experienced as pure presence. Rooted within language, even in its most holistic form, is the pregnant push toward sequencing, spacing, punctuation—differentiation in time and space. But differentiated language can

> never manifest the whole of the sign. Therefore there is no full speech, no absolute truth. (138)

But when the delusion of separateness is seen through, the "pregnant pressure" of the sign instantly evaporates as things, including verbal "things," reveal themselves to *be* precisely what they *mean*. Merrell-Wolff goes beyond Derrida[9] to a realization of the signifier as *itself* Presence, to a realization of Friedrich Schlegel's mystical notion of poetry in the famous *Athenäum* fragment 116: it is not a particular idiom or style or form but an experience of the ontological continuity of signifier and signified in whatever linguistic event happens to be occurring. It is the *coincidentia oppositorum* experienced linguistically.

This oneness of word and thing in the sense of a continuity of being is for Merrell-Wolff a spiritual fact of the utmost significance. It must be, for what else could cause this most scrupulously logical-rational of philosophers to insist on the superiority of the connotative to the denotative function of language? This self-confessed stranger to the charms of poetry before his awakening was absolutely convinced after it that what language suggests is far more important than what it "means": "Now, heretofore, throughout my life I have not been a lover of poetry and, much of the time, I had a decided distaste for it. Much less was I ever a writer of poetry. Yet now there comes a thought which requires poetry for its expression!" (*Pathways* 55). What words conjure up for us all on their own, without the least effort on our part, should not be obscured by our compulsive grasping for some phantom precision of "meaning" they might seem to be gesturing toward. (Some such inchoate realization, nagging at his staunch insistence on the bedrock nature of *différance,* must be the motive behind Derrida's frequent emphasis on the unique importance of poetic language.) It is the life bourgeoning "around" rather than looming "behind" the expression, life already present and not merely promised, that invites us to realize the ontological continuity between reality and its description. It is conceivable that one might totally "misread" Kant or Goethe or Kafka and yet be so attuned to the intensity of life hovering around their language as to achieve insight into those minds of an order superior to any "correct" reading. In his superb chapter in *Consciousness* on "Expression and Transcendent Consciousness," Merrell-Wolff characterizes this as awareness of the "subtle 'plus' value" of linguistic expression:

> The direct meaning of language does not express the actuality of the Higher Consciousness. We might say that the Actuality envelops the expression but is not directly contained in it. Thus

> the reader should strive not so much to understand the formal meaning contained in these writings, but to make a certain turn in his own consciousness toward a Matrix that surrounds the expression. He should concentrate upon faint stirrings in his consciousness which he cannot really express, even to himself. They constitute a certain "plus" quantity added onto the formal meaning. The formal meaning serves as a sort of focal point that entrains the subtle "plus" value. . . . Now, the "plus" quality at first is almost indistinguishable from nothing or emptiness. It is like a breath that has just escaped, a momentary gleam caught from the corner of the eye that disappears when the full focus of sight is turned upon it. It must be reached for very gently, as one must act in seeking the confidence of a defenseless and fearful creature of the wilds. One should reach out almost as though not reaching at all. (147)

At times in his writings Merrell-Wolff alludes to a certain "heat effect" as an actual physiological manifestation of a person's being in phase with the "plus" or connotative dimension of language. In his own case, he describes this heat as being noticeable by others and even contagious at certain times when he would be discoursing on ideas dear to him. He speculates that the heat might well be a manifestation of libido, not in Freud's reductionistic instinctual sense but in Jung's more open, spiritual sense of the term. In any case, it is clear that it cannot be accounted for as a symptom of mere meaning-driven cognitive activity: "No; the heat is a witness of the presence of something more than merely the intellectual content of consciousness. I repeat: This is something that can be observed and should be studied" (*Pathways* 258).

Merrell-Wolff did not think there was any necessary correlation between rational intelligence and sensitivity to this "plus" or symbolic functioning of language. Thus, even men acknowledged as brilliant by conventional academic standards might be virtually blind to it, which is precisely Merrell-Wolff's judgment on his towering philosophical contemporary, Bertrand Russell. This master of that most spiritual of languages, mathematics, had no inkling of the Pythagorean soul of his own discipline:

> Now, unquestionably, pure mathematics does afford a genuine road to Recognition, but it is not the kind of mathematics that remains after men like Bertrand Russell are through defining it. Mathematics in that sense becomes merely a formal definition of possibility, but it is stripped of all spiritual actuality. Mathematics is a spiritual power just because of that element in it that is stripped away in Russell's "Principles of Mathematics." Thinkers of this type do not see it because, however great their intellectual powers may be, yet in one dimension of themselves they are blind. They see the

> skeleton but do not Realize the soul of mathematics. And right here is the key to the failure of the coercive method [of demonstrating truth]. Without the Recognition of the Soul, in some sense, such as the soul of mathematics or of logic or in some other form, formal demonstration proves merely possibility or the hypothetical imperative but never arrives at a categorical imperative. (*Pathways* 125)

Russell claimed never to be quite himself again, intellectually speaking, after completing the monumental *Principles*. The intense, sustained effort had exhausted him and worn away something of that powerful "cutting edge" that had seen him through the ordeal of the work. Merrell-Wolff might say Russell had spent himself in a futile effort to force language (mathematical language) to *denote* or "nail down" what it can only *connote* or spontaneously conjure up by *its own* mysterious workings: Truth. This casts an oddly ludicrous light on the pretentiousness of all solemn Crusades for Truth that are mounted on the lance of language or any other system of signs meant to "pierce through" to a realm beyond themselves, ludicrous because, in Merrell-Wolff's eyes, the goal of the crusade is always already won, but goes unnoticed as it hovers modestly and inconspicuously right beside or behind the (ego-ideal of) Crusading Hero, just as the playfulness of the "plus" or connotative or symbolic value of language is lost to the "serious" thinker hell-bent on using language as equipment (in Heidegger's sense of *Ausrüstung* ) to get "beyond language."

The Awakened Merrell-Wolff, with his new-found appreciation for the spiritual power of the symbol and of poetic language generally, would certainly have applauded Kafka's metaphor on metaphor or meta-metaphor, "The Truth about Sancho Panza," which makes his point about the peripheral or "plus" value of language with brilliant aptness. Kafka's "take" on Cervantes casts the Don and Sancho in the roles of spiritually myopic Crusader for Truth and Truth itself, respectively.[10] The Don, having devoured all those medieval romances, is in love with the metaphor of the Quest, and of course with himself as Questing Hero. Since the metaphor, like any signifier, *seems* to direct one to some field of reality "away from here" (another of Kafka's slogans of futility), he is off to "real-ize" the metaphor, to replace the image with the "thing itself." Of course, there is no end to this, so the Don's campaigns fast become a sort of hypnotic repetition compulsion. Always hovering nearby, at best marginal to the Quest from Quixote's point of view, is Sancho, who, as the unnoticed "plus" value of the Don's self-absorbed life-metaphor, is the ever-overlooked key or bridge to Truth, that is, the Don's unrealized Higher Self. As such, he unobtrusively accompanies the Don on all his campaigns, waiting in patient amusement for his "master" to turn around one day and wake up to what has always been closest at hand.[11]

## INTROCEPTION AND THE HIGH INDIFFERENCE

When, in a moment of, say, "linguistic" Recognition, the mind moves from the metonymic "plus" value given off by a text, from its bourgeoning life of association, to what James called "its radiant core" of mystical meaning, what is happening? Merrell-Wolff's answer is that an actual third organ of cognition, one quite apart from sensation and reason, which he calls "introception," is going into spontaneous operation. "Introception" is the term coined by Merrell-Wolff for the mystical sense or faculty, which he believed to be inherent in all human beings but latent in most. As the word suggests, it involves the mind's "taking" or "turning" its attention away from the field of objects, its conditioned arena of interest, and focusing that attention on itself. As Merrell-Wolff puts it in his first definition in *Pathways,* it is "[t]he Power whereby the Light of Consciousness turns upon Itself toward Its Source" (228). Later on he elaborated this to

> a way of knowledge differing both from the empiric and from the conceptualistic, as those notions are currently understood. It also implies a function more profound than the conative principle of Will as understood by Schopenhauer. Thus I am calling this [my philosophic] view "introceptualism," in which the term *introception* is given a dual reference, (1) to a function of consciousness, and (2) to the content or state of consciousness rendered accessible by the function. (*Transformations* 143–44)

In terms of our linguistic example, this implies the perhaps sudden recognition of the associative life of the text as somehow one's own creation, this recognition in turn imploding back on itself ("introceiving") to the deeper recognition of the identity of associative or connotative life and denotative meaning: the text's surface or periphery, when properly, i.e., introceptively, viewed, *is* its radiant core. Put another way, in introception one experiences no break in ontological continuity between any of these categories and its complement: suggestion and meaning, surface and depth, periphery and core, and perhaps most significant, reader-subject and text-object—all commingle in a pellucid *coincidentia* superseding even the fundamental logically orienting categories of identity and difference. (It is interesting to consider Derrida's pronouncement, "There is nothing outside the text," from the viewpoint of introception so understood.)

Certainly, introception, both as function and insight resulting therefrom, is what Merrell-Wolff is convinced he gained from his pursuit of Shankara's advice to break the bondage of the mind to objects through the practice of actively isolating the mind's own conscious center with the bare attention. Leonard is quick to point out Merrell-Wolff's caution that this self-isolating act of the mind is to be "clearly distinguished from introspection, which has a necessarily objective orientation" (249):

> It is not the same as introspection, wherein consciousness merely short circuits itself to observe more subtle psychical objects that are generally unconscious for the extraverted attitude. Introception, when successful, leads to a state such that consciousness becomes its own content, that is, a consciousness that is divorced from its objective reference. By this means, the self as a source of consciousness can be Realized, without being transformed into a subtle object, as a *me*. (*Transformations* 104)

It is precisely "introception" that Merrell-Wolff offers in response to Kant's criticism of the foundationlessness of traditional rationalist metaphysics (*Consciousness* 182). He accepts the arguments in the *Critique* as to the impotence of the two human modes of cognition, sensation and conception, to give us knowledge of "things as they are in themselves," that is, knowledge of the so-called noumenal world. But then he proposes a "third organ," introception, this ability of consciousness to penetrate itself directly, as the foundation of true metaphysical understanding that traditional philosophy in particular and questing humanity in general has largely gone without. (An exception with respect to the former for Merrell-Wolff is the German idealist philosophers, especially Fichte and Hegel, who, perhaps even without fully appreciating their own innovativeness, responded to Kant's challenge with philosophical systems at least partially grounded in "introceptive" vision.)

Introception, then, is the long-lost "philosopher's stone," able to transmute base awareness into the pure gold of Recognition. Available in the Renaissance, neglected or even suppressed in the Enlightenment and subsequent scientific era, only the Romantic idealists, taking their lead from Kant, had briefly rediscovered it; and now Merrell-Wolff, again under Kant's guidance, but in this instance guidance toward ancient Eastern transpersonal psychologies with their highly elaborate technologies of the ego, was bent on reembedding the stone in the consciousness of the West. Of course, Kant's guidance here was generic, not specific. At the very end of *Consciousness* Merrell-Wolff seizes on a passage in the *Critique* which he takes to be a rare hint by Kant of the possibility of a mode of cognition that just might reveal the supreme knowledge man craves but from which he seems hopelessly cut off. It is this "speculative" hint, dropped by a mercilessly antispeculative philosopher but one in whose thought nevertheless the Recognition "lay deeply buried," that caused Merrell-Wolff to look Eastward, particularly to

Shankara, for further wisdom. The final third of the lines from Kant quoted by Merrell-Wolff, lines that became for the latter a virtual point of departure for a lifetime of self-exploration, runs as follows:

> But, in order that a noumenon may signify a *real* object that can be distinguished from all phenomena, *it is not enough that I should free my thought of all conditions of sensuous intuition, but I must besides have some reason for admitting another kind of intuition besides the sensuous,* in which such an object can be given, otherwise my thought would be empty, however free it may be from contradictions. (261; italics M-W's)

But introception did not merely give knowledge *of* the noumenon—that would simply be business as usual—it gave the *noumenon itself,* the *Ding an sich*! But what could this removal of mediation, of all prepositions "of," "about," or "concerning" reality, mean if not the utter identity of the knower with the known, the recognition of all true knowledge as Self-knowledge. Beneath the quotation from Kant, almost at the end of the book, Merrell-Wolff exults: "At last we are in a position to define 'Reality' as the noumenon that is immediately cognized by Introception, or Knowledge through Identity" (261).

Again and again Merrell-Wolff insists that his transcendental philosophy is not speculative, hence not vulnerable to the Kantian critique, but grounded in "introception," a valid third organ of human cognition providing genuine metaphysical knowledge. Of course, as he also grants, introception itself is not subject to rational proof or demonstration; it can only be known through immediate personal experience. But it is thus at least self-verifiable, and with a sense of certainty that accompanies *any* rational intuition (e.g., the taste of strawberries or of my own existence) that precedes reason-*ing*. One is reminded here of Pascal's famous aphorism to the effect that "The heart has its reasons, which reason does not know." Aware of the traditional liability of affectively based mysticisms to criticism and derision, Merrell-Wolff would doubtless substitute the more noetic "introception" for Pascal's "heart," but he would heartily endorse the aperçu. Perhaps even a certain defensiveness and need to head off potential charges of "ecstatic irrationalism," "unseemly fits and swoons," etc., made him partial to sober mathematical analogies in clarifying this subtle relation between prerational intuition and its rational extension:

> An analogous form [to the pure noesis occurring in introception] is to be noted in the groups of postulates that form the [prerational] bases of formally developed systems of mathematics that by themselves do not give an explicit logical whole, but rather

> provide the components from which a logical whole may be developed. (*Consciousness* 96)

However that may be, Merrell-Wolff saw clearly that it is the same essential intelligence that, at one end of the spectrum, engages feverishly and neurotically in an endless series of self-interetsed projects and, at the other end, frolics as it were in

> another kind of thought, dispassionate and self-directing, that stands in contrast with the thought that is guided by wishing. It may be said that this thought thinks itself, or tends to do so, depending upon the degree of its purity. It is not concerned with the preconceptions of the relative consciousness nor with the pragmatic interest of man. It tends to be authoritarian in its form, and while possessed of its own logic, yet ignores or tends to ignore that part of logical process oriented to objective referents. (*Consciousness* 96)

By Merrell-Wolff's own account, the deepest penetration ever of his power of introception occurred in his so-called Second Recognition, which took place in early September 1936, about a month after the first. We have already considered this second experience as a "linguistic event" (see above), but it cannot be overemphasized that any such categorization-by-aspect is of the most provisional nature since, in its deepest significance, this experience went for the philosopher well beyond all meaningful particularity to a realm of absolutely mutual ontic interpenetration, that is, to the realm of the *coincidentia oppositorum*.

Two circumstances prefacing the event are of particular interest, one for confirming the wisdom of the mystical manuals, the other for contradicting it. Merrell-Wolff says "the culminating Recognition came with the force of an unexpected bestowal without my having put forth any conscious personal effort toward the attainment of it" (*Consciousness* 61). Thus, as we are advised, the Spirit moveth as *it* will, deliberate pursuit tending to chase it away. However, contrary to the recommended "slowed down" or "psyched down" and ultimately "empty" mind as the ideal soil for the flowering of insight, Merrell-Wolff insists that on the evening in question, "[m]y mind, instead of being calm, as has been its dominant quality during the last month, was rather agitated" (*Pathways* 115). And what was the cause of this agitation? None other than an *intellectual* issue, a philosophical problem, traditionally the bane of mystical insight! "During the day preceding the final Recognition I had been busy writing and my mind was exceptionally clear and acute. In fact, the intellectual energy was of an unusual degree of intensity. The mood was decidedly one of intellectual assertion and dominance" (*Consciousness* 61). What mattered in Merrell-Wolff's state of mind that evening was not the presence or absence of intellectual or any other kind of "content," but the self-described intensity of that mind, a mind collected and poised to "take in" (introceive) anything it might discover. Philosophical problems that grip the mind in a deep and sustained way, in the manner, say, of Zen koans, can bring it into this kind of optimal psychospiritual focus.

The first phase of the Second Recognition involved Merrell-Wolff's experience of the oneness of sign and referent discussed above: "satisfaction" as Satisfaction, utter ontic fluency among term, concept, and experience. But he says that after a while he sensed a deepening of the experience as

> [g]radually the 'Satisfaction' faded into the background and by insensible gradation became transformed into a state of 'Indifference'. For while satisfaction carries the fullness of active affective and conative value, indifference is really affective-conative silence. It is the superior terminus of the affective-conative mode of human consciousness. There is another kind of indifference where this mode of consciousness has bogged down into a kind of death. This is to be found in deeply depressed states of human onsciousness. The High Indifference, however, is the superior or opposite pole beyond which motivation and feeling in the familiar human sense cannot reach. But, most emphatically, it is not a state of reduced life or consciousness. On the contrary, it is both life and consciousness of an order of superiority quite beyond imagination. The concepts of relative consciousness simply cannot bound it. In one sense, it is a terminal state, but at the same time, in another sense, it is initial. Everything can be predicated of it so long as the predication is not privative, for in the privative sense nothing can be predicated of it. It is at once rest and action, and the same may be said with respect to all other polar qualities. I know of only one concept that would suggest its noetic value as a whole, and this is the concept of "Equilibrium", yet even this is a concession to the needs of relative thinking. It is both the culmination and beginning of all possibilities. (*Consciousness* 63)

This "High Indifference" is for Merrell-Wolff the summum bonum, superior even to the Nirvanic or Self consciousness extolled by Shankara. For even *nirvana,* though supremely blissful, is for that very fact desirable, and therefore not yet beyond the net of desire. And so, just as a turning-away from the world of objects (including *nirvana* itself as a subtle object) had been requisite to his attainment of *nirvana,* an even more profound abandonment, this time of Nirvanic bliss itself, had been the "price of admission" for Merrell-Wolff's entrance into the ultimate Magic Theater, the theater of the *coincidentia oppositorum.*[12] Here spiritual freedom reigns absolutely since absolutely nothing either can or need be barred from the stage of consciousness on which all barring or, in Merrell-Wolff's term, "privative," impulses instantaneously trigger a mysterious alchemy of transformation: in a flash anything unseemly becomes its utterly "seemly" opposite. As Novalis has it, "And every pain will be a spur to blissful gain." His fellow Romantic E. T. A. Hoffmann's dramatic-allegoric metaphor for this inner alchemy, the bolts of fire hurled by Ignorance that turn into flowers upon impact with the princely mantle of Wisdom, highlights the seamless flow-effect of a freedom that is identical with creativity, both understood to be always arising *ex nihilo*. The very sobriety of Merrell-Wolff's tone as he describes this "tender entrapment" by a free-flowing creativity, this final "irrelevancy" of the principle of contradiction, only intimates the more subtly its supreme attraction:

> For to isolate any phase of the State was to be immediately aware of the opposite phase as the necessary complementary part of the first. Thus the attempt of self-conscious thought to isolate anything resulted in the immediate initiation of a sort of flow in the very essence of consciousness itself, so that the nascent isolation was transformed into its opposite as copartner in a timeless reality. Every attempt I made to capture the State within the categories of relative knowledge was defeated by this flow effect. (*Consciousness* 70)

Certain key terms to which Merrell-Wolff naturally inclines in his descriptions of the indescribable ring true, not only by virtue of their being direct crystallizations of his own experience, but also because they share a common core of inner significance with the idiosyncratic language of other Western mystic sensibilities. Thus, we think of Rilke's *Weltinnenraum* ("inner space of the world"), the intimate medium of the Enlightened poetic consciousness, when Merrell-Wolff describes himself at the moment of Recognition as "spreading everywhere and identical with a kind of 'Space' that embraced not merely the visible forms and worlds, but all modes and qualities of consciousness as well" (*Consciousness* 66). And when he uses the word *Presence* to characterize his awareness of the Mystery in moments when he is attempting to focus on it intellectually and is therefore "less blended in the Identity" (*Consciousness* 66), we are reminded precisely of Derrida's harangue against "Presence" as the delusion par excellence of Western metaphysics. But most evocative of all, perhaps, is Merrell-Wolff's settling on the conative-valuative term *indifference*, which he is careful to define in terms of its own peculiar polarity: the indifference of depression, "in which consciousness has bogged down into a kind of death," is the equal and inferior pole of the "High Indifference" of Enlightenment. But like all the pairs of opposites, these apparent antagonists are never far apart from each other. Just as Merrell-Wolff consciously submitted to the death of interest in the world of objects, and later the world of the Self, in order to go beyond those worlds, so too does Kafka's Gregor Samsa, in his last days in the asp-ridden bosom of his family, suffer through a "Gleichgültigkeit gegen alles" [indifference toward everything] and Kafka's Alexander the Great endure a riveting "Erdenschwere" [weight of the earth], both crucifixions metamorphosing, in the fullness of time, into the High Indifference of reconciliation with all. (Gregor's Enlightenment is narrated—by his emancipated narrative Self; Alexander's is not.) It is worth noting that the German *Gleichgültigkeit,* literally "equal validity" or "equal meaningfulness," is much more suggestive of the fertile ambiguity lying at the heart of the relationship between the "Low" and the "High Indifference" than is the nonchalant-sounding English "indifference."

But it is not only in conative terms, that is, from within the context of the psychology of desire, that Merrell-Wolff regards the High Indifference as superior to *nirvana.* It is also superior in the ontological sense in that it transcends the very principle of ontic particularity itself, compared, say, to *nirvana,* which is still identifiable with the subjective pole of consciousness and hence, at least from the standpoint of the former, derivative. Throughout his writings Merrell-Wolff equates his own High Indifference with the Buddha's anatmic Enlightenment, and both with such traditional Buddhist concepts as the *sunyata* and the *dharmakaya* (e.g., *Pathways* 281), all on the basis of the *coincidentia oppositorum* common to each. Pointing as they all do to a Reality that transcends all conceivable distinctions, polarities, and dualisms (even as It preserves these!), these terms direct the inner gaze past the self/other, even the Self/Other, dimension of existence to a realm, as Merrell-Wolff describes it in terms of his Second Recognition,

> wherein both that which I have called the Self and that which had the value of Divinity were dissolved in a Somewhat, still more transcendent. There now remained naught but pure Being that could be called neither the Self nor God. No longer was "I" spreading everywhere through the whole of an illimitable and conscious Space, nor was there a Divine Presence all about me, but everywhere only Consciousness with no subjective nor objective element. Here, both symbols and concepts fail. (*Consciousness* 73)

## THE MYSTICAL ARCHITECTURE OF THE "56"

The quintessence of Franklin Merrell-Wolff's philosophy is contained in the fifty-six aphorisms that make up chapter 4 of *The Philosophy of Consciousness without an Object.* He wrote reams before them to set them up and reams afterward in explication and elaboration, but the fifty-six pronouncements themselves, presented in chapter 4 in simple sequence without comment, as it were *in nuce,* are the virginal expression of the two Recognitions, which were themselves the fruit of a quarter-century's spiritual labor. "Virginal expression," in the sense of the natural "pre-press condensation" of the juice of the fruit, which is its purest essence, is quite in keeping with Merrell-Wolff's own view of them as spontaneous "precipitates" of *"the Thought of the Self"* (*Transformations of Consciousness* 127; italics M-W's). Mystical thought conceived as a kind of immediate precipitation or crystallization of a consciousness that, on its own terms, is beyond articulation is common to other Western mystics who, like Merrell-Wolff, have a culturally inbred tendency to intellectualize their experience. Thus, Novalis is fond of both *Krystallization* and *Niederschlag* (literally "a casting-down" in the sense of a deposit of rain or dew) when pinpointing the transition from mystical experience itself to its articulation. And even writers with an ax to grind against organized religion, such as Lichtenberg and Nietzsche, have had no trouble acknowledging and valuing the precipitous or "inspirational" quality of their own aphoristic thinking.

The mystic's recourse to the vocabulary of spontaneous natural processes such as ripening and condensation points up the sharp distinction to be made between mystical and ordinary thought, the latter usually carried on through willed and wearisome effort with little if any spontaneity. Merrell-Wolff himself distinguishes four basic levels of thought, connected by numerous gradations, ranging from the instinctual-organic (little more than "the grunt or the gesture") through the conceptual ("science, philosophy, mathematics, and much of art") and the conceptual-spontaneous ("[t]he best of poetry") to the transcendental (free-flowing and postconceptual in which "[e]very thought includes the whole of Eternity"; see also previous discussion of introceptive thought) (*Consciousness* 97–98).

This notion of a qualitative hierarchy of thought from gold to dross helps to clear away the confusion arising from the apparently antagonistic valuations of thought in Eastern and Western spiritual cultures, a confusion that Merrell-Wolff admits "caused me some years of needless misunderstanding" (*Pathways* 195). It is the lower forms of thought, the incessant need-based internal chatterings, that the Eastern manuals inveigh against. Unfortunately, due to the paucity of metaphysically subtle vocabulary in Western languages, the Sanskrit term usually used in the Eastern manuals for this base thought, *manas,* has most often been misleadingly rendered in English as "mind." This has led to false Western views of Eastern mystics as opposing thought per se. Once Merrell-Wolff learned a bit of Sanskrit, he realized that what he had been reading in translation had "violated what I felt intuitively and subsequently demonstrated to be the case" (*Pathways* 195), that is, the validity of his own noetic or "intellectual" approach to transformation.

Merrell-Wolff intends the fifty-six aphorisms as a kind of mini-manual of spiritual transformation. As "precipitates" of the Ineffable, the mysterious "perfume" of the latter still clings to them, as it were, yet as particularized or "condensed" forms they also "speak," thus appealing to the human need for meaning. They are thus potential bridges, symbols in Jung's sense, *Mittelglieder* (intermediaries) in Novalis's, and are characterized by Merrell-Wolff as such:

> In high degree, this [aphoristic] thought flows of itself, yet blends with verbal concepts. Here the conceptual thought and the transcendent thought combine in mutual action. But the lowly thought of the organic being has no part in this. It is a thought that is sweet and true, but fully clear only to him who has Vision.
>
> The best of poetry has much of this kind of thought . . . . But most of all, from this level of thought are born the aphorisms, that strange kind of thought that is both poetry and something more. For it stirs the thinking as well as the feeling and thus integrates the best of the whole man. Mystery is an inextricable part of this thought. (*Consciousness* 98)

Leonard echoes Merrell-Wolff's own characterization of the aphorisms as a group of utterances "with more or less dissociation of statement from statement" (147), analogous to a set of mathematical axioms "that by themselves do not give an explicit logical whole, but rather provide the components from which a logical whole may be developed" (*Consciousness* 96). This seems to me an overly modest appraisal on the part of both writers of the formal aspect of the aphorisms which, on close inspection, turns out to be most impressive in its intricacy; I would even venture that the architecture by which the "Group of 56" is held together is as much key to their transformative power as is their conceptual content. Indeed, as with all great art, the two aspects are indivisible, and we cannot say anything significant about form that does not in some way illuminate content.

Leonard sees a Neoplatonic circular structure, "[p]erhaps unintentional," symbolizing a cosmology of emanation away from and return to the One, and certainly there is something to this: the movement of the utterances is from pure Consciousness, Merrell-Wolff's fundamental principle ("1. . . Consciousness-without-an-object is" [*Consciousness* 101]); through manifestation or cosmic genesis in terms of a series of dichotomies (phenomenal universe versus *nirvana,* time versus eternity, etc.); thence through Liberation back to pure Consciousness, here conceived as "the GREAT SPACE, where none of the central categories of relative existence apply. . . . The end is identical to the beginning, in a sense cancelling the relevance of all between" (Leonard 148; see appendix).

But there is much more to the architecture, and to its subtle but powerful effect on the student, than this bare lapsarian outline, and, like Leonard, I find I must leave the question of Merrell-Wolff's deliberate aesthetic intention here moot, hazarding only the speculation that the very issue of mystical or inspired writing makes the question of aesthetic intention in a personal sense seem wrongheaded. What close study reveals is a highly elaborate structure every aspect of which seems to allude in some way to the ultimate Mystery of the High Indifference *(coincidentia oppositorum),* leaving the impression of an abiding Oneness amidst all the change and differentiation represented in the long middle or "manifestation" section of aphorisms. Surveying the whole, one first observes a sequence of ten subdivisions plus a summary-and-bridge aphorism between the ninth and tenth parts, each part consisting of between five and seven aphorisms. The first or "pre-manifestation" part is made up of the first five aphorisms:

> 1. . . Consciousness-without-an-object is.
>
> 2. . . Before objects were, Consciousness-without-an-object is.
>
> 3. . . Though objects seem to exist, Consciousness-without-an-object is.
>
> 4. . . When objects vanish, yet remaining through all unaffected, Consciousness-without-an-object is.
>
> 5. . . Outside of Consciousness-without-an-object nothing is. (*Consciousness* 101–02)

One notes here the mantra-like repetition of the primary symbol, linked in each case with the existential "is" (in the fifth aphorism by inversion). In number 2, the awkward illogic of the present tense of the "is" affirms the *nunc stans* or abiding present of Enlightenment that supersedes time and history as suggested by "were." The ancient Rinzai Zen koan on the *honrai-no-memmoku* or "Original Face" ("Show me your face before your parents were born") has the same thrust.

There follows the extended second phase expressive of manifestation. This encompasses sections two through nine (aphorisms 6 through 50), each section developing a different binary opposition as the Original Consciousness "steps down" into manifest existence. The sequence of antinomies is as follows: universe/*nirvana* (conceptually most "precipitous"); time/eternity; space/void; tension/equilibrium; agony/bliss; creativity/resistance; action/rest; and bondage/freedom. I will quote here the aphorisms of part eight, on action and rest (41 through 45), to give a sense of the repetitious, monolithic rhythmic structure that dominates each of these intermediate sections:

> 41. . . Ever-becoming and ever-ceasing-to-be are endless action.
>
> 42. . . When ever-becoming cancels the ever-ceasing-to-be then Rest is realized.
>
> 43. . . Ceaseless action is the Universe.
>
> 44. . . Unending Rest is Nirvana.
>
> 45. . . But Consciousness-without-an-object is neither Action nor Rest. (*Consciousness* 113–14)

As here, there is in each middle section the back-and-forth dialectic of an antinomy (some ground phenomenon vis-à-vis *nirvana* in one of its aspects) followed by an abrupt double denial, echoing the *neti, neti* style of the Upanishadic *via negativa,* that in effect affirms the essential Reality (Consciousness-without-an-object) common to each term, thus vaporizing the antinomy. Moreover, each climactic affirmation is directly preceded by an aphorism that defines *nirvana* in terms of the "positive" pole of the binary at issue, so that the final two aphorisms in each middle section reflect the supersession of Merrell-Wolff's two great Recognitions. The repetition of this pattern of tension followed by resolution over the nine middle sections of the aphorisms creates a powerful, mounting wave-like rhythm that is unmistakably erotic in its effect. And this is one of the quasi-covert aspects of the architecture of the aphorisms that grip the student, largely unconsciously, bringing his heretofore busy "manas" mind into taut focus, poised to make the introceptive leap at any moment. For the erotic rhythm of the aphorisms seamlessly complements their noetic value as pronouncements, creating an organic mind-and-body or mind-and-heart structure that becomes itself a manifestation of the Mystery.

I am struggling to suggest here something of the awe that overtakes one when in the presence of a construction of human hand that yet intimates by its endlessly layered complexity a power beyond the human. Merrell-Wolff's "56" give off the depth-beyond-depth, level-beyond-level aura of, say, Bach's *Goldberg Variations,* and the comparison of the form of that masterpiece by one performer to two double-sided mirrors that reflect each other, move toward each other, and ultimately pass through each other resulting in a "reflection of the whole piece inside and an eternity from outside" is not entirely out of place here (Feltsman 4–5). In fact, something of this ability of doubled mirrors to suggest the paradoxical two-yet-One nature of Reality occurred to Merrell-Wolff in the pages of *Consciousness* prefatory to the chapter containing the aphorisms:

> While it is affirmed that the essence of mind is unitary, yet in the process of manifestation mind becomes like a two-faced mirror, one face oriented to the objective, the other to the subjective. . . . But since both facets are of one and the same essence, there is a native affinity between them. (*Consciousness* 93–94)

A single aphorism, number 51, occurs between the last of the middle or "manifestation" sections (9) and the final section of triumphant return (10):

> 51. . . Consciousness-without-an-object may be symbolized by a SPACE that is unaffected by the presence or absence of objects, for which there is neither Time nor Timelessness; neither a world-containing Space nor a spatial Void; neither Tension nor Equilibrium; neither Resistance nor Creativeness; neither Agony nor Bliss; neither Action nor Rest; and neither Restriction nor Freedom. (*Consciousness* 115)

The longest aphorism by far, it seems to have several functions. It recapitulates and, in so doing, greatly intensifies the entire series of antinomous tensions built up over the long middle section, even as it bridges the gap between that and the final section by introducing the objective correlative (SPACE) of the primordial Consciousness-without-an-object. It is something like the sustained dominant chord in a musical cadence that gathers all forces to the brink of full tonic resolution. Seen in the context of the mounting waves of tension preceding it, it represents a profound climax of effort and struggle, a do-or-die spending of that final ounce of energy to break through the endless cycle of suffering generated by the pairs. If, passing over the obvious sexual analogy in silence, one be permitted a more interesting (and perhaps not entirely unrelated) one from meditational styles, it is somewhat reminiscent of the bamboo type of breathing recommended by Sekida for *zazen* (Zen sitting meditation) (*Zen Training* 71–73). If we imagine the entire aphorism as uttered in one long exhalation, with slight pauses punctuating the antinomies (like the succession of nodes on a bamboo stick), the effect is to turn the breath (and the concentration bound up with it) into a kind of battering ram smashing repeatedly against the confining gates of Ignorance and ultimately penetrating into the unfettered vastness of SPACE.

Merely announced in aphorism 51, that SPACE is celebrated in the loftiest devotional tone as the GREAT SPACE in the five aphorisms that make up the final section ten:

> 52. . . As the GREAT SPACE is not to be identified with the Universe, so neither is It to be identified with any Self.
>
> 53. . . The GREAT SPACE is not God, but the comprehender of all Gods, as well as of all lesser creatures.
>
> 54. . . The GREAT SPACE, or Consciousness-without-an-object, is the Sole Reality upon which all objects and all selves depend and derive their existence.
>
> 55. . . The GREAT SPACE comprehends both the Path of the Universe and the Path of Nirvana.
>
> 56. . . Beside the GREAT SPACE there is none other. (*Consciousness* 116–17)

God, gods, the Self, the Universe—absolutely anything we can conceive of, however vast, however lofty, however noble, is derivative of That which is beyond all conceiving. Since It cannot be conceived or named, the artist-philosopher-devotee must content himself with dumbly gesturing toward It with expressions of simultaneous affirmation and denial, bravely embracing the logical absurdity of contradiction, intimating Its essential nature as, somehow, zero, nothing at all, but a nothing at all that is a Nothing At All and, as such, the condition for anything at all.

So we have in the final section the object that cancels out the subject of the opening section. This sequential or "horizontal" cancellation is itself cancelled out by the "vertical" binary of mind (content)/heart (form) elaborated above. The suggestion is of an infinitely self-potentiating succession of binary cancellations, an endless game of illusions that linger for a while and go poof to make room for new ones. This is the free and bracing cosmic romp of the *coincidentia oppositorum.* Appropriately, Merrell-Wolff takes to heart Wittgenstein's renowned advice at the end of the following chapter of extensive discussion of the aphorisms, simply intoning number fifty-six and retiring without comment.

## MERRELL-WOLFF IN THE WAR OF THE PARADIGMS

At first blush it might seem that Franklin Merrell-Wolff is an anachronism on the contemporary philosophical scene. A retiree from the academy virtually at the beginning of his serious philosophical work early in the previous century, he retained basically a nineteenth-century perspective oriented to Kant and had little to say about this century's major developments, about Wittgenstein, Heidegger, or existentialism, not to mention the postmodern revolution. But here we must remember that his fundamental assertions as to the primacy of Consciousness issue, not from dialogic interaction with other minds, but directly from experience he insists is mystical or transcendental, in other words, from "the perennial philosophy." Like any other Western transcendental philosophy from Plato to positivism, his introceptualism inserts itself right into the midst of the current postmodern war against ahistorical "foundations." Is Merrell-Wolff's Consciousness-without-an-object, then, fairly characterized, in Kai Nielsen's phrase, as a fixed "Archimedian point" from which to conduct philosophical inquiry, or, in Richard Bernstein's, as "a permanent neutral matrix for assessing all forms of inquiry and all types of knowledge" (both qtd. in Leonard 297–98)? In other words, does Merrell-Wolff share the tradition's vulnerability to what Leonard calls "Richard Rorty's 'deconstruction' of Western philosophy" (297)?[13]

I would say that the answer to this question must remain as ambiguous as Merrell-Wolff's characterization of fundamental consciousness as the High Indifference, the principle that structures Reality (that is, Itself) as a *coincidentia oppositorum.* Thus, an ontological "Foundation" or epistemologically fixed "Archimedian point" or transcendent "Presence," each a quasi-demonized name for Rorty's target, is real or true only insofar as it is equally *not,* since the High Indifference is as far beyond the categories of reality or truth as any others. In other words, from the "vantage point" of the High Indifference, the very framing of such "fundamental" questions assumes a foundation that the questions themselves are calling into question. Thus, like Oscar Wilde's profound pose and shallow depth, God's lofty eye and man's historical myopia turn out, *mirabile dictu,* to be but another pair of opposites that, at some point, coincide. It is as if one were condemned to Freedom, despite one's best efforts to remain a prisoner of reason and logic.[14]

However Franklin Merrell-Wolff's introceptualism may fare in the current War of the Paradigms, we must at least grant with Leonard that the clarity and rigor of his thought have gone far to extend the relevance of mysticism beyond the precincts of religion to those of philosophy, particularly epistemology and metaphysics (268). He is, literally, the thinking man's mystic. Nevertheless, as we have seen, all the cogitation is intended to serve the fundamentally spiritual ideal of philosophy as a Way of Life the central concern of which is personal transformation. Never for a moment does he forget that the noetic way to Enlightenment, like the more traditional affective way or any combination of the two, is meant at some point to overcome itself, to become useless, as the Truth it gestures toward becomes manifest: "But scholarship . . . is a barrier when one is everlastingly hung up with the process of ideation. Remember that scholarship is only a tool. It is not the end; it is not the goal. The goal is another way of knowing" (Tape 34). This conception of philosophy as one way of knowing meant ultimately to yield to another way, which Merrell-Wolff sometimes calls "Knowledge through Identity" (e.g., *Consciousness* 50), places him in a tradition at least as old as Plato. Of course, in the postmodern view, Identity is just another shibboleth of foundationalism and, as such, represents psychologically a strategy of avoidance of the insuperable tension of difference that makes the world, which for man is a world of language, go round. But the Identity to which Merrell-Wolff refers, being one of opposites, is just as at home with its other as itself, since it *is* every bit its other as itself. When this Knowledge happens, difference makes no difference.

7

# *Ground:* German Romanticism, Zen, and Deconstruction

> No dog would endure such a curst existence!
> Wherefore, from Magic I seek assistance,
> That many a secret perchance I reach
> Through spirit-power and spirit-speech,
> And thus the bitter task forego
> Of saying the things I do not know,—
> That I may detect the inmost force
> Which binds the world, and guides its course;
> Its germs, productive powers explore,
> And rummage in empty words no more!
>
> —Goethe's *Faust*

In the broadest sense, it has been my aim in this study to show that German Romanticism, Zen Buddhism and the currently powerful deconstruction, for all their cultural difference, are three intimately related expressions of a universal vision or "perennial philosophy" known, among many other names, as the *coincidentia oppositorum.* I have tried to present these three cultural moments as "modulations" of an infinitely pliant mystical wisdom that, by dint of its transcendence of the mind's dualistic structure, is able to behold all things as aspects of the One. In spite of, or indeed by virtue of, the bafflement they cause rational inquiry—Romanticism eludes definition, Zen humors it, deconstruction spurns it—these three points of view are mutually illuminating;[1] they evidence man's irrepressible urge to go beyond himself, beyond any sense of his own "best interest," to a realization of the free flow of all beings into and out of one another. This final ontic freedom is termed by Zen *satori,* by Novalis *romantisieren* (as in "Die Welt muß romantisiert werden" [The world must be romanticized]), and is, I would argue, at least implied, wittingly or not, in such paradoxical notions of deconstruction as aporia.

The ground occupied by my subject is admittedly vast, and in the preceding chapters I have only been able to survey certain strategic areas of the overall terrain, specifically, areas in which inter- or comparative-cultural connections have been clear. In order, here in my concluding discussion, to fit it all into a manageable purview, I offer a narrowly focused synopsis of these three world views on the basis of four ideas pivotal to each. The four ideas I caption as follows: no self, no time, no meaning, and no thing, or, Nothing. It will be seen that each of the three profoundly questions the conventional Western wisdom as to the ontological validity of the ideas of self, time, and meaning when viewed "unilaterally," that is, as existing independently of their own opposites (i.e., not-self, eternity, signifier). It will then be pointed out that this dialectical logic implies the fourth idea, the idea of no thing (hence Nothing) as a Ground or Matrix for the infinite variety of differential pairs that "body forth" as modifications of It. This Ground, this Matrix, is the placeless place, the Utopia, where it all coincides. It is the *coincidentia oppositorum.*

## NO SELF

Contrary to the persistent stereotypic view, which confuses Romanticism with Storm and Stress (e.g., as in the archetypal "Romantic" artist Werther), the former does *not* glorify the ego or individual self; it is rather, if one must label it, meta-egocentric in upholding the fundamental validity of a state of consciousness superior to what it regards as the deluded egoic or subject-object level, indeed, a state that can only emerge to the extent that the ego surrenders its conventional psycho-spiritual hegemony. This is implicit in Friedrich Schlegel's ideal of *Symphilosophie* and *Sympoesie* and is made explicit in his wish for an appropriate empowering technique, quasi meditational perhaps, "an art," as he puts it, "of blending individuals" (M; 94).

For Romanticism then, as we have seen, the true self is the spirit of relationship, experienced and understood as ontologically prior to the terms of relationship. Ironically, the true self is not to be found in any "self" so-called, but in the connections *(coincidentia)* between "selves." This perspective goes against our ordinary way of viewing things according to which connections or relationships can never be more than attributes, or what the philosophers call "epiphenomena," of the things connected. But it is clear that Novalis, for example, holds the self, conceived as an autonomous entity, to be relatively unreal. Recent work in that poet[2] has highlighted his dynamic relational notion of the self, expressed in such recurrent themes as *Interesse* (interest) (in its literal Latin sense) and *Schweben* (hovering), as well as in his idea of the seat of the soul as located "there, where inner world and outer world touch" (M; *Novalis Schriften* 2:419).

This view of the self as dialectical oscillation rather than discrete entity, as reflexive verb rather then reifying noun, is also fundamental to Zen. Doctrinally it is rooted in the early anatmic Mahayana scriptures, particularly the "Diamond Sutra of Perfect Wisdom" wherein the Buddha is held to assert, "If in a Bodhisattva [an enlightened being dedicated to the spiritual liberation of others]. . . the conception of 'being', 'egotistic entity', 'personality' or 'separate existence' should take place, the Bodhisattva would not be an authentic Being of Wisdom and Compassion" (*Diamond Sutra* 14–15). That is to say, he would be deluded.

But authentic Zen only begins where doctrine ends. The Zen master insists that his student apply himself assiduously to the meditational koan of identity, the question "Who am I?", so that he might eventually, in the fullness of time, grasp the truth of no-self directly in the lightning flash of insight. As one master put it at the moment of his own enlightenment: "When I heard the temple bell ring, suddenly there was no bell and no I, just sound" (Kapleau 113–14). This "just sound" is the numinous interface between subject and object hinted at in Novalis's sense of *Schweben*. Of course, the heady freedom enjoyed in the experience of "just sound" comes at a price, the price of belief in one's own sovereign individuality, for as the medieval Rinzai master Bassui forewarned his disciples upon assigning them the koan, "Who is it that hears?", "Even though your questioning penetrates the unconscious, you won't find the one who hears, and all your efforts will come to naught. . . . Within yourself you will find no 'I,' nor will you discover anyone who hears" (Kapleau 171–72). Nevertheless, as Bassui says elsewhere, "should someone call your name, something from within will hear and respond. Find out this instant who *it* is!" (Kapleau 186).

As for deconstruction, its premiere voice, Jacques Derrida, is by now infamous for proclaiming the fictitiousness of the subject, whether conceived as writer, reader, or otherwise. As if that were not enough, he goes on to generalize that consciousness itself is an illusion with which Euro- and logocentric man has armed himself to fend off the dreaded consequences of a materialist conception of mind (Harland 146). For Foucault, the West's deep mistrust of the physical, especially its need to control the body and its pleasures, is just as illusion-driven as its endless pursuit of a pristine self (Harland 158–59); both sexual body and asexual self are "ghostly essences," the presumed rift between them giving them the steam of a quasi-substantiality. This polar rift between ghosts is often characterized by deconstructionists as a "privileging" of (that is, a profound attachment to) the subjective member of all the standard subject-object binaries: mind over body, mind over matter, *Geist* over *Natur* (Derrida, *Of Spirit*).

Simply put, we cling violently to the illusion of an autonomous self. Basically, the deconstructionist viewpoint is no different from that of the ego-transcending Romantic or the anatmic Buddhist. All three aim to awaken us to the narrowing effect upon consciousness of any cherished position, however lofty or noble the issue, and to the heady expansion of consciousness that comes with a surrendering of that position and a movement toward a synthesizing neutral or middle view capable of embracing the I/Not-I dichotomy in its entirety. Thus, Novalis's notion of the true self as a "hovering" between self and other or Friedrich Schlegel's ideal of Romantic poetry as a suspension "between the thing represented and the one representing" (M; 93) is unmistakably announced in Zen Master Rinzai's homage to the "true man without rank," that is, the Self that, neither preferring the I nor shunning the Not-I, "is brisk and lively with no roots at all" (qtd. in Dumoulin 193–94) and clearly echoed in deconstruction's fascination with undecidability and aporia (the contrapuntal dance of recurrent mutual annihilation enacted between the privileged and the marginal). It is interesting to me that this proclaimed exposure of the hoax of the individual self by contemporary French theorists should have aroused such rabid controversy among the educated Western community when the same proclamation has been issued by mystics from time immemorial without causing anyone undue concern. Perhaps the easiest way to defuse Derrida would be simply to call him a mystic.

## NO TIME

Our unconscious assumption of discrete, fixed entities and essences distorts our experience of time no less then of self. All three *Weltanschauungen* point to this assumption as underlying our hypnosis by what *appears* to be the transitory quality of time. In his treatise on "Being-Time," Zen's greatest metaphysician, the medieval Soto master Dogen, admonishes in this regard: "Do not regard time as merely flying away; do not think that flying away is its sole function. For time to fly away there would have to be a separation [between it and things]. Because you imagine that time only passes, you do not learn the truth of being-time" (Kapleau 311). Dogen's insight applies both to history, conceived as the grand forward march of time from past through present to future, and to the ordinary stream of individual life that all too often seems to be "passing us by." For hidden in all such views is the ghost of essence. For time to be passing, there would have to be some entity or telos that passes; likewise some entity that is passed by. But just as with the koan of identity, one can find no such entity, search as one may. It seems there is only passing itself, nothing that passes nor anything passed. But if there is *only* passing, then there is *no* passing, for passing is only possible with respect to something passed. In this way Zen insight makes its characteristic dialectical leap to a realization of the identity of opposites: passing and abiding, *Wechsel* and *Dauer, Werden* and *Sein, samsara* and *nirvana,* or, in Dogen's terms, time and being, are one. It is only man's bifurcating consciousness that separates them.

This aporetic congruence between time and eternity is also distinctive of Novalis's mystical understanding of time and takes him a crucial step beyond Fichte whose vision of history as an "unendlicher Progreß" [unending progress] leaves us, in the end, mired in a frustrated millenialism. Novalis's insight bores through to the other side of the time/eternity coin, revealing the temporal flux of the universe, in its very endlessness, to be its own infinitely fulfilling goal:

> Life is to be viewed as a beautiful, brilliant illusion, as a marvelous spectacle, . . . we can live in absolute delight and eternity right here in this mind.[3] (M; *Novalis Schriften* 2:667)

And in another place:

> What can only be recognized through activity and what is realized through perpetual deficit./ In this way eternity is realized through time, despite the fact that time contradicts eternity. (M; *Novalis Schriften* 2:270)

Finally, the simple affirmation:

> synthesis of eternity and temporality (M; *Novalis Schriften* 3:436)

Elsewhere, Novalis hints at the manner in which this mystical transcendence of time may occur: "Synthesis is realized within time whenever I seek to realize the idea of synthesis *successively* [Ger. *succesive*]" (M; *Novalis Schriften* 3:373). The key word here is the unusual Latinate "*succesive,*" by which I believe the poet refers to the chain of photic implosions that often betokens mystical illumination. The mind's sudden grasp of the identity of time and timelessness may react upon itself in a self-generating series of liberating flashes. Soto Zen Master Shunryu Suzuki alludes to this chain-reaction phenomenon when he says: "It is necessary for us to have enlightenments one after another, if possible, moment after moment. This is what is called enlightenment before you attain it and after you attain it" (86).

The contrapuntal structure of *Heinrich von Ofterdingen,* with its playful alternation between the timeless dream-cum-fairy-tale sequences and the time-bound narrative in which they are embedded, seems to issue from this mystico-aporetic insight of Novalis's. Other Romantic tales in which the precise temporal sequence of events is paramount, such as Hoffmann's proto-detective stories, "Mademoiselle de Scudéri" and "Councillor Krespel," likewise evoke the giddy sense that what is from one angle a careful reconstruction of a causal chain of events is, from another, simply an atemporal series of perspectival displacements without intrinsic connection, as though points of view were all there were, nothing viewed.

This radical perspectivism that shapes the narratives of Novalis and Hoffmann, particularly the latter, seems also to lie at the heart of Michel Foucault's archaeological theory of history. For him too all is point of view, interpretation, with no "outside" truth viewed or interpreted. History is a discontinuous succession of collective interpretations, which he calls "epistemes," that serve as unconscious promotions of the interests of a dominant social group. Even the claims of science to a disinterested objectivity in the tracing of chains of causality, be it in medicine or biology, are unconscious assertions of ideology. The nineteenth-century evolutionist thought that shaped biology and the nascent human sciences is just a bead in the string of discrete epistemes. If evolution is ideology, then so too must be history itself, at least in its modern conception as developmental process. For Foucault history reflects nothing but the belief in history. Essentially, there *is* no history.

But if all is point of view, what of Foucault's own? It seems to me that right here, at the point where his *Geschichtsphilosophie* is in jeopardy of being deconstructed by its very own terms, the mystic in Foucault fails him and he flinches, whereas it is precisely at this aporetic juncture, at the astonishing *coincidentia* of signifier (Foucault's presumably extra-epistemic discourse) and signified (episteme), that the Romantic and Zen sensibilities combust and take flight. Foucault, apparently unready to relinquish entirely his need for discourse to be referential, or for his own perspective to transcend epistemic limits, confesses at the end of *The Archaeology of Knowledge* to an imaginary interlocutor: "I admit that this question embarrasses me more than your earlier objections. I am not entirely surprised by it; but I would have preferred to leave it in suspense a little longer" (205). Romanticism and Zen would seem at times to be truer to the spirit of deconstruction than deconstruction itself. For them the view of a mysterious transpersonal Principle that is creating all of "history" moment by moment, *not excluding themselves,* is a source of delight rather than anxiety.

## NO MEANING

If Foucault does not quite surrender the need for discourse to point to something beyond itself, Derrida does. As the arch-spokesman for deconstruction, he shares with Romanticism and Zen a profound recognition of the ultimate resistance of language to extralinguistic human intention. We have yet to learn that "there is nothing outside the text" and that our insistence, fueled by delusive desire, that there be something final and abiding outside it to which it points, some "Sacred Signified," constitutes that pointing as a misery. This misery of pointless pointing Derrida calls "the movement of the signifier," a movement without beginning or end, "the indefinite referral of signifier to signifier . . . its force . . . a certain pure and infinite equivocality which gives signified meaning no respite, no rest, but engages it in its own *economy* so that it always signifies again and differs" (italics Derrida's; *Writing and Difference* 25).

This suffering of "dissemination," with its eternal scattering of meaning just beyond our grasp, I would like to call Derrida's version of Buddhism's wheel of desire, a metaphor of *samsara,* the ceaseless becoming of the phenomenal universe. Derrida's tight focus on language as such in no way diminishes or "miniaturizes" the vastness of the Buddhist concept, since for Derrida the behavior of language and the movement of the "things" that constitute the "world" are co-extensive (Harland 141). There is nothing but restless text, and that is what we are.

Zen scholar D. T. Suzuki puts the dilemma of language this way: "As soon as words are used, they express meaning, reasoning; they represent something not belonging to themselves; they have no direct connection with life, except being a faint echo or image [Derrida would say "trace"] of something that is no longer here" (*Essays* 300). Both Suzuki and Derrida implicate language in the mind's ironic—and fatal—distancing of itself from things in order to "get at them."

When we add Novalis's voice to these two, we have a most compelling synopsis indeed. In the "Monologen" he says: "What is unique about language, namely that it is only concerned with itself, no one knows. . . . Whenever someone speaks simply in order to speak, he pronounces just the most marvelous, original truths. But whenever he intends to speak of something in particular, capricious language causes him to utter the most ridiculous and perverse nonsense. . . . Words make up their own world—They play only with themselves" (M; *Novalis Schriften* 2:672).[4]

As usual with Novalis, dilemmas contain their own, aporetic, solutions: "Whenever someone speaks simply in order to speak, he pronounces just the most marvelous, original truths." It is the surrendering of intention itself, the letting-go of individual desire, the desire that *is* the false self, and the assumption of the space between—and spanning—desire and language that liberates man from the so-called "prisonhouse of language" and gives birth to poetic utterance. Somehow I must allow language to do its *own* mysterious bidding through the narrowing vortex of intention that "I" am. The poet sees through the delusion of linguistic reference, for he is aware of his expression as always already issuing from, even as it continues to abide with, that to which it points.[5] What is there to "refer" to?

D. T. Suzuki implies this aesthetic principle when he says: "An assertion is Zen only when it is itself an act and does not refer to anything that is asserted in it" (qtd. in Ross 258). Katsuki Sekida, a meditator and student of meditation for more than sixty years, describes a condition known in Zen as "language samadhi," which may overtake one while absorbed in a favorite poet, when "suddenly the passage will seem charged with infinite meaning, seeming almost to come as a revelation from heaven" (*Zen Training* 99). An implication of Sekida's example is that, when the ego is banished, the *reader* is as much a poet as the writer; or, to take it a step further, there are no readers or writers, not even any poets, just poetry itself.

It seems to me that, in order to reach the point where what Sekida calls "language samadhi" and Novalis calls "the most marvelous, original truths (of language)" can emerge, something like the traditional Great Mystical Death must occur—in other words, one must say to language, in effect, "Not my will but Thy Will be done." Whereas Romanticism and Zen do not resist this self-immolation—indeed, they espouse it as the gateway to oneness with the Absolute—deconstruction, at this point at least, seems yet to tremble on the brink of a *salto mortale* into the abyss of that meaninglessness that fulfills all meaning. Deconstruction knows full well that it has arrived at the outermost edge of a rational-linguistic understanding of the world and that any move it might assay to get outside language to see "what it might be up to," in Paul de Man's apt phrase, would inescapably be accompanied by language. It yet stands in terror of the apocalyptic insight that signifying is all there is, no one signifying and nothing signified. As de Man puts it in the context of criticism: "Any question about the rhetorical mode of a literary text is always [itself] a rhetorical question which does not even know whether it is really questioning. The resulting pathos is an anxiety (or bliss, depending on one's momentary mood or individual temperament) of ignorance, not an anxiety of reference" (*Allegories* 19). Here I would suggest two things: first, that de Man's "ignorance" is the beginning of mystical wisdom;[6] and second, that if this ignorance/wisdom is in any way resisted, it falls back to the anxiety of "*différance*"; if, on the other hand, it is affirmed as our true fundamental condition, it can shift into a rapture (intuited by de Man) ushering in the aporetic coalescence of signifier and signified. This coalescence is the *coincidentia* manifesting as language, the apprehension of which is nothing less then spiritual emancipation: when one at last throws off the delusive burden of referential meaning, all things suddenly mean simply themselves—and that is enough, and more then enough. It would seem that deconstruction is not quite yet a mature mysticism.[7]

## NO THING

As stated above, this fourth idea, that "there is no thing," or that "no thing is real," is not, properly speaking, the last in a sequence but an implication of the first three. From a psychological point of view, one might call it a comprehensive state of mind that any one of them can inaugurate when fully realized. A simple exercise in logic may perhaps give an inkling of this condition: if there is no self, then there is no other, for each of these defines its counterpart. If neither self nor other, then nothing at all, for the terms are all-inclusive. The same holds for the pairs time/eternity and signifier/signified. What we are left with is nothing.

While the West, caught in a kind of aporia anxiety,[8] generally dreads this prospect as a privative absence or vacuousness, in Zen it is fervently sought as the highest goal of spiritual practice, for in Zen's wholehearted embrace of the *coincidentia oppositorum* this nothing is found to be the Absolute Nothing that is everything, the fertile void or *sunyata* that is forever bodying forth as all beings. This Nothing, then, is not at all to be viewed as a solipsistic subjectivity devoid of objects (a lopsided attitude) but rather as a dynamic ground-zero state of consciousness that is perfectly at one with either the presence or absence of objects, being as it is beyond all conceivable dualisms.

Ordinary consciousness is, however, dualistic or binary and is thus by nature condemned, as it were, to a pursuit of the unreal in the sense that things are constituted for it in only the most provisional way by the very absence or deferral of their counterparts. When, however, both part and counterpart are beheld together, that is, when they coincide as in Zen *satori,* a kind of ontological leveling pervades the moment as both are realized to be without substance, or without "foundation," to borrow a current term from Stanley Fish (342–55). However, they are not on that account tragically vacuous, as the foundationalists among us are too quick to conclude; quite the contrary, they are exhilaratingly free, free to make and unmake, construct and deconstruct, each other again and again in a playful mutual interpenetration. This is the full implication of Novalis's *Schweben* as well as his injunction to us to "romanticize" the world. It is also, I would suggest, the other side of the coin of deconstruction's *différance*. When Derrida waxes soulful over the elusiveness of things, whether in lamenting the ubiquity of the trace or the endless movement of the signifier away from itself, one senses behind the elegiac tone a decidedly puckish tongue-in-cheek, almost as if he were parodying what strikes him as our misguided need for things to be stable, or at the very least to have stable essences. He seems to be searching for a new way to teach an age-old lesson of Romanticism and Zen.

## CONCLUSION

One could, were one so inclined, trace an arguable chain of historical influence linking our three subjects together. The general configuration of this chain might be as follows: Buddhism, transmitted to the East as Zen and to the West in the Neoplatonism of Plotinus; thence through St. Augustine, medieval German mysticism (especially Meister Eckhart), Cusanus, Spinoza, German Romantic Idealism, and Nietzsche to poststructuralism, particularly deconstruction. Interesting as these extrinsic connections are, the intrinsic connection is to me far more so, for I am convinced that what truly accounts for the synoptic viewpoint of our three subjects is an undaunted passion to explore the territory of mind directly, without the buffer of conceptual maps. Insofar as it is mystical, Zen *is* the mind's direct confrontation with itself, the single eye, as Eckhart put it, through which God and man view each other; the Romantics, for their part, are known to have cultivated an intense introspection of their own states of consciousness (Walzel 12); and Derrida's writings are replete with meditational analogies and metaphors (Harland 149–51). If Romanticism, Zen, and deconstruction are alike, it is mainly because their direct insights overlap in a fundamental way. All three have glimpsed something vital, something "perennial," in Huxley's term, of the elusive nature of mind. All three, to borrow a verse from that most uncompromising of Western seekers, Goethe's Faust, bear potent witness to the *coincidentia oppositorum* as "the inmost force/Which binds the world, and guides its course."

# Appendix

## MERRELL-WOLFF'S APHORISMS ON CONSCIOUSNESS-WITHOUT-AN-OBJECT

1. Consciousness-without-an-object is.
2. Before objects were, Consciousness-without-an-object is.
3. Though objects seem to exist, Consciousness-without-an-object is.
4. When objects vanish, yet remaining through all unaffected, Consciousness-without-an-object is.
5. Outside of Consciousness-without-an-object nothing is.
6. Within the bosom of Consciousness-without-an-object lies the power of awareness that projects objects.
7. When objects are projected, the power of awareness as subject is presupposed, yet Consciousness-without-an-object remains unchanged.
8. When consciousness of objects is born, then, likewise, consciousness of absence of objects arises.
9. Consciousness of objects is the Universe.
10. Consciousness of absence of objects is Nirvana.
11. Within Consciousness-without-an-object lies both the Universe and Nirvana, yet to Consciousness-without-an-object these two are the same.
12. Within Consciousness-without-an-object lies the seed of Time.
13. When awareness cognizes Time then knowledge of Timelessness is born.

14. To be aware of Time is to be aware of the Universe, and to be aware of the Universe is to be aware of Time.
15. To realize Timelessness is to attain Nirvana.
16. But for Consciousness-without-an-object there is no difference between Time and Timelessness.
17. Within Consciousness-without-an-object lies the seed of the world-containing Space.
18. When awareness cognizes the world-containing Space then knowledge of the Spatial Void is born.
19. To be aware of the world-containing Space is to be aware of the Universe of Objects.
20. To realize the Spatial Void is to awaken to Nirvanic Consciousness.
21. But for Consciousness-without-an-object there is no difference between the world-containing Space and the Spatial Void.
22. Within Consciousness-without-an-object lies the Seed of Law.
23. When consciousness of objects is born the Law is invoked as a Force tending ever toward Equilibrium.
24. All objects exist as tensions within Consciousness-without-an-object that tend ever to flow into their own complements or others.
25. The ultimate effect of the flow of all objects into their complements is mutual cancellation in complete Equilibrium.
26. Consciousness of the field of tensions is the Universe.
27. Consciousness of Equilibrium is Nirvana.
28. But for Consciousness-without-an-object there is neither tension nor Equilibrium.
29. The state of tensions is the state of ever-becoming.
30. Ever-becoming is endless-dying.
31. So the state of consciousness of objects is a state of ever-renewing promises that pass into death at the moment of fulfillment.
32. Thus when consciousness is attached to objects the agony of birth and death never ceases.
33. In the state of Equilibrium where birth cancels death the deathless Bliss of Nirvana is realized.
34. But Consciousness-without-an-object is neither agony nor bliss.

35. Out of the Great Void, which is Consciousness-without-an-object, the Universe is creatively projected.
36. The Universe as experienced is the created negation that ever resists.
37. The creative act is bliss, the resistance, unending pain.
38. Endless resistance is the Universe of experience; the agony of crucifixion.
39. Ceaseless creativeness is Nirvana, the Bliss beyond human conceiving.
40. But for Consciousness-without-an-object there is neither creativeness nor resistance.
41. Ever-becoming and ever-ceasing-to-be are endless action.
42. When ever-becoming cancels the ever-ceasing-to-be then Rest is realized.
43. Ceaseless action is the Universe.
44. Unending Rest is Nirvana.
45. But Consciousness-without-an-object is neither Action nor Rest.
46. When consciousness is attached to objects it is restricted through the forms imposed by the world-containing Space, by Time, and by Law.
47. When consciousness is disengaged from objects, Liberation from the forms of the world-containing Space, of Time, and of Law is attained.
48. Attachment to objects is consciousness bound within the Universe.
49. Liberation from such attachment is the State of unlimited Nirvanic Freedom.
50. But Consciousness-without-an-object is neither bondage nor freedom.
51. Consciousness-without-an-object may be symbolized by a SPACE that is unaffected by the presence or absence of objects, for which there is neither Time nor Timelessness; neither a world-containing Space nor a Spatial Void, neither Tension nor Equilibrium; neither Resistance nor Creativeness; neither Agony nor Bliss; neither Action nor Rest; and neither Restriction nor Freedom.
52. As the GREAT SPACE is not to be identified with the Universe, so neither is It to be identified with any Self.
53. The GREAT SPACE is not God, but the comprehender of all Gods, as well as of all lesser creatures.
54. The GREAT SPACE, or Consciousness-without-an-object, is the Sole Reality upon which all objects and all selves depend and derive their existence.

55. The GREAT SPACE comprehends both the Path of the Universe and the Path of Nirvana.
56. Beside the GREAT SPACE there is none other.

OM TAT SAT

# Notes

## OVERVIEW

1. Or, in the Latin coinage of the late-medieval German mystic, Nicholas Cusanus, the *coincidentia oppositorum*. See his tract, *De visione Dei* (1443). Throughout this study I will generally refer to my theme with Cusanus's Latin designation.

2. "Difference," of course, is a conceptual category. No need to belabor here the implication that the opposites that, according to the idea, coincide are categories, the verbal tools by which we structure experience, the "pairs" of the Gospel of Thomas that we are to go beyond to enter "the Kingdom," and not things in nature, except insofar as categories are themselves (verbal) things. What come together in coincidence or conjunction, then, are the categorical terms of the illusion of separate things and groups of things in nature. The illusion goes "poof." Thus, the coincidence also implies the recovery of something that has always been there but was blocked from view, ironically, by the very organizing concepts that make up "understanding."

3. See *The Origin of Consciousness in the Breakdown of the Bicameral Mind* (1978).

4. See Wheelwright's *The Burning Fountain: A Study of the Language of Symbolism* (1968).

5. Ironically, it is none other than the most "left-brained" of modern Western cultural enterprises—science—that in recent times has evidenced on some fronts a distinct tendency away from the linear-causal and toward the "bilateral" spirit of the *coincidentia oppositorum*. Even apart from the recent breed of "mystic-physicists" such as David Bohm, who flirts with the idea of coincidence in his theory of the interplay of holistic implicate and fragmented explicate orders that supposedly make up the universe (*Wholeness and the Implicate Order,* 1980), there is the emerging science of chaos with its fascinating use of computer graphics that give us the ability to model, in effect to see with mathematically precise eyes, natural processes heretofore thought to be random and thus imponderable such as the weather, the thermodynamics of fluids, or the waves of electrical activity coursing through heart muscles. The visual image that has become an emblem of the new science, the so-called "Lorenz attractor" or "butterfly wings" (the computer-generated double spiral describing the play of

forces rotating a waterwheel that keeps turning back on itself like an infinity sign, *but never tracing quite the same course*), bears an uncanny resemblance to certain ancient dynamic symbols of the *coincidentia* such as the Chinese *yin/yang* mandala. This striking image of "sameness-within-difference-within-sameness, etc." threatens to confound traditional notions of order and disorder to the point of conflation, indeed, to the point of a coincidence of the opposites. See Gleick.

Ronald McKinney sees a War of Reality Paradigms currently being waged between "centripetal" scientists such as Bohm and the chaoticians on the one hand, who "opt for just such a mystical vision of the identity of opposites as a way of experiencing the ultimate unity of reality" (305) and the postmodernist linguistic philosophers and theorists (including Bakhtin) who "choose the centrifugal realm of difference, multiplicity, contradiction, ambiguity, uncertainty, relativity, and becoming" (307). As one might expect, McKinney reaches the vertiginous conclusion, though one quite in keeping with the theme of this book: "[W]hat is most striking in the visions of these two paradigms is their common allegiance to the fundamental notion of a non-hierarchical, dynamic interplay of opposites. . . . Holism and Postmodernism are simply complementary facets of one reality" (310).

6. See the opening of *Civilization and Its Discontents* (1930). Interestingly, a younger Freud, in an essay of 1910 entitled "The Antithetical Sense of Primal Words," revealed a fascination with the tendency of certain words in certain ancient languages to convey directly opposite meanings: "Thus in this extraordinary language [ancient Egyptian] there are not only words which denote both 'strong' and 'weak', or 'command' as well as 'obey'; there are also compound-words like 'oldyoung', 'farnear', 'bindloose', 'outsideinside'" (57). Freud claims that this discovery, of the comparative philologist Karl Abel, enabled him finally to understand his own observation, in *The Interpretation of Dreams* (1900), of "[t]he attitude of dreams towards the category of antithesis and contradiction. . . . This category is simply ignored; the word 'No' does not seem to exist for a dream. Dreams show a special tendency to reduce two opposites to a unity or to represent them as one thing" (55). One can only wonder what revelations Freud might have enjoyed had he pursued this nascent dialectical insight in subsequent research.

7. For more on this, see Valente.

8. Another interesting superficial figuration of the *coincidentia* occurs in the literature featuring doubles, Doppelgängers, or alter egos. This, the "divided-self" motif, is especially prominent since Romanticism. However, contrary to the norm of dialectical synthesis in Romanticism, Michael Neve (22–23) sees the vast Romantic literature on doubles from E. T. A. Hoffmann to Dostoyevsky as the reduction of an old and dynamic Christian-trinitarian archetype to a static dualism. According to Neve, the alter ego character was originally intended as a necessary stage of a character's confrontation of his own inner demons preparatory to psychospiritual rebirth. By the time of Romanticism, however, the third stage of resolution and redemption had dropped out, locking the "doubled" character into a grotesque and interminable psychopathology.

9. I intend expressions such as *core of this core* or *meta-core* or *womb* in the same provisional sense as the term *meta-archetype* above. As will become apparent in the essays that follow, any logocentric term applied to the *coincidentia* is strictly analogical. Since the *coincidentia* is the "no man's land" where all the pairs of opposites touch,

including the pair core/circumference (or periphery or Derridean supplement), it is in no sense opposed to these logical opposites.

10. I know of no other study comprehending all three. There are, however, several two-way comparisons of deconstruction with either of the other two. See note 1 of the final chapter here.

## CHAPTER 1

## *FIGURE:* WHAT IS GERMAN ROMANTICISM

1. Notable exemplars of such traditional progressivist-millenialist readings would include, e.g.: Korff, who paraphrases F. Schlegel's thinking on the imminent Golden Age as follows: "Um dieses innere Zentrum [i.e., the new Idealist philosophy] wird sich langsam eine Welt herumbilden" (303); Mähl, who, though sensitive to the Romantics' understanding of the ultimately Orphic, aporetic relationship between time and eternity, still falls back to a relativist, futurist position in speaking of Novalis's "Wissen darum, daß die Ewigkeit die Zeit durchwirkt und am Ende in sich zurücknehmen wird" (386); Walzel, who describes the Romantic as one who, though he "cast his eyes upon the glory of the past, . . . nevertheless heralded a spiritually quickened golden age of the future" (3); and Haym, the prototypic scholar of Romanticism, who sees Novalis as joyfully certain "daß die Einheit von Welt und Gemüth in einer zu erwartenden Zeitperiode einst thatsächlich eintreten, sich als ein allgemeiner Zustand offenbaren werde" (384).

2. Close to Kuzniar's view is that of Lacoue-Labarthe and Nancy, who argue for the Romantic *Weltanschauung* as in many ways intuitively anticipating the Derridean differential or nonclosural "un-paradigm." Supposedly, Romanticism is all about creatively coming to terms with the tension generated by the awareness of the impossibility of ever achieving what is variously termed "Totality," "Identity," "Sameness," or "the [Platonic?] Idea." We may take these terms as poststucturalist coinages for what the Romantics refer to as "the Absolute" or "the Golden Age": "From the outset, we have attempted to point out not the place, but the play of a difference *[écart]* that separates romanticism from idealism (from the metaphysics that perfects itself therein). This difference appears in a supplementary complexity, hesitation, hovering—or *schweben,* to use a word that these [Romantic] texts are immoderately fond of, a word that may correspond to romanticism's infamous 'vagueness,' but that at times may also mean that romanticism constitutively involves a certain impossibility of exactly *accommodating* the vision of the Idea" (122).

3. See the Overview, note 1.

4. Others have, of course, read Romanticism, German and non-German, in terms of its preoccupation with dialectical synthesis. See, e.g., Jones (182), Robertson (360–61) and Kluckhohn (16–17). My point is that such a reading, if consistently maintained, problematizes the unilateral nature of *all* views *(not excluding itself),* and, in the case of diametrically opposed views such as the millenialist and the poststructuralist, in a particularly interesting and ironic way, one that reveals, as I hope to show here, the limits of scholarly understanding.

5. Notwithstanding the apparent disaffection of poststructuralism, and particularly of deconstruction, from Romanticism on some fronts, there is good reason to compare the two. See the concluding essay below.

6. Throughout this book my own translations of foreign-language sources, as in this instance, are referenced parenthetically in the text by "M" ("McCort"); this is followed in the same parentheses by a reference to the original source used. Although in these pages, for the sake of scholarly completeness, the original German is occasionally quoted above its English translation, it is only in chapter 2, which deals pointedly with issues of translation and interlinguistic understanding generally, that both original and translation are consistently presented together. Translations done by others are referenced in the usual way.

7. Indeed, the trinitarian implications of the discovery of positive and negative electricity, as of the positive and negative poles of the magnet, could only have served to validate the Romantics' inner perceptions.

8. Interestingly, Lacoue-Labarthe and Nancy suggest that the Romantics' fondness for the verb *schweben* may be an anticipation of the key deconstructionist concept of *différance*. (See note 2.) For other recent views on Novalis's sense of *schweben,* see Newman; Kuzniar, "Reassessing Romantic Reflexivity"; von Molnár; and the concluding chapter below.

9. See Mahl (236–37), esp. note 176, and Walzel (5–8).

10. On this see Harland's explanation of Derrida's "unorthodox logic of supplements, where what's added on later [culture] is always liable to predominate over what was there in the first place [nature] . . . . Derrida goes all the way with the separation between historical and conceptual priority. He overturns our assumptions about origins in culture no less than our assumptions about origins in nature" (130–31).

11. The poet is the central Romantic personification of what Jung would later identify as the Self archetype, the numinous unifying force of ego, unconscious, and world. As I hope to have indicated here, it is possible to give a Jungian reading of Hoffmann's tale without capitulating to the pessimistic views of his student, Aniela Jaffé, for whom Hoffmann's Anselmus is the prototype of the Romantic "escape artist," i.e., the spineless aesthete who cannot wait to shuffle off this mortal coil and dissolve into some transcendental archetypal cloud: "Anselmus, the young hero, decides to renounce life and love in reality, and a split results between the magical and the real worlds; it is a split between consciousness and the unconscious, and characteristic of the heroes of Hoffmann's stories. Anselmus typifies all idealistic and unrealistic youths who take flight from the reality of the moment. They live entirely for their longing for the transcendent, and in the process, they elevate this yearning to a goal in itself. Such flight from the real world is genuinely Romantic" (31). I beg to differ.

12. See note 14.

13. See note 11.

14. Some recent scholarship has emphasized Novalis's relational notion of the self, e.g., Newman; Kuzniar, "Reassessing Romantic Reflexivity"; and von Molnár. I part company with Kuzniar, however, when she argues that Novalis views the self

as "a fictional construct" (81). Rather, it is the ego, the product of self-reflection, that Novalis regards as fictional ("ein Kunstwerck" [*Novalis Schriften* 3: 253]), in the sense that there is no autonomous entity it can be said to reflect. Unlike Novalis, Kuzniar fails, I believe, to distinguish consistently between (artificial) ego and (genuine) self as, respectively, the constructed object of reflection and the relationship or axis between that object and the other (i.e., what it excludes). To the extent that Newman, in her own elaboration of Novalis's relational notion of the self, adopts uncritically Kuzniar's argument as to its "fictional" status (62, 70), I must disagree with her as well. Moreover, Newman, it seems to me, compounds the confusion over the term *fictional* when she says, in one sentence, that Novalis posits "a self that exists in the fictional congruence between the two realities [i.e., subjective and objective]" and, in the next, contrasts the fictional to an "absolute congruence" (61–62). Alas, we are left in the dark as to whether "fictional" (and hence the self so described) is to be taken as "invented" (hence "unreal") or "constituted by the *(real)* act of writing fiction."

15. It is the Self as *Interesse* or *Teilnahme* ("taking part"), with its capacity to empathize with the other, indeed to become the other, that Paul de Man, in my view, mistakes for its opposite, the so-called anaesthetizing (and therefore potentially violent) "distance" he cites as the hallmark of idealist aesthetics. See *The Rhetoric of Romanticism* 279–81.

16. While deconstruction uses the term *aporia* in its narrow rhetorical sense to denote various types of contradiction inherent in texts (e.g., semantic, figural, grammatical, etc., including contradictions *between* these modes), some forms of mysticism, such as Rinzai Zen with its koan tradition, expand the phenomenon (if not the term) to include any psycho-spiritual contradiction powerful enough to push the mind into a higher condition of synthesis or Enlightenment. An unresolved aporia or koan entraps the logical mind, but according to Zen, this very trap, if endured and, eventually, affirmed, can liberate the latent dialectical consciousness and thus be the gateway to Absolute Freedom itself. The trap is thus its own principle of emancipation *(coincidentia oppositorum).* De Man, I think, has an inkling of this liberating power of the aporia (see next note).

17. This is so despite Paul de Man's vociferous opposition to Romantic transcendence (or, for that matter, transcendence in any hue), alluded to in the opening paragraph of this chapter. What we have here, in my opinion, is a classic case of psychological projection: de Man, having repressed his own strong mystical tendencies, unconsciously projects them onto the Romantics (easy screens) and then attacks. Nevertheless, these denied impulses "leak out" here and there at "aporetic junctures" in his writings, e.g., in the introduction to *Allegories of Reading* where he intuits the simultaneous terror and rapture that may accompany penetration of the delusion of linguistic reference. I would even venture to "read" the recent revelations of de Man's collaborative activities during the Nazi era as part and parcel of this massive repression of a profound religious sensibility. De Man strikes me as a dramatic illustration of the inscrutable intimacy that binds even such mythic antagonists as light and darkness, a sort of abortive Faustian/Mephistophelian *coincidentia oppositorum,* enmeshed in self-struggle somewhere on the level of Schlegel's "chemischer Geist."

18. Here and elsewhere in this study (e.g., p. 45, 83, 93, 173–174), I either state or imply the limitation of my own point of view, a limitation necessarily *imposed by the very thesis I am arguing:* that ultimate truth is the *coincidentia oppositorum* cannot be stated without falsifying that truth, for to state that this is so is to deny that it is *not* so, and such a denial violates the *coincidentia.* But, lo and behold, if this is the case, if the truth as asserted turns out to be false, the opposites do indeed coincide and the validity of my thesis is immediately reinstated. Logic cowers!

19. Setting off and yet supporting Wilpert's "eloquent inarticulateness" in the face of the unanswerable question as to the nature of Romanticism is the subtly and brilliantly elucidated position of Ernst Behler, unquestionably the premier living scholar of the early Jena circle. Wilpert's implicit suggestion of silence on the question speaks volumes; in differential symmetry, Behler's "middle" position between pro-transcendental millenialists and anti-transcendental poststructuralists approaches silence. It seems to me that Behler, in true Romantic spirit, comes closest to transcending the either/or terms of the debate itself in his illuminating discussion of the contribution to Friedrich Schlegel's philosophy of history of Condorcet's idea of "infinite perfectibility" (an oxymoron itself suggesting the coincidence of opposites): "In a subtle double gesture, the new Romantic conception of perfectibility maintains both scepticism towards any achievable final goal and belief in the pursuit of such a goal" (*GRLT* 70–71). For Behler, living with contradiction or "operating between opposites without overcoming them" (*GRLT* 60) is the "essence" of Romanticism, a notion of "essence" that I think fruitfully problematizes the term. Behler no doubt takes his key here from Friedrich Schlegel's frequent assertion as to the necessity of literally realizing the impossible (exactly the goal, incidentally, of Rinzai Zen koan meditation), as when he characterizes irony in the *Lyceum* fragments as a *coincidentia oppositorum:* "ein Gefühl von dem unauflöslichen Widerstreit des Unbedingten und des Bedingten, der Unmöglichkeit und Notwendigkeit einer vollständigen Mitteilung" (86). But it is precisely here where I believe Behler falls short: in viewing the Romantic sensibility as one "operating between opposites *without overcoming them*" (emphasis mine), he does not take literally enough Schlegel's insistence on the ultimate *absolute identity* ("vollständigen Mitteilung") of the pairs, e.g., conditional and unconditional, course and goal of history, time and eternity, immanent and transcendent, real and ideal. To stop short of overcoming the tension between the pairs is to remain mired in dualism (precisely Novalis's complaint against Fichte's philosophy of history). But it is just this overcoming, the overcoming of any and all pairs of opposites, that I say Romantic transcendence is. And since it is beyond all conceivable dualisms, not excluding the dualism transcendence/immanence, it can occur *right in the midst of dualism,* right in the midst of the oscillation between poles. It is, in other words, an overcoming that is only realized through absolute ontological identification with that which is overcome (time, space, world, reality, etc.). This is a going-beyond that is truly a remaining-with, a transcendence rising not a hair's breadth above immanence. Behler's position hovers, I think, on the brink of this paradoxical final step that is a non-step.

## CHAPTER 2

## MERTON'S "RILKE," RILKE'S "MERTON"

1. E.g., under the general editorship of Merton's friend and fellow monk, Patrick Hart, four of a projected seven volumes of *The Journals of Thomas Merton* (San Francisco: HarperSanFrancisco-HarperCollins, 1995–1996) have thus far appeared.

2. Both Rilke's German and Merton's translation are contained in Thomas Merton, Notebook 4, ms., Thomas James Merton Papers, 1960–1968, Syracuse University, Box 3, 50–51. Hereafter cited parenthetically in the text and notes of this essay by page reference only.

3. Thomas Merton, "Poetry and Imagination," *The Voice of Thomas Merton Recorded Live at Gethsemani,* Credence Cassettes, AA2076, n.d. Precise dating of this and other Credence Cassettes on which Rilke is featured is uncertain. Although the monk who introduces the tapes dates them from "the early nineteen-sixties," it is my strong sense that they were recorded from around February 1966 onward, immediately following the months of Merton's intense preoccupation with Rilke covered in the notebook. I am supported in this view by Professor John E. King of the University of Arkansas, who is presently chronicling sources both by and on Merton. Credence Cassettes are hereafter cited parenthetically in text and notes as "CC."

4. For clarity's sake Merton's cancellings and erasures have been omitted from my transcription and his punctuation minimally edited.

5. Though Merton concentrated in modern languages throughout his formal education, German seems to have played poor cousin to English, French, and Italian. He is known to have read some Goethe and even some Spinoza during his prep school years in England and vacations in Germany in the early 1930s, but as he moved on through Cambridge and Columbia Universities, at first German, and eventually the Romance languages, were dropped in favor of English. (See Kountz 24–61.)

6. For further discussion of these particular points, see the concluding chapter below. For more on the basic affinities between German Romanticism and postmodernism, see Helfer, O'Brien, Kuzniar, and Frank.

7. See, e.g., Paul de Man's *Allegories of Reading.*

8. For an elaboration of this argument from a somewhat different slant, which would substitute the Christian concept of *adventus* or sudden, unexpected breakthrough for my "always already here" point of view, see Kuzniar, *Delayed Endings* 29–50.

9. August Stahl (270) speaks for mainstream current opinion, I would say, in his reading of Rilke's *Narziss* as a symbol rather of self-containment, in the sense of spiritual equanimity, than of egotistical or self-absorption.

10. In a letter to R. H. Prince written several months later (Dec. 18, 1965), Merton seems to have settled the matter to his own satisfaction: "I have been studying Rilke, who is very interesting from this point of view. He is a great poet, and had tremendous insights into the reality of spiritual experience, and yet I think he rarely if ever got beyond his narcissism. I can think of only one or two places where he might

have done so. Otherwise, there is in him a magnificent regressive narcissism in full bloom, fully expressed, and wrong. Or, rather, misleading if you read it as mysticism, which only few do" (Shannon 495–96).

11. Merton read both Holthusen and Guardini in English translations.

12. See, e.g., his long autobiographical letter of Oct. 21, 1924, to Professor Hermann Pongs, in *Letters* 352–63.

13. According to Paola Mayer, "[B]y following Franckenberg in presenting Boehme as a saintly figure, Tieck and Novalis enlisted him in their battle against the growing marginalization of the sacred. At the same time, by insisting that Böhme was a poet, they aimed to fuse the personae of poet and prophet, and so to sacralize Romantic literature, that is, to invest it with the dignities traditionally conferred on religion" (iii). What Mayer calls the "marginalization of the sacred" has been traditionally characterized as the tendency of the analytical aesthetics of the Enlightenment (e.g., G. E. Lessing, K. P. Moritz, and Kant) to separate the categories of the sacred and the poetic.

14. That Rilke felt such pessimism about his own age is reflected in many letters written from Muzot between the end of the Great War and the burst of inspiration that led to the completion of the *Duineser Elegien* in 1922. See, e.g., *Letters* 280. Interestingly, Merton cites four such letters (23). Rilke, the modern poet, as "Enterbter" (the disinherited one), i.e., as a lone spark of inspiration struggling to stay lit in a benighted culture, is the perspective taken by Erich Heller in his great book, *The Disinherited Mind.* The image of disinheritance is, of course, from Rilke's classically cadenced lines in the "Seventh Duino Elegy," cited by Heller as epigraph on his title page: "Jede dumpfe Umkehr der Welt hat solche Enterbte, /denen das Frühere nicht und noch nicht das Nächste gehört" [Each and every prosaic reversal of the world has its disinherited,/ Who no longer the old and not yet the new possess].

15. Kramer says that the young Merton had problems concerning "how to combine contemplation and poetry—doubts about whether such a combination was even possible. Such questions continued well into his mature career—into the late 1950's" (12). More optimistically, Woodcock argues that by the time he was at work on the journal, *The Sign of Jonas* (1952), Merton had "finally reconciled his two vocations, and . . . recognized the kinship of the aesthetic and the spiritual and how they serve each other" (69). In light of the 1965–1966 manuscript under discussion here, I would have to side with Kramer, perhaps even going him one better to opine that the issue was never fully resolved in Merton's mind until his visit to Ceylon in December 1968. (See the section, "Epiphany," below.)

16. Some weeks later, in the previously cited taped talk on Rilke to the novices, Merton would make a point of reiterating this separation between poetic and mystical insight: "He's [Rilke's] a poet, not a mystic" (CC AA2076).

17. This, and the other *Dinggedichte* contained in the *Neue Gedichte,* held a special appeal for Merton. He elaborates his appreciation and understanding of the poet's intent in "Poetry and Imagination" (CC AA2076).

18. Marxist critic Georg Lukacs was perhaps the first to note the sociocultural paradox of the German situation in the late eighteenth and nineteenth centuries:

while German Idealistic philosophy was cutting-edge, indeed intellectually revolutionary, the political environment in which it flourished was, compared with developments in France and England, reactionary in the extreme: "Wir [Deutsche] sind *philosophische* Zeitgenossen der Gegenwart, ohne ihre *historischen* Zeitgenossen zu sein" (6).

19. Earlier in the notebook (14), Merton fills an entire page with quotations from two of Rilke's prose vignettes, "Erlebnis I" and "II" (1913), which relate the poet's experiences of being (as Merton translates) "completely absorbed into nature in a state of almost unconscious contemplation" (14). In expressing admiration for Rilke's ability to capture with such nuance this pure or mystical experience of nature ("He reflects on it very articulately!" [14]), Merton leaves no doubt as to his skepticism toward any "hygienic intervention" that might jeopardize such an ability. For an interesting discussion of Merton's personal and theoretical ambivalence toward psychoanalysis, see Kountz (42).

20. While it is true that Merton has deep intellectual roots in Blake, having written his Master's thesis on that poet at Columbia, still a true mystical empathy is hard to pin down. For example, the young thesis writer seems to applaud Blake's dialectical integration of good and evil, characterizing him as possessed of "a faith which dialectically embraces both extremes . . . moving freely between dialectical poles in a wild chaos, integrating sacred vision in and through the experience of fallenness as the only locus of creativity and redemption" (qtd. in Bailey 46). Yet the Merton of 1968 (presumably much closer in outlook to the man under study here), in a review of Thomas J. J. Altizer's book, *The New Apocalypse: The Radical Christian Vision of William Blake* (1967), chides the author for "reading into" Blake the idea of divine immanence and thereby missing the paradoxical quality of Blake's vision of God as being somehow both *in* and yet *over against* His creation. I would suggest that Merton's lingering attachment to this "over against" idea caused him to "read" a dualism "into" Blake that is not there and that, in general, it caused him anxiety when confronted with mystical visions of genuine dialectical synthesis such as those of Blake and Rilke. Daggy (280) makes what I believe is a telling observation in this connection: upon completion in the mid-1960s of a translation from the Latin of a tract by the fifteenth-century mystic, Nicholas of Cusa, who in his *De visione dei* (1443) defines God outright as a *coincidentia oppositorum,* Merton strangely lost all interest in that dialectical absolutist.

21. Interestingly, doubts about the seriousness, or shall we say the monolithic logocentrism, of Fichte's Idealism (represented in its traditional mode, e.g., by Lewis) have recently been raised. Helfer argues that Fichte was rhetorically and semiotically savvy and that he hints at the aesthetic conflation of philosophical and fictive discourses in his early *Practical Philosophy* of 1793–1794. If this is so, then his student Novalis is to be seen rather as developing than transforming Fichte's perspective.

22. He writes to Aziz on Dec. 9: "Recently I sent you two small books on Böhme, his confessions and another. I like his confessions. Unfortunately his work is so full of abstruse terminology borrowed from alchemy, etc., that I find it hard to follow him. But when I do make contact with his mind, I like his spirit very much indeed" (Shannon 60).

23. As for the place of postmodernism, particularly of Derrida's deconstruction, in this discussion of the Fall from Grace, one's initial assumption is that it has none, inasmuch as it regards all such preoccupation with "openness" (Rilke's "das Offene") or "pure experience" as our linguistic-delusive nostalgia for a metaphysics of Presence. That said, it is nevertheless remarkable how reminiscent Derrida's discussion of certain key concepts, such as that of the trace, is of the middle, or Fallen, phase of the grand triadic Christo-Romantic myth of Paradise Lost. For Derrida our state of exile is our damnable sense of our own experience as forever something "second-hand," something always already recorded, inscribed, or written even while we are having it. In *Writing and Difference* he makes delightful use of the metaphor of the child's mystic or magic writing pad (borrowed from Freud who uses it to make a point about habit as a laying-down of neurological pathways) to express this unshakable feeling of alienation from our own experience: the writing that appears on the pad's surface (perception) is never a direct registering of the world "out there" ("das Offene") but only of the trace incisions already made by the stylus on the pad's wax base. "Writing," asserts Derrida, "supplements perception before perception even appears to itself" (qtd. in Harland 144). We are doomed to register the traces of things, never things themselves *(das Ding an sich)*. But then again, as mentioned above, the tongue-in-cheek tone in which Derrida laments our plight seems to hint at some ironic-esoteric understanding of the trace, or signifier, or mask, as its own Experience, or Signified, or Face. If there is nothing "behind" any of these pointers, then, eureka, they must be pointing to themselves, and that must be enough, and more than enough.

## CHAPTER 3
## KILLING KAFKA KOANS

1. Lee claims Kafka's personal library contained no fewer than twenty-five books on Chinese religion and philosophy (274–75). By Whitlark, see both the article, "Kafka and the Taoist Sages," and his more recent book, *Behind the Great Wall.* As for Kafka's "Sinophilia" in general, the reader is referred to Rolf J. Goebel's recent study, *Constructing China: Kafka's Orientalist Discourse.* Regarding Kafka's overall knowledge of Buddhism, Whitlark says, "he owned Karl Neumann's version of *Die letzten Tage Gotamo Buddhos* and there is reason to suspect that Kafka also knew another Buddhist book translated by Neumann, *The Light of Asia* [by Edwin Arnold]" (*Behind the Great Wall* 51). Notwithstanding the uncanny spiritual affinities between the Kafkan and Zen points of view and the pervasive presence of "Kafuka" in postwar Japanese culture (see, e.g., Kuroiwa), there has been little exploration of the Zen-Kafka connection. Apart from occasional comparative observations in Whitlark's book, I have unearthed only Rickert and Tsukakoshi. The former is a study of the ways in which both Kafka's *Prozeß [Trial]* and Prometheus legend on the one hand, and Zen painting, on the other, can be said to be about the nature and limits of the interpretive act.

The latter is a provocative general discussion of parallels to Zen in modern Western philosophy and literature. Kafka's "Bericht für eine Akademie" ["Report to an Academy"] is mentioned as an astute parable on European man's condition of alienation from his own deepest being. I disagree with the author, however, when he concludes from this single piece that "Kafka glaubt, man könne lebend die Bewußtseinsschranken nicht durchbrechen: keine Freiheit des Seins gewinnen" (26). As I hope to show in these pages, Kafka was, at least at times, deeply aware of the possibility of perfect ontic freedom for man in this life.

2. Throughout this essay quotations of English translations of Kafka's parables are cited by parenthetical page references alone. These references are to the dual-language edition, *Parables and Paradoxes*. Quotations of other writings of Kafka are cited by reference to the appropriate edition.

3. This symbolic view of the crucifixion as the conscious and agonizing fusion of the opposites that the psyche by nature tends to keep apart is shared by Jung. See Clift (67–78).

4. In his tract, *De Visione Dei* (1443).

5. The pairs of opposites, that is, by which men in their ignorance are bound, as the *Bhagavad Gita* has it in its characterization of the Enlightened Man: "Content with getting what arises of itself/Passed beyond the pairs, free from envy,/Not attached to success nor failure,/Even acting, he is not bound./He is to be recognized as eternally free/Who neither loathes nor craves;/For he that is freed from the pairs,/Is easily freed from conflict" (qtd. in Wilber 27).

6. Here and elsewhere I use the more familiar (to Westerners) Japanese transliterations of the names of the early Chinese Zen masters. Hence, for example: "Joshu" for "Chao-chou," "Mumon" for "Wu-mên," "Rinzai" for "Lin-chi."

7. Whitlark, reading *The Metamorphosis* from a Taoist perspective, also sees the desire to fix a position, *any* position, as the nub of Gregor's identity-problem: Gregor suffers only because he insists on deciding what he is, or better—because he insists on being anything in particular at all, a futile endeavor:

> The situation has a few points in common with the most famous Taoist parable: Chuang Tzu dreamed that he was an insect (a butterfly); on awakening, he wondered whether he was Chuang Tzu, who had dreamed himself a bug, or a bug that now dreamed it was Chuang Tzu. He concluded, "This is a case of what is called the Transformation of Things". . . . In other words, all phenomena are merely states of mind ever changing into one another, for existence is no more real than a dream. ("Kafka" 30)

8. See Zen Master Yasutani's commentary on *Mu* in Kapleau 84.

9. The psycho-spiritual death that is prior to biological death, both in time and significance, also characterizes Rajneesh's provocative view of Jesus, often cited as a prototype for Gregor: "The moment he said, 'Let thy kingdom come, let thy will be done,' he surrendered his ego with all its expectations, his mind with all its desires. That *yes,* that total *yes*! And it could only be total at the last moment when he was

dying. What was there to hold back? He totally surrendered; that was let-go. In that let-go he became Christ" (205).

10. See Sokel, *Franz Kafka* 19. No less in recent articles do Sokel's otherwise brilliant and enriching analyses of Kafka's fiction continue to rest on the assumption therein of the protagonist's problematic "self," "subjectivity," or "ego," ironically the very assumption—indeed, delusion—to which that fiction points as man's fundamental predicament. See, e.g., "Kafka's Poetics" and "Frozen Sea." A further irony resides in the fact that Sokel, in the former article, appeals to some of the most suggestive concepts of Jacques Derrida (e.g., "metaphysical nostalgia" [8] and "trace" [12]) to elucidate Kafka's connection to the *Sprachkrise* pervading German and Austrian letters at the turn of the century, the same Derrida whose most strident and powerful message is the very death of the self.

In a still more recent article, "Between Gnosticism and Jehovah," Sokel continues to impute to Kafka various forms of dualism (e.g., between two aspects of "a divided self" [73], between "essence and actuality" [74], between "the true and highest God" and Jahwe [75], between God and man [passim]), which, I would argue, is precisely what Kafka in his most insightful moments is at pains to expose as the terminal disease *par excellence* of the human mind. Thus, while Sokel views Kafka's pronouncement about there being plenty of hope for God but none "for us" as "dismal" (75), I take it as a mot of mischievous koan-like subtlety in which what is truly insinuated is the end of all human suffering with the explosion of the delusive belief that there ever *was* an "us" in the first place.

11. Thus, the policeman's response, "Gibs auf!" [Give it up!], to the persona's request for directions to the railroad station in Kafka's posthumously published "Kommentar" [Commentary] is, in its perfect ambiguity, the stuff of oracles. One possible deciphering: "You can't get there from here, that is, *you as you* can't get there. But, should it ever occur to you that you are not really the 'you' you think you are, you would see that you are already there, and have never left." A state of affairs that more than warrants the oracular policeman's laughing up his sleeve in the narrative's final image.

Heinz Politzer's use of "Gibs auf!" as a motto of Kafka-interpretation is, in my view, exactly right and could serve, as well, as the only sound advice for the solution of any koan. Man, as the paradoxical point of contact between natural and supernatural, indeed, as the nucleus of tension between all the whirling pairs of opposites, is not meant to resolve the *double-entendre* of his own nature in favor of one side or the other. On the contrary, he must "give up!" all effort to "get there" unilaterally. It is precisely through this dying to the need for a "decision" that the issue is at last decided: giving up the way *is* the way; uncertainty *is* the only certainty, in ontological fact; the nonstop flow between and among the various options (phenomena) *is* the only freedom; or, in Politzer's terms, "the incomprehensibility of the incomprehensible" (21) *is* the only comprehensibility. "Further clarification" of things is not merely impossible but, more importantly, unnecessary. The opposites are, after all, One. Politzer, it seems to me, does not pick up on Kafka's occasional flashes of insight into this liberating paradox of paradoxes or metaparadox, the prized *kensho* or *satori* of Zen. See Politzer 1–22.

12. For an introduction to Hakuin's system of koan study, see Miura and Sasaki.

13. Lest I be accused by deconstruction of imputing to Kafka a transcendental concept, substance, or self-entity, let me hasten to reiterate that Kafka's overseeing "part" and my own "True Self" are unavoidable concessions to reifying language and are to be taken strictly as pointers to a fundamental Reality understood as ongoing process without boundaries of *any* kind.

14. Zen insists upon the unavailability of this awareness to even the most astute dualistic rational mind. See, e.g., the opening stanza of the "Song of Enlightenment" by Yoka Daishi (died 713), disciple of Hui-neng, sixth patriarch of Zen Buddhism (89):

> Knowest thou that leisurely philosopher who has gone beyond learn ing and is not exerting himself in anything?
>
> He neither endeavors to avoid idle thoughts nor seeks after the Truth;
>
> [For he knows that] ignorance in reality is the Buddha-nature,
>
> [And that] this empty visionary body is no less than the Dharma-body.

15. The identification of Kafka's Law with the Tao has also been made by Max Brod (174–75): "The chief theme [in Kafka] remains the enormous danger that we may lose the right way, a danger so grotesquely out of proportion that it is really only an accident—'gratia praeveniens'—that can bring us to the point of entering into 'The Law,' i.e. the right and perfect life, into 'Tao.' How much more probable it is, on the contrary, that we miss the way altogether."

16. This is also the point of view taken by Ralf R. Nicolai, who comes at the problem via the Kafka-Kleist connection ("'Ein altes Blatt'"; "Zur Stagnierung").

17. As noted at the beginning of this chapter, on at least one occasion Kafka seems to have gone considerably beyond a mere dim sense of Enlightenment. See Sokel's fascinating account of the author's ecstatic experience in writing "Das Urteil" ["The Judgment"] ("Frozen Sea" 75–79).

## CHAPTER 4

## *INTERFACE:* IDENTITY/DIFFERENCE/PRESTIDIGITATION

1. At least according to Althusser in *For Marx*: "The ruling class does not maintain with the ruling ideology, which is its own ideology, an external and lucid relation of pure utility and cunning" (235).

2. Another, very interesting, example of a discipline, on the American scene at least, currently playing "catch-up" with poststructuralism is psychotherapy. In several recent books Steve de Shazer has outlined what might be termed a differentialist mode of individual and group psychotherapy. De Shazer calls what he does "solution-focused therapy." As the term suggests, the emphasis in the therapeutic hour is on a collaborative endeavor between patient and therapist actively to create or "construct," rather than strictly speaking to "discover," solutions to the problems presented. The

implication here, as revolutionary as poststructualist thinking itself, is that psychological histories, like any other kind, are not so much remembered as unconsciously *created* ex post facto. This being the case, they can be consciously discreated or deconstructed and replaced by "versions of the past" one prefers. The past is no longer an—in any case—illusory foundation for the present, something one takes as autonomous and forever fixed "way back there," and therefore containing "objective" personal truths to be tediously excavated, but rather a kind of timeless inner theater for which one can write or rewrite, and then enact, any "historical drama" that suits one. (See the Magic Theater episode in Hermann Hesse's *Bildungsroman, Steppenwolf,* for a literary foreshadowing of this approach.) Putting it in more familiar deconstructionist terms, the patient is a text to be read, not backward "against the grain" in search of some primordial, mist-enshrouded psychological "Truth" or "Origin," but forward into the future as an ongoing, freely self-composing narrative. (It is this profound shift in perspective, from past truth to future fiction—or shall we say, to the "truth" of future fiction—, that emancipates Gregor Samsa in Kafka's *Metamorphosis* from infernal confinement within the loathesome insect-identity and restores him to the free, because now self-aware, status of the narrator of the story that he has been from the beginning.) Thus, for de Shazer versions of a person's past, like any nexus of signifiers, have a lateral, differential relationship to one another rather than separate potentially historical (i.e., "recessive," in keeping with the directional metaphor) connections to a psychological first cause or *Ursache.* See *Words Were Originally Magic* (1994), *Putting Difference to Work* (1991), and *Clues* (1988). Paralleling de Shazer's psychotherapeutic differentialism on the current American philosophical front is the self-creationist neopragmatism of Richard Rorty. See, e.g., *Consequences of Pragmatism* (1982) and, especially, *Contingency, Irony, and Solidarity* (1989).

The question whether Jacques Lacan belongs in any discussion of poststructuralist psychotherapy is, I think, moot. Granted, his linguistic differential-structural notion of the unconscious speaks for his inclusion (in which case my observation of psychotherapy as coming late to the "poststructuralist party" is certainly compromised). But his attachments to Freud and Lévi-Strauss, particularly his sense of the unconscious as itself a monolithic and objective foundational principle, would seem to place him in the older modernist-structuralist camp. (On this see Harland 3.)

One could speculate that the entrance of differentialist thinking into mainstream psychotherapy (individual, group, marital, family) represents the beginning of its expansion beyond intellectually elite academic precincts into popular Western culture. Should we look forward to a time when people will cease to search their unconscious and start to rewrite their "personal narratives" or restage their "private-historical dramas"?

3. Be it noted that the Nietzsche to whom Foucault points here is the author of the still relatively early *Human, All Too Human* (1878–1879). Between then and the publication of *The Joyful Science* three years later, the philosopher would undergo a period of intense psychospiritual experience, culminating in August 1881, that would prompt him to develop insights into the historical consciousness superseding these earlier views. These insights grew primarily out of the notions of "eternal recurrence," partially inspired by speculations of the poet Heinrich Heine (Hayman 232–35), and the necessity of the true historian to penetrate the quality or *Geist* of a past age not

only through his mastery of factual sources but, more importantly, through a quasi-artistic intuition or creative sympathy. The latter idea, which Nietzsche derived from his friend and colleague at Basel, the cultural historian Jacob Burckhardt (Heller 55), indirectly alludes to Nietzsche's career-long struggle to find a *coincidentia oppositorum* between philology or factual scholarship (his training) and speculative philosophy (his vocation).

It is clear that Nietzsche's later works *(On the Genealogy of Morals* [1887] and the posthumous *Ecce Homo* [1907] and *The Will to Power)* remove him even further from the "differentialist historiography" poststructuralists like to appeal to. The ecstatic heraldings of the apocalyptic *Blitzschlag* (thunderbolt) of the "Umwertung aller Werte" [revaluation of all values] are mystical pronouncements on the fundamental deludedness of *all* historical views, not just logocentric ones, since such views can never divest themselves of ideological self-interest. While Nietzsche's explicit target is Christianity and its self-presentation as chiliastic history or *Heilsgeschichte,* there is obviously implied the ultimate bankruptcy, not only of all historiographical, but of all explicit moral principles as well (including "differentialist historiography" as a quasi-moral principle of poststructuralist philology) precisely because their explicitness makes them one-sided, which amounts to a lapse from the "ground of high indifference" occupied by the *coincidentia oppositorum.* This is why, as Walter Kaufmann says, the revaluation is for Nietzsche "not a new value-legislation but a reversal [today read: deconstruction] of prevalent valuations" (111). Obviously, substituting "new" values for old is not the answer; rather, the problem for Nietzsche is that of the partial nature of human valuation itself, regardless of what is valued: *"'[T]he highest values devaluate* [again read: *deconstruct*] *themselves,'"* as Kaufmann quotes from *The Will to Power,* then adding a comment that clearly reads Nietzsche's insistence on the necessity of affirming this partiality as the very leap—a decidedly un-poststructuralist leap—to its transcendence in consciousness, that is, to the *coincidentia oppositorum.* "This [self-devaluation of the highest values] Nietzsche can call the revaluation—in the same note in which he defines it as 'a courageous becoming conscious'—a '*saying Yes* to what has been attained' (W[ille zur] M[acht] 1007)" (112).

A good Foucauldian like Bernard Faure may conceive of his radical critique of the history of Chan and Zen Buddhism (*The Rhetoric of Immediacy,* 1991) as the *Blitzschlag* of revaluation of Zen that Nietzsche's *Genealogy* was with respect to Christianity. If he does, I would argue that he is mistaken, as the above remarks imply. Nietzsche's critique of a particular form of spirituality came ultimately out of spiritual insight and was, in Kaufmann's Hegelian expression, "a negation of a negation" (112). The illuminating lightning bolts were Western glimpses of what Eastern traditions call "sunyata," the fundamental emptiness underlying all phenomena, historical no less than other kinds. Faure's critique, on the other hand, is positioned on the side of "difference" as over against "unity" or "purity of origin." This very positioning makes it an instance of the kind of "new value-legislation" Nietzsche knew to be futile.

4. The place, however, might well be David Wood and Robert Bernasconi's *Derrida and "Différance,"* a collection of six essays by American and British philosophers.

5. Whitlark (*Behind the Great Wall* 212–13), in pursuit of the Zen-poststuctural-ist connection specifically, makes the same paradoxical point in a somewhat different

way: "Mahayana, a later form of Buddhism, proclaims that, taken to their limits, the opposites, Samsara (the world of differ*a*nce) and Nirvana (its antithesis) are identical. . . . In Zen (a sect of Mahayana Buddhism) this means that the adept has an experience of extreme differ*a*nce [say, in the throes of practice], followed by a vision of sameness, *Byodo-kan,* the realization that all beings are identical in their Buddha-nature, the potential to attain Nirvana. Eventually, the Zenist is able to experience *satori,* radical sameness, and difference simultaneously."

## CHAPTER 5

## EAST MEETS WEST

1. *Catcher* 13; hereafter in this essay referenced parenthetically in text by page number only.

2. Thus the epigraph to *Nine Stories* (1953) quoting the well-known koan of Rinzai master Hakuin: "We know the sound of two hands clapping. But what is the sound of one hand clapping?", and the occasional detailed discussions of Zen philosophy in "Zooey" (1957) and "Seymour: An Introduction" (1959). Alsen (158–59) lists some nine scholars who, during the years 1957–1971, took up the Zen theme in these post-*Catcher* works. I would add Davis (1963) and Finkelstein (1965) and, by way of updating the list, Brinkley (1976), Lundquist (1979), Takeda (1983), and Tae (1985).

3. E.g., S. and B. Goldstein, "Zen and Salinger" and "Some Zen References in Salinger," Rosen throughout, and Lundquist 52–53, 70–74.

4. Lundquist (69–114) views *Nine Stories* as a synthesis of Zen aesthetic principles and the art of the short story.

5. For the compositional chronology of *Catcher,* see Hamilton (113–16). See also p. 124 above. Suzuki's source for the anecdote is the famous *Hekigan-roku (Blue Rock Collection),* an eleventh-century case book of one hundred koans, in which it is listed as number 53: "Hyakujo and a Wild Duck."

6. A few commentators have read the ducks as reflecting, in one way or another, Holden's preoccupation with the problems of change (hence, also death) and permanence: e.g., Light, Lundquist (40), Rosen (23), and Howell (86). No one, however, has heretofore recognized the Zen source of the episode.

7. Hakuun Yasutani, as quoted in Kapleau 76.

8. This, according to Donna Slawsky, currently reference librarian for HarperCollins, in a telephone interview with the present author on Oct. 27, 1995.

9. According to Hamilton (126–27), in 1953 Salinger gave a Zen booklist to writer-friend Leila Hadley.

10. As Alsen (130) points out, it is Suzuki's *Manual of Zen Buddhism,* in its 1950 Rider edition, from which Salinger quotes that religion's Four Great Vows in "Zooey." Moreover, Alsen includes the *Essays* as among those works used by Salinger in forming "the basis of Seymour's eclectic religious philosophy" (257–58) in the Glass stories.

11. There is an allusion to the fourth of Rilke's "Duino Elegies" in "Franny" (*Franny and Zooey* 6).

12. For a comparison of the two carousels, see Stone, with whose judgment that "Salinger took the [carousel] ride itself not for its meaning but merely as a point of departure" (523) I beg to differ. For the Rilke-Salinger connection in the broader sense, see Gwynn and Blotner.

13. It is interesting to note that, although Rilke was probably not acquainted with Zen, he did have an avid interest in neighboring spiritual practices, such as Hindu yoga, as pathways to expanded consciousness (see Carossa 333). His early *Dinggedichte,* including "Das Karussell," are well known as creative products of some sort of intense sustained contemplation or meditation.

14. Similarly, the German-Romantic view of the poet as spiritual adept in essence and wordsmith only by accident or convention characterizes Buddy's "rehabilitation" of his brother Seymour's image: "not one Goddamn person . . . had ever seen him for what he really was. A poet, for God's sake. And I mean a *poet.* If he never wrote a line of poetry, he could still flash what he had at you with the back of his ear if he wanted to" (*Raise High* 60).

15. The line from Eckhart down to Rilke would include, among others, the "Philosophical Eye" or "Mirror of Wisdom" of the great Baroque mystic Jacob Böhme and the flower-calyx-eye symbolism of such mystically inclined Romantic poets as Novalis and E. T. A. Hoffmann. Contemporary to Rilke is, of course, the archetypal psychology of Carl Jung for whom the Eye signifies the ideal Self that is to be realized, or at least approached, through the psycho-spiritual process of individuation.

16. The problem of sustaining the creative tension of the dialectic between paradigmatic poles that may be termed variously implicit/explicit, subtextual/textual, or aesthetic/intellectual (as here), immediate/mediate or sudden/gradual (the Zen Enlightenment paradigm), or, in Jacques Derrida's recent parlance, poetic/rabbinical, without allowing oneself to be pulled too closely to the one pole or the other, is, of course, inescapable, not only for Salinger but for anyone taking a serious interest in Zen, or, for that matter, in the free-flowing quality of consciousness typically associated with creative expression of any kind. Zen has always construed itself as the realization of "immediate experience." Questions from students that engage discriminative thought (e.g., "What is the highest principle of Buddhism?") are usually roundly rebuffed by masters, particularly in the Rinzai tradition, with a shout ("Kwatz!"), a clout or a nonsensical expletive. Yet even the most sincere intention or effort to "experience immediately" only lands one back in shallow intellectual modeling. The question for us as beings blessed with/condemned to self-reflection is: how can we possibly have immediate experience without, at the same time, suppressing its intellectualization; or, conversely, allowing such intellectualization to occur as it will, how can we "preserve" the immediacy of the experience? This paradox constitutes a koan every bit as challenging as Holden's. (It is, in fact, a variant of it.) One might call it the author's koan and be inclined to judge that Salinger, with his gradual "Fall" into Zen intellectualism, dealt with it rather less successfully than did his protagonist with his. For a most thoughtful reflection on this paradox in terms of the complex relationship that obtains between the writer—be he scholar or novelist—and the religio-cultural tradition about which he writes, see the "Prologue" to Faure's *Rhetoric of Immediacy.*

## CHAPTER 6

## WITHOUT AN OBJECT, WITHOUT A SUBJECT

1. On this, the often-overlooked respect, even reverence, of the German Romantics for reason, see also Huch, who cites Friedrich Schlegel's characterization of reason as "das Vermögen der Ideale; er nannte sie einen Grundtrieb, den nach dem Ewigen" (12).

2. Apart from an article by Thomas J. McFarlane published on the Internet, "The Spiritual Function of Mathematics and the Philosophy of Franklin Merrell-Wolff" (http://www.integralscience.org/sacredscience/SS_spiritual.html), Ronald Leonard's dissertation, soon to appear as a book by SUNY Press, is, at this point, the only extended study of Merrell-Wolff's philosophy. To be sure, I regard Merrell-Wolff as a most apt and fascinating inclusion under the governing idea of this book, but I also offer this chapter as a general introduction to, and an encouragement to pursue, the thought of a man who I believe deserves to, and in time surely will, become better known.

3. On the psycho-spiritual importance of the analogy between "going within to work on oneself" and doing physical work in a cave, Merrell-Wolff had the following to say a few years after the event: "The real gestation of the new Birth is in the womb of the Unconscious, and for this the literal entering of the earth facilitates the process. To find a rationale for this, one must turn to the recurring content of mystical thought. The mystic ever finds the world in complete correspondential relationship with inner psychical realities. Hence, objective relations are not irrelevant, though the degree to which they are determinant varies from individual to individual" (*Consciousness* 80).

4. *Pathways* was first published in New York by R. R. Smith in 1944. *The Philosophy of Consciousness without an Object* did not appear until 1973, issued then by Julian Press in New York. The original manuscript form of *Consciousness* contained a good deal more material than its subsequent published version. This "extra" material was published as a separate volume by Phoenix Philosophical Press in 1980 under the title, *Introceptualism: The Philosophy of Consciousness without an Object*—Vol. II. Recent reissuings of Merrell-Wolff's works, taken in conjunction with Leonard's forthcoming study mentioned above, may signal an incipient groundswell of general recognition that is certainly due this important American mystic and religious philosopher: in 1994 SUNY Press put out an indexed volume containing both *Pathways* and *Consciousness*, titling it *Franklin Merrell-Wolff's Experience and Philosophy: A Personal Record of Transformation and a Discussion of Transcendental Consciousness*, adding to it a year later a companion volume, *Transformations in Consciousness: The Metaphysics and Epistemology*, which is a new edition of *Introceptualism*, edited by Leonard.

5. The other three marks listed by James are ineffability, transiency, and passivity.

6. Among the many minor influences worthy of mention, most prominent are Plato and Plotinus ("[idealistic] exceptions to the sensuous-materialisitc orientation of the ancient Greeks" [Leonard 37]); the Buddha, whose emphasis on the more objective

"Enlightenment" (vis-à-vis Shankara's subjective "Liberation") makes him "the one genuine spiritual World Teacher that has been known in historic times" (*Pathways* 278); Jesus, whose profound appeal to "the more active consciousness of the Occidental" (*Pathways* 278) makes him Shankara's Western counterpart; and Sri Aurobindo Ghose, a rare contemporary influence, whom Merrell-Wolff discovered relatively late and whose main importance consequently is "to reinforce and confirm certain insights which Wolff attained independently" (Leonard 38). One notes here Merrell-Wolff's interesting self-aware distinction between spiritual teachers deemed of relatively greater importance to the world at large than to himself (the Buddha) and vice versa (Shankara).

7. This is the same Paul Deussen who was a lifelong friend of Nietzsche's and who, through his commentaries on and translations of Hindu and Buddhist sacred texts, gave the philosopher access to the Eastern wisdom traditions. Interestingly, however, the Deussen connection in no way endeared Nietzsche to Merrell-Wolff, who had read him only superficially in terms of a political and ruthlessly anti-Christian "Will to Power": "All Caesar-power, whether in the specifically political sense or in the military form, is essentially a manifestation of the time-power [i.e., power that is time-bound, hence subspiritual]. Nietzsche, as one of the prime exponents of time-power, saw this point clearly, and both frankly and aggressively taught anti-Christ. He exalted the time violence of the will and hated the potency of the Christly non-resistance. All rulers whose souls are identical with political power are consciously or unconsciously disciples of Nietzsche, and with respect to them, all men and women who incarnate something of the Christly principle stand in counter relationship" (*Pathways* 234). By his own admission, Merrell-Wolff as a mystic was something of an anomaly, being inclined neither by training nor temperament to poetic expression. Had he been so inclined, he might have lingered over Nietzsche's masterpiece, *Also sprach Zarathustra,* and recognized therein striking similarities between Zarathustra's proclaiming of victory over the seemingly incontrovertible logical principle of noncontradiction ("I unite all contradictions within myself") and his own bedrock mystical principle of the High Indifference (taken up at length below). Merrell-Wolff's early retirement from academic life largely cut him off from the great "academic-philosophical conversation," resulting in a basically nineteenth-century philosophical orientation that more or less ended with William James's pragmatism and did not at all entertain the prominent movements of the twentieth-century such as British analytic philosophy and continental phenomenology cum existentialism, not to mention the explosion of interest, including spiritual interest, in Nietzsche occurring since around mid-century. On the other hand, since Merrell-Wolff's philosophy is essentially grounded in his own personal religious experience, it is doubtful that even an intricate engagement with these contemporary movements would have had more than a tangential effect on it.

8. Merrell-Wolff's description here resembles that of the ancient sage Patanjali for the eighth and highest stage of Yogic meditation known as samadhi.

9. This assertion is, admittedly, moot as there is reason to question whether the arch-deconstructionist himself does not occasionally go beyond the hard-line differential position with which he is largely identified. See chapter 4 above.

10. For more on this, see chapter 3.

11. This seems the appropriate place to make one critical comment on a generally excellent job of editing carried out by Leonard in his recent edition of Merrell-Wolff's *Introceptualism,* originally the second half of the manuscript of *Consciousness*. Leonard's claim that "the original manuscript was able to benefit from [his own] careful editing and revision, particularly as the early twentieth-century language and style would have posed unnecessary barriers to contemporary and future readers" (*Transformations in Consciousness* xviii) is to me an unfortunate irony, overlooking as it does Merrell-Wolff's own emphasis on the importance of the personal idiosyncratic element of style to the "plus" value of the writing. Certainly, a good deal of Merrell-Wolff's own "plus" value is lost in Leonard's well-intentioned "updating" of his quaint, self-deprecatingly polite, ever so slightly late-Victorian style and tone. The style and tone themselves, expressive of a certain guileless devotional purity, tend *on their own* to lead one nearer to the Mystery. One has to consider carefully the sort of trade-off that occurs when any part of these "peripheral," yet somehow ultimately essential, stylistic values is sacrificed, even to philosophical-conceptual clarity. An editor can unwittingly create barriers more serious than those he presumes to overcome.

12. Whether—and if so, the extent to which—the relationship between the High Indifference and the Self as described by Merrell-Wolff reflects that between *Brahma* and *atma* in Hinduism must remain a matter of speculation. Merrell-Wolff himself does not speculate on it, concerned, I suspect, to present his experience and philosophy in a distinctly modern Western light.

13. As carried out in Rorty's by now classic *Philosophy and the Mirror of Nature* (1979).

14. For a good discussion of the tension between unitary-holistic and differential-postmodern paradigms of reality in contemporary philosophy and physics, see McKinney.

## CHAPTER 7
## *GROUND:* GERMAN ROMANTICISM, ZEN, AND DECONSTRUCTION

1. Though I am aware of no other three-way synopses, comparisons of deconstruction with either of the other two begin to burgeon in recent scholarship. For the Zen-deconstruction connection, see the brilliantly eccentric study of Magliola, as well as those of Coward and Loy *(Healing Deconstruction)*. Both latter link Derrida to Zen via Nagarjuna's Madhyamika philosophy of absolute negation. For the Romanticism-deconstruction/poststructuralism connection, see: Frank, *Was ist Neostrukturalismus?,* and Kuzniar, *Delayed Endings,* both whose arguments I take up below; and, above all, Behler, who in recent years has pursued the topic with the intellectual passion and vast scholarly breadth we have come to expect from him: *Die Aktualität der Romantik,* edited with Hörisch, is an anthology of uniformly excellent essays, the best of which, "Friedrich Schlegels Theorie des Verstehens: Hermeneutik oder Dekonstruktion?", by

Behler himself, elucidates Schlegel's early theory of understanding as a dynamic, fundamentally inexhaustible act transcending intellect and one that would thus seem to characterize him as "einen Repräsentanten jener Wende in der modernen Ideengeschichte . . . , die heute gern als 'postmodern' ausgegeben wird" (157). Behler's book, *Irony and the Discourse of Modernity,* views irony, the fundamental need to "say it otherwise," as the essential link between Romanticism and postmodernism (see esp. ch. 2, "The Rise of Literary Modernism in the Romantic Age"); while the conclusion of *German Romantic Literary Theory* credits the Jena Romantics with that initial move of literature "away from the model of representation to that of creation, from mimetic imitation to creative production" (301) that is by now a commonplace of poststructuralist orientation. Other important contributions to the topic include: Gadamer's essay, "Frühromantik, Hermeneutik, Dekonstruktivismus," in the Behler-Hörisch anthology, which is at pains to identify the author's own hermeneutic phenomenology as just as much a child of early Romantic thought, even considered apart from Schleiermacher, the father of hermeneutics, as is Derrida's deconstruction inasmuch as both philosophies have inherited Friedrich Schlegel's idea of the fundamental independence of the literary work from authorial intention; Lacoue-Labarthe and Nancy, whose *Literary Absolute* I comment on in the opening chapter, notes 2 and 8; and O'Brien, who argues in *Novalis: Signs of Revolution* that the poet really read his philosophical mentor Fichte from a proto-semiotic perspective and that perhaps any claims of German Idealistic philosophy to "truth value" are to be taken as made with tongue in cheek.

2. See the opening chapter above, esp. note 14. For a comprehensive and penetrating discussion of German Idealism as the beginning of the turn against the Cartesian notion of the subject that was to culminate in poststructuralism, see Frank, *Was ist Neostrukturalismus?*

3. Although she offers, in *Delayed Endings,* a deeply probing and sensitive reading of Novalis, Kuzniar ultimately pulls back from an aporetic view of the poet's sense of time, e.g., in such statements as, "Time is endless *(unendlich)* [for Novalis] because it never reaches or coincides with eternity" (88) and "Novalis also maintains that this epiphanic consciousness [of eternity] is illusory" (90). But Novalis's sense of *Täuschung* or *Schein* is itself mystico-aporetic: "Schein und Wahrheit zusammen machen nur eine eigentliche Realität aus" (*Novalis Schriften* 2:181). The "illusion" of eternity is not opposed to the "truth" of temporality but rather cooperates with it to form the Grand Illusion that is Truth itself. It seems to me that Kuzniar's tendency to overstate the case for temporal nonclosure in Novalis causes her to miss the crucial aporetic point. The same might be argued with respect to Frank's assertion, in *Das Problem "Zeit" in der deutschen Romantik,* that "Die Idee des 'goldenen Zeitalters' ist eine in sich widersprüchliche Bestimmung, für die Novalis nur Spott übrig hat. *In* der Zeit—etwa als Zukunft—läßt sich ein prinzipiell Außerzeitliches weder verwirklichen noch träumen" (224). Quite the contrary, it is precisely *within* time, as the utterances of Novalis quoted in these pages make clear, that the Eternal is to be realized.

4. Friedrich Schlegel shares Novalis's insight into the self-contained, "systemic" nature of language as well as his skepticism regarding the referential function of words, a skepticism that presumably led Schlegel to deny metaphor in his own poetics the privileged position it had enjoyed in that of the eighteenth century. See Menninghaus.

5. For a most provocative article on the Romantic theory of the aesthetic symbol, see Flax. Kuzniar ("Reassessing Romantic Reflexivity") also notes Novalis's assertion of the nonreferential nature of language but, in my view, misses his aporetic insight into the wholeness attained through the perfect coalescence, in poetry, of individual intent and transindividual linguistic behavior when she observes: "Language [as Novalis sees it] sports with itself and with the illusions it creates. It is a pure 'Verhältnisspiel.' But it is a misconception to then surmise that this self-reflexivity is or even attempts to be successful and that poetry possesses absolute knowledge of itself" (82).

6. Cf. the opening chapter, note 17.

7. What one might term "aporetic anxiety," i.e., fear of the ground-zero condition implied by the conflation of any pair of opposites, is also in evidence in Spivak, e.g., in her characterization of aporia as a "stalling" (158) and her retreat to a spacious middle ground between *différance* and aporia, "to a position that moves beyond stalled-out paralysis" (159). In Zen practice, however, it is precisely this dreadful "stalled-out paralysis" of the aporia that is sought, for it is only when the mind fully realizes its utter entrapment within its own categories that it has any chance of transcending those categories. All forty-eight koans contained in the famous medieval collection, entitled, with aporetic aplomb, *The Gateless Gate (Mumonkan),* are calculated to jolt the mind into the sudden realization that its own structure-by-contradiction ("gatelessness") is, in truth, the "gateway" to spiritual freedom.

8. See previous note.

# Works Cited


Allert, Beate. Review of *Herder and the Poetics of Thought: Unity and Diversity in "On Diligence in Several Learned Languages,"* by Michael Morton. *German Quarterly* 64 (1991): 247-48.

Alsen, Eberhard. *Salinger's Glass Stories as a Composite Novel.* New York: Whitston, 1983.

Althusser, Louis. *For Marx.* Trans. Ben Brewster. London: New Left Books, 1969.

Altizer, Thomas J. J. *The New Apocalypse: The Radical Christian Vision of William Blake.* East Lansing: Michigan State UP, 1967.

Bailey, Raymond. *Thomas Merton on Mysticism.* Garden City, NY: Doubleday, 1975.

Behler, Ernst. *German Romantic Literary Theory (GRLT).* New York: Cambridge UP, 1993.

———. *Irony and the Discourse of Modernity.* Seattle: Washington UP, 1990.

Behler, Ernst, and Jochen Hörisch, eds. *Die Aktualität der Frühromantik.* Paderborn: Ferdinand Schöningh, 1987.

Blake, William. *The Portable Blake.* 1946. Introd. Alfred Kazin. New York: Penguin, 1976.

Borges, Jorge Luis. *A Personal Anthology.* Ed. Anthony Kerrigan. New York: Grove, 1967.

Brinkley, Thomas Edwin. "J. D. Salinger: A Study of His Eclecticism—Zooey as Existential Zen Therapist." Diss. Ohio State U., 1976.

Brod, Max. *Franz Kafka: A Biography.* Trans. G. Humphreys Roberts and Richard Winston. 2nd, Enlarged, ed. New York: Schocken, 1960. Trans. of the original German ed. 1937.

Carossa, Hans. "Begegnung mit Rilke." *German Literature since Goethe.* Ed. Ernst Feise and Harry Steinhauer. Vol. 2. Boston: Houghton Mifflin, 1959. 330–37. 2 vols. 1958–1959.

Cirlot, J. E. *A Dictionary of Symbols.* Trans. Jack Sage. 2nd ed. New York: Philosophical Library, 1971.

Clift, Wallace B. *Jung and Christianity: The Challenge of Reconciliation*. New York: Crossroad, 1982.

Coward, Harold. *Derrida and Indian Philosophy*. Albany: State U of New York P, 1990.

Daggy, Robert E. "The Continuing Tsunami: 1989 in Merton Scholarship and Publication." *The Merton Annual: Studies in Thomas Merton, Religion, Culture, Literature & Social Concerns* 3 (1990): 277–89.

Daishi, Yoka. "Song of Enlightenment." *Manual of Zen Buddhism*. Ed. and trans. Daisetz Teitaro Suzuki. New York: Grove, 1960. 89–103.

Davis, Tom. "J. D. Salinger: 'The Sound of One Hand Clapping.'" *Wisconsin Studies in Contemporary Literature* 4 (1963): 41–47.

Deleuze, Gilles, and Felix Guattari. *Kafka: Toward a Minor Literature*. Theory and History of Literature 30. Trans. Dana Polan. Minneapolis: U of Minnesota P, 1986.

de Man, Paul. *Allegories of Reading: Figural Language in Rousseau, Nietzsche, Rilke, and Proust*. New Haven: Yale UP, 1979.

———. *The Rhetoric of Romanticism*. New York: Columbia UP, 1984.

Derrida, Jacques. *Of Spirit: Heidegger and the Question*. Trans. Geoffrey Bennington and Rachel Bowlby. Chicago: U of Chicago P, 1989.

———. *Speech and Phenomena*. Trans. D. B. Allison. Evanston: Northwestern UP, 1973.

———. *Writing and Differance*. Trans. Alan Bass. Chicago: U of Chicago P, 1978.

*The Diamond Sutra; With Supplemental Texts*. New York: Concord Grove, 1983.

Dumoulin, Heinrich. *Zen Buddhism: A History*. Trans. James W. Heisig and Paul Knitter. Vol. 1. New York: Macmillan, 1988. 2 vols. 1988–90.

Eckhart. *Meister Eckhart. A Modern Translation*. Trans. Raymond Bernard Blakney. New York: Harper, 1941.

Ellenberger, Henri F. *The Discovery of the Unconscious: The History and Evolution of Dynamic Psychiatry*. New York: Basic Books, 1970.

Faure, Bernard. *The Rhetoric of Immediacy: A Cultural Critique of Chan/Zen Buddhism*. Princeton: Princeton UP, 1991.

Feltsman, Vladimir. Jacket notes. *J. S. Bach: Goldberg Variations*. Rec. 26 Oct. 1991. Musical Heritage Society, 1993.

Finkelstein, Sidney. *Existentialism and Alienation in American Literature*. New York: International, 1965. 219–34.

Fish, Stanley. "Anti-Foundationalism, Theory Hope, and the Teaching of Composition." *Doing What Comes Naturally: Change, Rhetoric, and the Practice of Theory in Literary and Legal Studies*. Durham: Duke UP, 1989. 342–55.

Flax, Neil M. "The Presence of the Sign in Goethe's *Faust*." *PMLA* 98 (1983): 183–203.

Foucault, Michel. *The Archaeology of Knowledge*. Trans. A. M. Sheridan Smith. New York: Pantheon-Random House, 1972.

———. *Language, Counter-memory, Practice: Selected Essays and Interviews*. Trans. Donald F. Bouchard and Sherry Simon. Ed. Donald F. Bouchard. Ithaca: Cornell UP, 1977.

Frank, Manfred. *Das Problem "Zeit" in der deutschen Romantik: Zeitbewußtsein und Bewußtsein von Zeitlichkeit in der frühromantischen Philosophie und in Tiecks Dichtung*. Munich: Winkler, 1972.

———. *Was ist Neostrukturalismus?* Frankfurt: Suhrkamp, 1984.

Freud, Sigmund. *On Creativity and the Unconscious: Papers on the Psychology of Art, Literature, Love, Religion*. Ed. Benjamin Nelson. New York: Harper and Row, 1958.

Gleick, James. *Chaos: Making a New Science*. New York: Penguin, 1987.

Goebel, Rolf J. *Constructing China: Kafka's Orientalist Discourse*. Columbia, SC: Camden House, 1997.

Goldstein, Bernice and Sanford. "Zen and Salinger." *Modern Fiction Studies* 12 (1966): 313–24.

———. "Some Zen References in Salinger." *Literature East and West* 15 (1971): 83–95.

Gras, Vernon W. "Deconstruction." *The New Princeton Encyclopedia of Poetry and Poetics*. 1993.

Guardini, Romano. *Rainer Maria Rilkes Deutung des Daseins: Eine Interpretation der Duineser Elegien*. 2nd ed. Munich: Kösel, 1961.

Gwynn, Frederick L., and Joseph L. Blotner. *The Fiction of J. D. Salinger*. Pittsburgh: U of Pittsburgh P, 1958.

Hamilton, Ian. *In Search of J. D. Salinger*. New York: Vintage, 1989.

Hardenberg, Friedrich von (Novalis). *Werke, Tagebücher und Briefe Friedrich von Hardenbergs*. Ed. Hans-Joachim Mähl and Richard Samuel. Vol. 2. Munich: Hanser, 1978. 2 vols.

Harland, Richard. *Superstructuralism: The Philosophy of Structuralism and Post-Structuralism*. London: Methuen, 1987.

Hart, Patrick, ed. *The Journals of Thomas Merton*. 4 vols. to date. San Francisco: HarperSanFrancisco-HarperCollins, 1995–.

Haym, Rudolf. *Die romantische Schule. Ein Beitrag zur Geschichte des deutschen Geistes*. 1870. Hildesheim: Olms, 1961.

Hayman, Ronald. *Nietzsche: A Critical Life*. New York: Penguin, 1982.

Hederer, Edgar. *Deutsche Dichtung des Barock*. 3rd ed. Munich: Hanser, 1961.

Heidsieck, Arnold. *The Intellectual Contexts of Kafka's Fiction: Philosophy, Law, Religion*. Columbia, SC: Camden House, 1994.

Helfer, Martha B. Rev. of *Novalis: Signs of Revolution*, by William Arctander O'Brien. *GQ* 70 (1997): 198–99.

Heller, Erich. *The Disinherited Mind: Essays in Modern German Literature and Thought*. Philadelphia: Dufour and Saifer, 1952.

Holthusen, Hans Egon. *Der späte Rilke*. Zurich: Die Arche, 1949.

Howell, John M. "Salinger in the Wasteland." *Critical Essays on Salinger's "The Catcher in the Rye."* Ed. Joel Salzburg. Boston: G. K. Hall, 1990. 85–92.

Huch, Ricarda. *Die Romantik: Blütezeit, Ausbreitung und Verfall*. Tübingen: Wunderlich, 1951.

Humphreys, Christmas. *Buddhism*. 3rd ed. Harmondsworth, Eng.: Penguin, 1962.

Jaffé, Aniela. *"Was C. G. Jung a Mystic?" and Other Essays*. Trans. Diana Dachler and Fiona Cairns. Ed. Robert Hinshaw. Einsiedeln, Switzerland: Daimon, 1989.

James, William. *The Varieties of Religious Experience. A Study in Human Nature*. New York: Mentor, 1958.

Jofen, Jean. *The Jewish Mystic in Kafka*. American University Studies: Germanic Languages and Literature, Series 1, 41. New York: Peter Lang, 1987.

Jones, John A. "The 'Reconciliation of Opposites' in Romantic Poetry and Classical Style Music: Some Relations."*Centennial Review* 28 (1984): 159–84.

Jung, C. G. *Aion: Researches into the Phenomenology of the Self*. 2nd rev. ed. Princeton: Princeton UP, 1968. Vol. 9, II of *The Collected Works of C. G. Jung*. Trans. R. F. C. Hull. Ed. Herbert Read et al. Bollingen Series 20. 20 vols. Princeton: Princeton UP; London: Routledge and Kegan Paul, 1953–83.

———. *Memories, Dreams, Reflections*. Trans. Richard and Clara Winston. Ed. Aniela Jaffé. New York: Vintage, 1965.

———. *Psyche and Symbol: A Selection from the Writings of C. G. Jung*. Ed. Violet S. de Laszlo. Garden City, New York: Anchor-Doubleday, 1958.

Kafka, Franz. *Briefe, 1902–1924*. New York: Schocken, 1958.

———. *Die Erzählungen*. 1935. n.p.: Fischer, 1961.

———. *Hochzeitsvorbereitungen auf dem Lande und andere Prosa aus dem Nachlaß*. Frankfurt am Main: Fischer, 1953.

———. *Parables and Paradoxes: In German and English*. 1935. New York: Schocken, 1961.

Kapleau, Philip, comp. and ed. *The Three Pillars of Zen: Teaching, Practice, and Enlightenment*. Rev. ed. Garden City: Anchor-Doubleday, 1980.

Kaufmann, Walter. *Nietzsche: Philosopher, Psychologist, Antichrist*. 3rd Rev. ed. New York: Vintage, 1968.

Keenan, Terrance. "Standing Where Roads Converge: The Thomas Merton Papers at Syracuse University." *Syracuse University Library Associates Courier* 30 (1995): 157–62.

Kermode, Frank. "Paul de Man's Abyss." Rev. of *Wartime Journalism, 1939–1943*, by Paul de Man, *Critical Writings 1953–1978*, by Paul de Man, *Paul de Man: Deconstruction and the Critique of Aesthetic Ideology*, by Christopher Norris, and *Reading de Man Reading*, ed. Lindsay Waters and Wlad Godzich. *London Review of Books* 16 Mar. 1989: 3–7.

Klein, Anne C. "Mental Concentration and the Unconditioned: A Buddhist Case for Unmediated Experience." *Paths to Liberation: The Marga and Its Transformations in Buddhist Thought.* Studies in East Asian Buddhism 7. Ed. Robert E. Buswell, Jr., and Robert M. Gimello. Honolulu: U of Hawaii P, 1992. 269–308.

Kluckhohn, Paul. *Das Ideengut der deutschen Romantik.* 5th ed. Tübingen: Niemeyer, 1966.

Korff, H. A. *Frühromantik.* 7th ed. Leipzig: Koehler & Amelang, 1966. Vol. 3 of *Geist der Goethezeit: Versuch einer ideellen Entwicklung der klassisch-romantischen Literaturgeschichte.* 4 vols. 1964–1966.

Kountz, Peter. *Thomas Merton as Writer and Monk: A Cultural Study, 1915–1951.* Chicago Studies in the History of American Religion 11. Brooklyn: Carlson, 1991.

Kramer, Victor A. *Thomas Merton: Monk and Artist.* 1984. Cistercian Studies Series 102. Kalamazoo: Cistercian, 1987.

Kuroiwa, Junichi. "Japan." *Kafka-Handbuch.* Ed. Hartmut Binder. Vol. 2. Stuttgart: Kröner, 1979. 732–43. 2 vols.

Kuzniar, Alice A. *Delayed Endings: Nonclosure in Novalis and Hölderlin.* Athens: U of Georgia P, 1987.

———. "Reassessing Romantic Reflexivity—The Case of Novalis." *GR* 63 (1988): 77–86.

Lacoue-Labarthe, Philippe, and Jean-Luc Nancy. *The Literary Absolute: The Theory of Literature in German Romanticism.* Trans. Philip Barnard and Cheryl Lester. Albany: State U of New York P, 1988.

Lee, Joo-Dong. *Taoistische Weltanschauung im Werke Franz Kafkas.* New York: Lang, 1985.

Leonard, Ron. "The Transcendental Philosophy of Franklin Merrell-Wolff." Diss. U of Waterloo, 1991.

Lewis, C. S. *Surprised by Joy: The Shape of my Early Life.* New York: Harvest-Harcourt Brace Jovanovich, 1955.

Lewis, Leta Jane. "Novalis and the Fichtean Absolute." *GQ* 35 (1962): 464–74.

Light, James F. "Salinger's *The Catcher in the Rye.*" *Explicator* 18 (1960): Item 59.

Loy, David. "The Clôture of Deconstruction: A Mahayana Critique of Derrida." *Indian Philosophical Quarterly* 27.1 (1987): 59–80.

———. *Healing Deconstruction: Postmodern Thought in Buddhism and Christianity.* Atlanta: Scholars Press, 1996.

Lukacs, Georg. *Deutsche Realisten des 19. Jahrhunderts.* Bern: Francke, 1951.

Lundquist, James. *J. D. Salinger.* New York: Ungar, 1979.

Mähl, Hans-Joachim. *Die Idee des goldenen Zeitalters im Werk des Novalis.* Probleme der Dichtung: Studien zur deutschen Literaturgeschichte 7. Ed. Adolf Beck and Karl Ludwig Schneider. Heidelberg: Karl Winter, 1965.

Magliola, Robert. *Derrida on the Mend.* West Lafayette, IN.: Purdue UP, 1984.

Maybury-Lewis, David. "The Quest for Harmony." *The Attraction of Opposites: Thought and Society in the Dualistic Mode.* Ed. David Maybury-Lewis and Uri Almagor. Ann Arbor: U of Michigan P, 1989. 1–17.

Mayer, Paola. "Reinventing the Sacred: The Romantic Myth of Jakob Böhme." *GQ* 69 (1996): 247–59.

McKinney, Ronald H. "Towards the Resolution of Paradigm Conflict: Holism Versus Postmodernism." *Philosophy Today* 32 (1988): 299–311.

Megill, Allan. *Prophets of Extremity: Nietzsche, Heidegger, Foucault, Derrida.* Berkeley: U of California P, 1985.

Menninghaus, Winfried. "Die frühromantische Theorie von Zeichen und Metapher." *GQ* 62 (1989): 48–58.

Merrell-Wolff, Franklin. *Franklin Merrell-Wolff's Experience and Philosophy: A Personal Record of Transformation and a Discussion of Transcendental Consciousness.* Albany: State U of New York P, 1994.

———. *Pathways through to Space: A Personal Record of Transformation in Consciousness.* 2nd ed. New York: Julian, 1973.

———. *The Philosophy of Consciousness without an Object: Reflections on the Nature of Transcendental Consciousness.* New York: Julian, 1973.

———. *Transformations in Consciousness: The Metaphysics and Epistemology.* Albany: State U of New York P, 1995.

Merton, Thomas. *The Asian Journal of Thomas Merton.* Ed. Naomi Burton, Patrick Hart, and James Laughlin. New York: New Directions, 1973.

———. *Conjectures of a Guilty Bystander.* Garden City, NY: Image-Doubleday, 1968.

———. *The Hidden Ground of Love: The Letters of Thomas Merton on Religious Experience and Social Concerns.* Ed. William H. Shannon. New York: Farrar, Straus, Giroux, 1985.

———. *The Literary Essays of Thomas Merton.* Ed. Patrick Hart. New York: New Directions, 1981.

———. "Love and the Search for God." *The Voice of Thomas Merton Recorded Live at Gethsemani.* Credence Cassettes, AA2078, n.d.

———. Notebook 4, ms. Thomas James Merton Papers, 1960–1968. Box 3. Syracuse University.

———. "Poetry and Imagination." *The Voice of Thomas Merton Recorded Live at Gethsemani.* Credence Cassettes, AA2076, n.d.

Miller, David L. *Three Faces of God: Traces of the Trinity in Literature and Life.* Philadelphia: Fortress, 1986.

Mitchell, Stephen, ed. and trans. *The Selected Poetry of Rainer Maria Rilke.* New York: Random House, 1982.

Miura, Isshu, and Ruth Fuller Sasaki. *The Zen Koan: Its History and Use in Rinzai Zen.* New York: Harvest-Harcourt, 1965.

Molnár, Géza von. *Romantic Vision, Ethical Context: Novalis and Artistic Autonomy.* Theory and History of Literature 39. Minneapolis: U of Minnesota P, 1987.

Morton, Michael. *Herder and the Poetics of Thought: Unity and Diversity in "On Diligence in Several Learned Languages."* University Park: Pennsylvania State UP, 1989.

Neve, Michael. "Triples." Rev. of *The Double in 19th-Century Fiction,* by John Herdman, *Romanticism and the Sciences,* ed. Andrew Cunningham and Nicholas Jardine, and *Schizophrenia: A Scientific Delusion?,* by Mary Boyle. *London Review of Books* 8 Nov. 1990: 22–23.

Newman, Gail. "The Status of the Subject in Novalis's *Heinrich von Ofterdingen* and Kleist's *Die Marquise von O . . .*" *GQ* 62 (1989): 59–71.

Nicolai, Ralf R. "'Ein altes Blatt' als Beispiel für Kafkas Weltanschauung." *Akten des VI. Internationalen Germanisten-Kongresses Basel 1980.* Bern: Lang, 1980. 481–85.

———. "Zur Stagnierung im Werk Kafkas und Kleists: Dreistufigkeit." *Franz Kafka. Eine Aufsatzsammlung nach einem Symposium in Philadelphia.* Ed. Maria Luise Caputo-Mayr. Berlin: Agora, 1978. 194–201.

Nishida, Kitaro. *Intelligibility and the Philosophy of Nothingness.* Trans. Robert Schinzinger. Honolulu: East-West Center, 1958.

Novalis. *Werke in einem Band.* 3rd ed. Hamburg: Hoffmann and Campe, 1966.

———. *Novalis Schriften; die Werke Friedrich von Hardenbergs.* Ed. Paul Kluckhohn and Richard Samuel. 2nd rev. ed. 5 vols. Stuttgart: Kohlhammer, 1960–1988.

O'Brien, William Arctander. *Novalis: Signs of Revolution.* Durham: Duke UP, 1995.

Politzer, Heinz. *Franz Kafka: Parable and Paradox.* Ithaca: Cornell UP, 1966.

Rajneesh, Bhagwan Shree. *Philosophia Ultima: Discourses on the Mandukya Upanishad.* n.p.: Rajneesh Foundation International, 1983.

Reps, Paul, ed. *Zen Flesh, Zen Bones: A Collection of Zen and Pre-Zen Writings.* New York: Anchor-Doubleday, n.d.

Rickert, Richard Frederick. "Aesthetic Interpreting and Describing: Their Functions in Regard to the 'Transinterpretive' Art of Kafka and of Zen." *DAI* 33 (1973): 4480 A. U of North Carolina, Chapel Hill.

Rilke, Rainer Maria. "Rainer Maria Rilke, 1875–1926." *German Literature since Goethe.* Ed. Ernst Feise and Harry Steinhauer. Vol. 2. Boston: Houghton Mifflin, 1959. 223–30. 2 vols. 1958–1959.

———. *Letters of Rainer Maria Rilke, 1910–1926.* Trans. Jane Bannard Greene and M. D. Herter Norton. New York: Norton, 1969.

———. *Werke in drei Bänden.* 3 vols. Frankfurt: Insel, 1966.

Rilke, Rainer Maria, and Marie von Thurn und Taxis. *Briefwechsel.* Vol. 1. Zurich: Niehans and Rokitansky, 1951. 2 vols.

Robertson, J. G. *A History of German Literature.* Ed. Edna Purdie et al. 4th rev. ed. New York: British Book Centre, 1962.

Rosen, Gerald. *Zen in the Art of J. D. Salinger*. Modern Authors Monograph Series 3. Berkeley: Creative Arts, 1977.

Ross, Nancy Wilson, comp. and ed. *The World of Zen: An East-West Anthology*. New York: Random House, 1960.

Salinger, J. D. *The Catcher in the Rye*. 1951. Boston: Little, Brown, 1991.

———. *Franny and Zooey*. 1961. Boston: Little, Brown, 1991.

———. *Nine Stories*. 1953. Boston: Little, Brown, 1991.

———. *Raise High the Roof Beam, Carpenters and Seymour: An Introduction*. 1963. Boston: Little, Brown, 1991.

Schillemeit, Jost. "Chancen und Grenzen der Willensfreiheit. Fragen der Ethik und Religionsphilosophie bei Max Brod, Felix Weltsch und Kafka (1920)." *Prager deutschsprachige Literatur zur Zeit Kafkas*. Ed. Österreichische Franz Kafka-Gesellschaft Wien-Klosterneuburg. Vienna: Braumüller, 1989. 165–81.

Schlegel, August Wilhelm. *Schriften*. Munich: Goldmann, n.d.

Schlegel, Friedrich. *Schriften und Fragmente: Ein Gesamtbild seines Geistes*. Ed. Ernst Behler. Kröners Taschenausgabe 246. Stuttgart: Kröner, 1956.

Sekida, Katsuki, trans. and ed. *Two Zen Classics: Mumonkan and Hekiganroku*. New York: Weatherhill, 1977.

Sekida, Katsuki. *Zen Training: Methods and Philosophy*. Ed. A. V. Grimstone. New York: Weatherhill, 1975.

Senzaki, Nyogen, and Paul Reps, ed. and trans. *The Gateless Gate*. Los Angeles: John Murray, 1934.

———. ed. and trans. *101 Zen Stories*. Philadelphia: McKay, 1939.

*The Shambhala Dictionary of Buddhism and Zen*. Ed. Ingrid Fischer-Schreiber et al. Trans. Michael H. Kohn. Boston: Shambhala, 1991.

Shibayama, Zenkei. *Zen Comments on the Mumonkan*. Trans. Sumiko Kudo. New York: Harper, 1974.

Skow, John. "Sonny: An Introduction." *Time* 15 Sept. 1961: 84–90.

Slawsky, Donna. Telephone interview. 27 Oct. 1995.

Sokel, Walter H. "Between Gnosticism and Jehovah: The Dilemma in Kafka's Religious Attitude." *Germanic Review* 60 (1985): 69–77.

———. *Franz Kafka-Tragik und Ironie: Zur Struktur seiner Kunst*. München: Albert Langen Georg Müller, 1964.

———. "Frozen Sea and River of Narration: The Poetics behind Kafka's 'Breakthrough.'" *Newsletter of the Kafka Society of America* 7 (1983): 71-79.

———. "Kafka's Poetics of the Inner Self." *Modern Austrian Literature* 11.3–4 (1978): 37–58. Rpt. in *From Kafka and Dada to Brecht and Beyond*. Ed. Reinhold Grimm, Peter Spycher, and Richard A. Zipser. Madison: U of Wisconsin P, 1982. 7–21.

Spivak, Gayatri Chakravorty. *The Post-Colonial Critic: Interviews, Strategies, Dialogues*. Ed. Sarah Harasym. New York: Routledge, 1990.

Stahl, August. *Rilke: Kommentar zum lyrischen Werk*. Munich: Winkler, 1978.

Stone, Edward. "Salinger's Carrousel." *Modern Fiction Studies* 13 (1967-68): 520–23.

Sublette, Jack R. *J. D. Salinger: An Annotated Bibliography, 1938–81*. Garland Reference Library of the Humanities 436. New York: Garland, 1984.

Sussman, Henry. *Franz Kafka: Geometrician of Metaphor*. Madison: Coda, 1979.

Suzuki, D. T. *Essays in Zen Buddhism (First Series)*. 1949. New York: Evergreen-Grove, 1961.

———. *Manual of Zen Buddhism*. 1935. New York: Evergreen-Grove, 1960.

Suzuki, Shunryu. *Zen Mind, Beginner's Mind*. Ed. Trudy Dixon. New York: Weatherhill, 1970.

Tae, Yasuhiro. "Between Suicide and Enlightenment." *Kyushu American Literature* 26 (1985): 21–27.

Takeda, Katsuhiko. "Uchi naru Zen v.s. Soto naru Zen." *J. D. Salinger Bungaku no Kenkyu*. Ed. Hisashi Shigeo and Ayako Sato. Tokyo: Tokyo Shirakawa Shoin, 1983.

Tsukakoshi, Satoshi. "Zen im Osten und Westen." *Alles Lebendige Meinet den Menschen. Gedenkbuch für Max Niehans*. Ed. Irmgard Buck and Georg Kurt Schauer. Bern: Francke, 1972. 24–40.

Valente, Luiz Fernando. "Variations on the Kenotic Hero: Tolstoy's 'Ivan Ilych' and Guimarães Rosa's 'Augusto Matraga.'" *Symposium* 45 (1991): 126–38.

Wagenbach, Klaus. *Franz Kafka in Selbstzeugnissen und Bilddokumenten*. Rowohlts Monographien 91. Reinbek bei Hamburg: Rowohlt, 1964.

Walzel, Oskar. *German Romanticism*. Trans. Alma Elise Lussky. 1932. New York: Capricorn, 1966.

Whitlark, James. *Behind the Great Wall: A Post-Jungian Approach to Kafkaesque Literature*. Rutherford, NJ: Fairleigh Dickinson UP; Toronto: Associated University Presses, 1991.

———. "Kafka and the Taoist Sages." *Journal of the Kafka Society of America* 8 (1984): 28–34.

Wilber, Ken. *No Boundary: Eastern and Western Approaches to Personal Growth*. Boulder: Shambhala, 1981.

Wilpert, Gero von. *Sachwörterbuch der Literatur*. Kröners Taschenausgabe 231. 3rd rev. ed. Stuttgart: Kröner, 1961.

Wolff, Franklin F. [Franklin Merrell-Wolff]. *Introceptualism: The Philosophy of Consciousness without an Object*—Vol II. Phoenix: Phoenix Philosophical Press, 1980.

———. The Power of the Will. Audiotape. Rec. 18 Sept. 1973. Lone Pine, CA. Tape #34: R/R 0-140.

Woodcock, George. *Thomas Merton, Monk and Poet: A Critical Study*. New York: Farrar, Straus, Giroux, 1978.

# Index